PROGRESSIVISM AND MUCKRAKING

Bibliographic Guides for Contemporary Collections
Series Editor, Peter Doiron
Anatomy of Wonder: Science Fiction by Neil Barron
Cities by Dwight W. Hoover
Cooking for Entertaining by Nancy Tudor and Dean Tudor
Progressivism and Muckraking by Louis Filler

PROGRESSIVISM AND MUCKRAKING
LOUIS FILLER

FOR

R. R. BOWKER COMPANY
A Xerox Education Company
New York & London, 1976

Published by R. R. Bowker Company (A Xerox Education Company)
1180 Avenue of the Americas, New York, N.Y. 10036
Copyright © 1976 by Xerox Corporation
Printed and bound in the United States of America

Library of Congress Cataloging in Publication Data

Filler, Louis, 1911-
    Progressivism and muckraking.

(Bibliographic guides for contemporary collections)
Includes indexes.
1. United States—Social conditions—Bibliography.
2. Social reformers—United States—Bibliography.
3. Social problems—Bibliography.
4. Progressivism
(United States politics) I. Title.
Z7164.S66F54 [HN64]   016.3091'73   76-950
ISBN 0-8352-0875-3

Contents

Foreword

The concept of the Bibliographic Guides for Contemporary Collections Series was derived from a realization that many librarians, students, teachers, and laypersons lack indepth guidance to subjects of current interest. Too often, librarians are faced with inadequate, or even a total lack of selection assistance when developing specific areas for their libraries or individual studies. "Contemporary Collections" seeks to help fill this need. The word "contemporary" refers to a subject, old or new, that is now experiencing a high level of interest throughout America and across the educational spectrum. A sudden upsurge of interest in a specific area emphasizes the lack of guidance, in many instances, to the best and most necessary materials for reading and research. The "Contemporary Collections" series will attempt to meet such information crises by presenting the reader with a selective basic guide to the literature. Each book will be written by an expert or group of experts who will develop each subject through selection, annotation, and commentary. The emphasis is on in-print materials but, obviously, some subjects cannot be adequately explored without citing titles of landmark quality and some of these may be out of print. Where appropriate media other than books will be included for most titles in the series. These bibliographic guides will give librarians, students, scholars, and the general public a frame in which to approach certain immediate topics with solid organization.

In *Progressivism and Muckraking* Dr. Louis Filler (Professor of American Civilization, Antioch College) demonstrates the difficult art of melding bibliographic form and function. He has achieved two goals: a bibliographic essay in book-length form and a cogent perspective of an indigenous American activity currently practiced by such people as Ralph Nader, Tom Wolfe, Hunter Thompson, and the Watergate journalists who ferreted out the sordid details. Dr. Filler has studied, taught, and written about America for more than twenty years and in this book he shares a rare accumulation of knowledge.

PETER DOIRON
Series Editor

OTHER WRITINGS by LOUIS FILLER

BOOKS

Appointment at Armageddon: Muckraking and Progressivism in the American Tradition (1975)

Randolph Bourne (1965 ed.)

The Crusade Against Slavery, 1830–1860 (1960 ff.)

A Dictionary of American Social Reform (1963; Greenwood ed., 1969)

The Unknown Edwin Markham (1966)

The Muckrakers: Crusaders for American Liberalism (rev. ed., 1976)

EDITED WORKS

The New Stars: Life and Labor in Old Missouri, Manie Morgan (1949)

Mr. Dooley: Now and Forever, Finley Peter Dunne (1954)

American Liberalism of the Late Nineteenth Century (1961), anthology

The Removal of the Cherokee Nation: Manifest Destiny or National Dishonor? (1962)

The World of Mr. Dooley (1962)

The Anxious Years (1963), anthology of 1930's literature

Horace Mann and Others, Robert L. Straker (1963)

A History of the People of the United States, John Bach McMaster (1964)

The President Speaks (1964), major twentieth-century addresses

Horace Mann on the Crisis in Education (1965), Spanish translation, 1972

Wendell Phillips on Civil Rights and Freedom (1965)

The Ballad of the Gallows-Bird, Edwin Markham (1967)

Old Wolfville: The Fiction of A. H. Lewis (1968)

Slavery in the United States of America (1972)

Abolition and Social Justice (1972)

Preface

The purpose of this interpretive bibliography is to make a vital and varied subject readily available to as wide a reading public as possible. It might seem strange that an admittedly popular topic of standard consequence in our history could be treated in esoteric terms. Yet it has been so treated in a number of modern studies. Although some studies give due notice, under one or another aspect, to muckraking or Progressivism, these subjects are not explored in a survey like the present one which intends to recognize the many ways in which the themes have been viewed and over the years activated in society.

Obviously, subtopic leads on to subtopic. I have made efforts to ensure that the reader may find his or her preferred way through references without difficulty. There are cross-references and indexes to guide the reader to whichever writing may serve personal or class purpose. A list of audiovisual aids appears at the end of each chapter.

A major concept directing the preparation of this bibliography has been to indicate continuity from the past to the present, so that current muckraking, for example, when it can be identified, is seen as comporting with or deviating from the greater American tradition. Also involved in this concept is the idea of relevance. Numerous works that were once treated seriously have been shelved or depreciated. In some cases, I have indicated such changes in critical temper, and have reminded the reader that certain books are available and may be judged anew for modern purposes. Generally accepted opinions of this writing or that have been reversed in the past, and in some instances could be reversed again. Thus, Populism is today in the news, and much more so than Progressivism. The very latest of books, *The Genteel Populists* (1974)—written by Simon Lazarus, a follower of Ralph Nader and Nicholas Johnson, an associate of Bess Myerson, and other "public interest" workers, upbraids the the old Progressives as frauds and progenitors of "A New Deal That Never Really Happened." Yet Progressivism had once been seen as a grand fulfillment, a national movement with stride and substance, as compared to "western" Populism which had echoed old dreams and outmoded political fancies. It is not impossible that further changes in national temper may materialize. This bibliography takes such possibilities into consideration.

DEFINITIONS: THE CHALLENGE OF A PAST PROGRESSIVISM

During its great days, Progressivism seemed to be carving out a record which would thrill successive generations. Progressive reformers numbered literally in the thousands; the following discussion will no more than indicate contrasting progressive types in order to open roads to further study of them and their social missions. They worked in every associated field, from vitalized politics to civic pursuits. They concerned themselves with a spectrum of problems which included the wants of the poor and also the dilemmas of the rich. They satirized marriages for money or foreign titles, lavishly empty outlays on houses and trousseaus—what Thorstein Veblen called "conspicuous consumption"—and other expenditures which showed social irresponsibility. The legitimate needs of the sick and the crippled, the challenge of new immigrants held down by lack of language and victimized by conditions alien to their upbringing, the special rights of women and children of every group and circumstance subject (usually negatively) to changing industrial and familial relations—such were a few of the aspects of American life which stirred the progressive reformers.

William English Walling, an influential socialist of the time and one of the remarkable breed of "millionaire-socialists" which a vibrant democracy produced, in his *Progressivism and After* (1914) saw the Progressive drive as so well established that the transition to a socialist state could be predicted. Capitalism stood to lose too much by impeding the march to the classless society. The forces calling for it were too many and too great. Thus, as he said:

> [For] the first time in history, the ballot will be used to secure an advance of the lower half of the population towards equal opportunity. And both the ballot and the use of it will be secure, for the various ruling class factions will each want to use the masses for their purposes, and the slight advance the latter make on each occasion will not be enough to unite their political masters against them.

Obviously, something went wrong with Walling's calculations, and the following narrative will in part display the conditions which blighted them. Nevertheless, it remains true that the Progressive era was a time of hope, and that hope was not based on intangibles. Our present less optimistic outlook could prove to be as unfounded in an opposite direction. An effort will be made to spell out components of our social attitudes, past and present. In any event, it behooves us grasp why the public of the time responded with such enthusiasm to the Progressive argument and adherents. Progressivism existed in politics and society before the Progressive era. Yet the public drive toward and support of Progressives from 1900 through the 1910s was of unprecedented proportions. It resulted in remarkable sensations and a large framework of laws.

There were revelations of official chicanery in the cities and the countryside, as well as in Washington, touching important individuals, as well as agencies and organizations. There was news of secret deals among businessmen and politicians to seize or hold public property on false grounds or inadequate payment, or to sell goods or services on shoddy terms. Sorrowful conditions afflicting the helpless, cruel treatment of child workers, the mulcting of their parents by what should have been public services—gas, transportation, police protection—all this was reported by journalists who came to be called muckrakers. Investigatory reporters there had been before, but never in such number or operating with such sophisticated skills of communication. Never before had they been as closely associated with men of affairs and reformers in politics.

Their arts roused indignation and a continuous stream of demands for action which seemed to establish a pattern of public need. Their explanations of conditions were directed to the general populace, which put pressure upon legislators for redress of grievances. Behind the journalists and the politicians grew research and action institutions—settlement houses, social work associations, foundations, professional publications—to set down bases of fact and experience for further developments.

The Progressive era posited a moral stance on the part of the public and its leaders. It reached its height in a leader who was first of all a moral spokesman. Woodrow Wilson thrilled the nation in his Inaugural Address with such words as:

> This is not a day of triumph; it is a day of dedication. Here muster, not the forces of party, but the forces of humanity. Men's hearts wait upon us; men's lives hang in the balance; men's hopes call upon us to say what we will do. Who shall live up to the great trust? Who dares fail to try? I summon all honest men, all patriotic, all forward-looking men, to my side. God helping me, I will not fail them, if they will but counsel and sustain me!

As president, Wilson sponsored a program then deemed the most sweeping in the nation's history. He then, in 1917, turned from domestic concerns to lead Americans into a war which was intended to extend the crusade for democracy abroad. It turned out to be technologically a triumph, but catastrophic insofar as American hopes and expectations of a progressive sort went. The country suffered relatively little compared to the multimillion dead and wounded in devastated lands abroad. The United States enjoyed a wartime prosperity to boot. But it also experienced a reaction of disillusionment which seriously affected its morale. Postwar prosperity was succeeded by a cancerous economic depression which widely shook faith in American destiny and ideals; see *American Dreams, American Nightmares* (1970), edited by David Madden.

Traditional American pride was not revived by what should have seemed a holy crusade against a bestial Nazism. The triumphs of World War II were succeeded by a fatuous prosperity featuring a proliferation of ranch houses and fish-tailed automobiles, all juxtaposed with "foreign aid": a strange and unexamined giant expenditure. By then the goals of Progressivism seemed simple and remote indeed. New domestic turmoil, a debilitating war in

---

*Filler, ed., *The President Speaks* (New York, 1964), 93.

Vietnam, and unresolved efflorescences in areas of sex, drugs, and free expression further suggested even to forthright and self-respecting elements of the American population that the world had changed drastically since the days of Theodore Roosevelt and Woodrow Wilson—too drastically for Progressivism to find an area of usefulness within it.

The devastating events of recent times suggest that the millenium is not about to happen. With national programs and their sponsors largely discredited or put in doubt, it is unlikely that a tidal wave of public opinion will form either favoring or derogating the national prospect. It appears to be a time for reconsidering one's political and social beliefs. A new emphasis is likely to be put on the individual, who will be expected to assess information for content and accuracy, to examine carefully people who demand attention, to measure national needs irrespective of race, creed, or color.

This was what Progressivism in its time claimed to do. Its title to respect has been challenged, as will be seen, in the interests of other programs, with what accuracy or goodwill may be judged. Both muckraking and Progressivism thus return to the stage, once more to learn what they have to contribute to the well-being of their countrymen.

LOUIS FILLER
Professor of American Civilization
Antioch College

Producers of Audiovisual Aids

The superscript numbers in the text refer to the list of audiovisual aids at the end of each chapter. Following is a list of the abbreviations used in the listings and the addresses of the producers. Thanks are due Edward Clark, Director of Instructional Systems, Antioch College, for aid in compiling this material.

AMIP	American Institute of Planners 917 15th Street, N. W. Washington, D. C.	EBEC	Encyclopedia Brittanica Educational Corp. 425 N. Michigan Ave. Chicago, Ill.
AZRELA	Azzrella Unlimited 207 E. 74 Street New York, N. Y.	ERS	Educational Record Sales 157 Chambers Street New York, N. Y.
BBC	British Broadcasting Company 630 Fifth Avenue New York, N. Y.	FCE	Film Classics Exchange 1926 Vermont Avenue Los Angeles, Calif.
BFA	BFA Educational Media 2211 Michigan Avenue Santa Monica, Calif.	FOX	Twentieth Century-Fox Film Corporation 444 West 56 Street New York, N. Y.
CBS	Columbia Broadcasting System 383 Madison Avenue New York, N. Y.	HEARST	Hearst Metrotone News 450 West 56 Street New York, N. Y.
COL	Columbia Pictures 711 Fifth Avenue New York, N. Y.	ILGWU	International Ladies' Garment Workers Union Educational Dept. 1710 Broadway New York, N. Y.
CORF	Coronet Films 65 East South Water Street Chicago, Ill.	JTS	Jewish Theological Seminary of America 3080 Broadway New York, N. Y.
DOUGLS	Douglass Productions Box 878 Sedona, Ariz.		
EAV	Educational Audio Visual Inc. Pleasantville, N. Y.	MAGNUM	Magnum Films 72 West 45 Street New York, N. Y.

MGHF	McGraw-Hill Films 330 West 42 Street New York, N. Y.	PATHE	Pathe News Inc. 835 Broadway New York, N. Y.
MOT	Time-Life Films 43 West 16 Street New York, N. Y.	PSP	Project Seven Productions 331 N. Maple Drive Beverly Hills, Calif.
NBC	National Broadcasting Company 30 Rockefeller Plaza New York, N. Y.	SAUDEX	Robert Saudex Associates, Inc. 689 Fifth Avenue New York, N. Y.
NET	National Educational Television Audiovisual Center Indiana University Bloomington, Ind.	TFC	Teaching Film Custodians 25 West 33 Street New York, N. Y.
NFBC	National Film Board of Canada 680 Fifth Avenue New York, N. Y.	USDA	U.S. Dept. of Agriculture Motion Picture Services Room 1850, South Bldg. Washington, D. C.
NSCCA	National Society for Crippled Children and Adults 2023 Ogden Avenue Chicago, Ill.	USDD	U. S. Dept. of Defense Pentagon Washington, D. C.
		WB	Warner Brothers 4000 Warner Burbank, Calif.
PAR	Paramount Pictures Corporation 1 Gulf & Western Plaza New York, N. Y.	WOLPER	Wolper Productions 8489 West Third Street Los Angeles, Calif.
		WTTWTV	WTTW Television 5400 N. St. Louis Chicago, Ill.

PROGRESSIVISM
AND
MUCKRAKING

i

A Meaning for Modern Times

1. The Progressive Impulse

Progressivism may be traced in a score of movements preceding the Progressive era proper. It expressed itself in uprisings and broader political movements, raising questions among historians as to where Progressivism ended and revolution began. See, for example, E. C. Rozwenc, ed., *The New Deal: Revolution or Evolution?* (1959), composed of essays which answered that precise question from opposite ends. The problem of the difference between reform and revolution is implicit in John F. Jameson's famous *The American Revolution Considered as a Social Movement* (1926): a pioneer effort to see beneath mere slogans to class interests.

In general, Progressivism has involved popular protest and unrest, and efforts to cross class and group lines for greater social impact. Progressivism has sought a common denominator for disparate elements of the American population. It is no accident, as will be seen, that the popular and the progressive became interwoven. Inevitably, however, they required a leadership, and that which had proclaimed itself of the populace found itself communicating with peers: a new elite.[1]

An overall view of American life of classic dimensions which honors American dissent is *The Rise of American Civilization* (1927) by Charles A. Beard and Mary R. Beard. The hope of freedom implicit in the Beards' treatment is doubted in *The Decline of American Liberalism* (1955) and *Progressivism in America* (1974) both by Arthur A. Ekirch, Jr.

Early expressions of popular feeling include Nathaniel Bacon's 1676 uprising against Virginia authorities, as told richly and authoritatively in T. J. Wertenbaker's *Torchbearer of the Revolution* (1940). Another landmark in social dissatisfaction was the crisis in Rhode Island which, for a moment, saw two state governments all but engaging in civil war. Marvin E. Gettleman's *The Dorr Rebellion: A Study in American Radicalism 1833–1849* (1973) caps a remarkable literature about a memorable event.

A broader and more national movement was that led by Andrew Jackson in 1828. It was significant that Arthur M. Schlesinger, Jr.'s recounting of this movement in his *The Age of Jackson* (1945) was less a history than a reaffirmation of Democratic party principles: a kind of *carte de visite* from New Dealers to post-World War II voters. Schlesinger read a Franklin D. Roosevelt into Jackson, as he would later, in books on the New Deal, read a species of

3

Jackson into Roosevelt. *The Age of Jackson* ensured its then young author of a public and literary career. Jackson has since sunk in general esteem, partly because he was a slaveholder and thought like free-wheeling democratic slaveholders. This fact prepares us for later criticism of post-slavery and patently egalitarian Progressives of the early decades of the twentieth century (*see* Chapter II-20) who, in their time, seemed secure against criticism from all but strict conservatives and uncompromising reactionaries. In 1970 it was possible for several types of "activists" to declare that "the liberal is our worst enemy," and yet be treated with respect in liberal journals. For a judicious survey of the subject's dimensions, see Joseph L. Blau, ed., *Social Theories of Jacksonian Democracy* (1954).

Andrew Jackson, like other prototypes of Progressivism, may yet recapture for some of us a good deal of his old charisma. After all, we do not hold it against the Elizabethan Age that its Virgin Queen was an unmitigated despot.[2]

2. Progress and Progressivism

The concept of "progress" seemed important to crusaders of the early twentieth century, in the same way that *justice* and *religious faith* had once motivated and inspired earlier social movements.

This is not to say that a need for psychological reassurance was not present in the progressive movements of our own century up to recent times. It is clear, however, that Progressivism — twentieth-century Progressivism — was much firmer in spelling out material and egalitarian goals than were older affirmations of American ideals.

Aspects of the subject are treated in Raymond Aron, *Progress and Disillusion: The Dialectics of Modern Society* (1968); Charles A. Beard, ed., *A Century of Progress* (1933); Robert Briffault, *Rational Evolution (The Making of Humanity)* (1930); Shmuel Noah Eisenstadt, *Modernization: Protest and Change* (1966); Joseph Kirk Folsom, *Culture and Social Progress* (1928); Bernard J. James, *The Death of Progress* (1973) — this last, a bold statement of a contemporary attitude.

Norman Hapgood's *Industry and Progress* (1911) is of particular interest as expressing a faith in the inevitability of an expanding industrial democracy which directed much progressive thinking in its time. Hapgood's autobiographical *The Changing Years* (1930) is optimistic, despite his disappointments with World War I. He was especially proud of his brother William's experiments in business sharing, as exemplified in his canning works in Indianapolis, where employees for a number of years all but ranked beside management; see Filler, introduction to William Hapgood, *The Columbia Conserve Company* (new ed., 1975). See also W. Jett Lauck, *Political and Industrial Democracy 1776-1926* (1926), which includes a discussion of the Hapgood company.

Progressivism is today much less in the news, much less an inspiration to action than is muckraking, intended to implement justice and democracy. This may be because our faith in progress has been impugned. Many moderns would be ready to settle for survival or a little more: a belief that though individuals may be expendable, they need not be soured on humanity or without dignity.

Muckrakers we have in plenty, sometimes having the impact of a Drew Pearson, whose life has been told in Oliver Pilat's *Drew Pearson* (1973), and even more revealingly in his own *Drew Pearson Diaries 1949–1959*, edited by Tyler Abell (1974). His successor, Jack Anderson, has also provided something of his own record in *The Anderson Papers* (1973), compiled with George Clifford. The quality and substance of their work needs to be compared not only with classical muckraking, but also with such other works as that of Walter Winchell, one of the greatest of the gossip columnists who in eras of his career actually touched on the public interest in some of his revelations; see, for example, St. Clair McKelway, *Gossip* (1940), and Edward H. Weiner, *Let's Go to Press* (1955). See also Bob Thomas, *Winchell* (1972). In general it can be suggested that Winchell's columns and radio talks contained too little of larger issues and philosophic import to rate as muckraking, let alone Progressivism.

It is unrealistic not to note as soon as possible that "muckraking" has had and must doubtless continue to have two meanings, one relating to public service efforts to expose wrong or evil situations, the other involving exploitation of the thirst of popular readerships for sensational writing and subject matter. The most famous (or notorious) editor in this respect was William Randolph Hearst, whose personality and publications conjured up storms of controversy for decades. He was undoubtedly unscrupulous and a purveyor of misleading articles and campaigns. Yet he also employed some of the most famous writers and civic personalities to lead and express themselves in his papers on vital issues. There is no single book which wholly separates the worthwhile from the shoddy in Hearst's career, but much can be gleaned from the following works: W. A. Swanberg, *Citizen Hearst* (1961); Oliver Carlson and Ernest Sutherland Bates, *Hearst, Lord o,ʿSan Simeon* (1936); *Selections from the Writings and Speeches of William Randolph Hearst*, ed., E. F. Tompkins (1948); Ferdinand Lundberg, *Imperial Hearst* (1936); Mrs. Fremont Older, *William Randolph Hearst, American* (1936); John Tebbel, *The Life and Good Times of William Randolph Hearst* (1952).

Filler, *Crusaders for American Liberalism* (1939, and later editions) discusses Hearst in chapter XI. Oliver Carlson's *Brisbane* (1937) is devoted to Hearst's chief editorial assistant. Raymond Gram Swing's *Forerunners of American Fascism* (1935) voices the fears which Hearst inspired in some of his foes.

The problem of sensationalism emerges from a variety of works, such as Silas Bent, *Ballyhoo* (1927), John Wheeler, *I've Got News for You* (1961); Hugh

Cudlipp, *Publish and Be Damned! The Astounding Story of the Daily Mirror* (1953), though dealing with a British publication, is useful; Emile Gauvreau, *My Last Million Readers* (1941); Ben Hecht (with Charles MacArthur), *The Front Page* (1928), which stereotyped the unscrupulous newspaper office and editors.

Worthy of separate mention is Charles Carver's *Brann* [William Cowper Brann] *and the Iconoclast* (1957). This editor and his paper were sensational in their charges of moral turpitude and religious hypocrisy in the southwestern town of Waco, Texas. Brann died in 1898 in a duel growing out of his flamboyant writing which, though not muckraking in its later sensational sense, exemplified the vivid prose and personality factors which contributed to it.

The problem of standards in social deportment affects even the most apparently serious essays in social service. *The Pentagon Papers* (1971), made public by Daniel Ellsberg, are doubtless the most formidable unread five-volume revelations in our era. They make it clear that our military and political leaders had secrets, and were less than candid with the general public. This fact is glaring in Sanford J. Ungar, *The Papers & The Papers: An Account of the Legal and Political Battle over the Pentagon Papers* (1972). But whether they should have been more candid — and can be expected to be more candid in "post-Watergate" diplomacy and military maneuvers, remains to be determined.

The basic question is how much exposure a working society can endure. Secrets there must be. Public servants may be flawed in competence and character, and yet be useful. Moreover, an interesting muckraking requires an interested public. We have yet to determine what the public truly wants.

A "new morality" is clearly in the making. Concern for environment, the "energy crisis," jobs, security in the cities — such issues oppose the lax social attitudes which once gave us the fraudulent $64,000 Question, Payola, "featherbedding" in unions, the soft-sell in advertising, and the empty-spirited Willy Loman in Arthur Miller's *Death of a Salesman* (1949). We can no longer afford such self-deceptions.

But can we recapture a faith in progress? And if we can't, what can we derive from study of the Progressive era? Its essential characteristic was a belief that all social problems could be mastered by exercise of the collective will. Although it was evidently wrong in so thinking, it had created *techniques* for social change which could serve beset people like ourselves. We may yet try to adopt some of the progressive methods for improving our lot, even if we lack the belief that we are necessarily "progressing."[3]

3. The Effect of Darwinism

Darwinism had a momentous effect on reform because it raised questions about the nature of man and his proper prospects. Some intellectuals it made pessimists, as in the case of the journalist-fiction writers Ambrose Bierce and Theodore Dreiser. Some it made turbulent, sometimes envisioning socialist cooperation, at other times becoming grim admirers of strength as a vital ingredient of life. This ambivalence confused Jack London and inspired him to write his masterpiece, *Martin Eden* (1909), as well as his enigmatic *The Iron Heel* (1907) which has been interpreted as both proto-socialism and proto-fascism. Ultimately this ambivalence led to Jack London's suicide in 1916, thus carrying out the prophecy of *Martin Eden*.

Others saw Darwinism as evolution: evolution in society as well as nature. Social Darwinism, defined by the British philosopher Herbert Spencer, saw a world in which classes and nations competed for domination, with the most fit attaining their goals. Militarists like Captain Alfred T. Mahan of the United States Navy foresaw Americans as either becoming a dominant power or sinking into ignominious inconsequence. Theodore Roosevelt agreed, but added a momentous reform component stipulating that the nation would honor all who served.

The literature of Darwinism and Social Darwinism is enormous, and aspects of them shadow or make glow much of what follows in this book. Richard Hofstadter's *Social Darwinism in American Thought 1860–1915* (1944) is of general interest, as is Bert J. Loewenberg's *Darwinism, Reaction or Reform?* (1957). The British passed on their insights to the Americans; see Hiram B. Glass, ed., *Forerunners of Darwin, 1745–1859* (1959). A remarkable pre-Darwin and pro-religious account is Hugh Miller's *The Foot-Prints of the Creator. . .with a Memoir of the Author by Louis Agassiz* (1850). Professor Agassiz never gave up his campaign in following years to disprove Darwin. Thomas Henry Huxley in effect created Darwinism, Darwin himself having little philosophic interest in the implications of his research. Huxley was a literary stylist as well as a scientist, and passed on both traits to his grandchildren, Sir Julian Huxley and Aldous Huxley; see Thomas Henry Huxley's *Evolution and Ethics and Other Essays* (1896) for a defense of the theory's civilizing effects.

William Graham Sumner, pioneer Yale sociologist, was the foremost Social Darwinist in America. His *What Social Classes Owe to Each Other* (1883) said in effect, that they owed nothing. Classes were to prove their power in competition, and without government intervention. Yet, also, Sumner hated war as barbarous and destructive of civilization; see his *War and Other Essays* (1911). Sumner's panacea for war was free trade, guaranteed to provide enough for all, competitively and without war.

David Starr Jordan, as president of Stanford University, not only endorsed evolution, as in his *Footnotes to Evolution: A Series of Popular Addresses on the Evolution of Life* (1898); he also wholeheartedly endorsed peace. Henry Ward Beecher in his *Evolution and Religion* (1885) led the way for ministers to reconcile the two; for a broad view of the controversy and its results, see Henry Higgins Lane's *Evolution and Christian Faith* (1923).

Many writers felt impelled to develop the positive, helpful qualities in evolution. One of the most successful was Henri Louis Bergson, as in his *Creative Evolution* (1911). John Elof Boodin's *Cosmic Evolution* (1925) provided the outlines of cosmic ideals, essentially pursuing the same path. John Burroughs, a follower of Walt Whitman, writing of the "divine abyss" and "scientific faith," extended his master's thought as he saw it, in *Time and Change* (1912). In more recent times another God-seeker and reformer, Gerald Heard, offered "a new outlook on evolution and the future of man," in his *Pain, Sex and Time* (1939). For an overall view of the subject and its unfoldings, see Stowe Persons, ed., *Evolutionary Thought in America* (1956).

One of the greatest of popularizers as writer and lecturer in historical studies and social attitudes, in his time preceding Progressives, was John Fiske, whose *Excursions of an Evolutionist* (1883) praised both Protestantism and industrialists as furthering progress. Fiske's *A Century of Science and Other Essays* (1899) was in praise of Edward Livingston Youmans and his "positive" influence on thought through popular scientific publications. (*See also* Chapter I-9.) John Dewey, speaking for the new pragmatists, wrote *The Influence of Darwin on Philosophy* (1910).

4. Morality and Expediency

Our great moral reformers are well remembered as names, though how much they affect our daily lives is matter for interpretation. Chaplains and priests have made efforts in recent years to affect events, as in anti-Vietnam War protests. In this way they have continued a tradition running from religiously-motivated abolitionism through "Christian socialism," in post-Civil War decades. Religious leaders were, still later, active in the Prohibition drive which gave us the Volstead Amendment and rum-runners. How much of moral reform can be related to Progressivism and how much to anti-Progressivism?

Progressivism can be traced in Alice Felt Tyler's *Freedom's Ferment* (1944) which shows religious feelings infused in causes ranging from woman's suffrage to abolition. Moral and religious feelings are intertwined in the work of reformers. Horace Mann, for example, was less interested in clothing and feeding children than ministering to their spiritual wants; see Louis Filler, ed., *Horace Mann on the Crisis in Education* (1965). Some abolitionists *opposed* purchasing the slaves from their owners with public or private funds because doing so would seem to accept the validity of human bondsmanship. Such a position, though no doubt moral and high-minded, did contribute to ensuring a civil war of great devastation and doubtful morality.

Yet those who sought to avert the Civil War by condoning slavery, as told in Robert W. Johannsen's *Stephen A. Douglas* (1973), were not more realistic or progressive in the sense that they broadened definitions of freedom. Edward

Pessen's *Jacksonian America* (1969) concludes that there were indeed egalitarian ideas in pre-Civil war America, but that the nation was run by "uncommon" leaders whose achievement — to the extent that it can be identified as progressive — was in mobilizing unprecedented popular participation behind often specious slogans; see Edward Pessen's *Most Uncommon Jacksonians, the Radical Leaders of the Early Labor Movement* (1967).

Religious leaders like William Ellery Channing, orators of the stature of Wendell Phillips, socially-minded businessmen such as Lewis Tappan of New York have been criticized as frustrated elitists, neurotics, and hypocrites; see, for example, David H. Donald, "Toward a Reconsideration of Abolitionists," in *Lincoln Reconsidered* (1956), Hazel C. Wolf, *On Freedom's Altar: The Martyr Complex in the Abolition Movement* (1952), and Bertram Wyatt-Brown, *Lewis Tappan and the Evangelical War against Slavery* (1969). Although it is dangerous for authors living in glass characters to throw charges too indiscriminately at other mortals, it can be readily agreed that the great men and women treated in these and other works were complex and deserving of understanding.

It can also be agreed that those who dealt with such earlier causes as imprisonment for debt, the ten-hour day, and even free trade and the right and wrong of the Second Bank of the United States were closer to the actual troubles of the American majority than to their spiritual state, and so touched the roots of American Progressivism more immediately; see Bray Hammond's *Banks and Politics in America from the Revolution to the Civil War* (1957), for an unblurred view of the real men and measures affected.

Abraham Lincoln is an important example of a conservative who can, in the context of his times, be judged a Progressive in that he sought to ensure the continuation of the Union, being even willing to endure the persistence of slavery while he sought curbs on its spread. The key fact was that he held on to the moral component in life and government. As he said:

> This declared indifference. . .for the spread of slavery, I cannot but hate. I hate it because of the monstrous injustice of slavery itself. I hate it because it deprives our republican example of its just influence in the world; enables the enemies of free institutions with plausability to taunt us as hypocrites; causes the real friends of freedom to doubt our sincerity; and especially because it forces so many good men among ourselves into an open war with the very fundamental principles of civil liberty, criticizing the Declaration of Independence, and insisting that there is no right principle of action but self-interest.*

It would be unfaithful to Lincoln not to quote him further on the limits he imposed on his capacity for action, as in the following passage:

> Let reverence for the laws be breathed by every American mother to the lisping babe that prattles on her lap; let it be taught in schools, in seminaries, and in

---

*Quoted in J. G. Randall, *Lincoln the Liberal Statesman* (New York, 1947), p. 196.

colleges; let it be written in primers, spelling-books, and in almanacs; let it be preached from the pulpit, proclaimed in legislative halls, and enforced in courts of justice. And, in short, let it become the political religion of the nation; and let the old and the young, the rich and the poor, the grave and the gay of all sexes and tongues and colors and conditions, sacrifice unceasingly upon its altars.[†]

Considering that Lincoln himself pushed civil liberties hard during the war crisis, abrogating *habeas corpus,* and otherwise finding qualifications on his adherence to rigid law, one must realize that neither has hatred of slavery nor his reverence for legality settled anything. Both suggested standards of morality which continued to trouble Progressives, even at the high point of their crusade.

It helps one to cope with the dilemmas of American life to realize that Progressivism could be found along with anti-Progressivism, often in the same person. The question was always how much of the one, how much of the other could be discerned in his or her career. For example, Lewis Tappan was, in pre-Civil War decades, as useful a citizen as could be found in all New York or anywhere else. He was outstanding in his campaign against slavery, furthered education with aid and encouragement which created Oberlin College in Ohio and Berea College in Kentucky, and advanced the careers of scores of reformers. He helped found such valuable journals as the *National Era*, in which Harriet Beecher Stowe's *Uncle Tom's Cabin* first appeared. There was almost no field of reform which Tappan did not influence in his time.

Yet he was also suspicious of Catholics, and eager to help resist what he felt to be their untoward conversion activities in the West. He was a rigid moralist and total prohibitionist, and in various ways intolerant of others' preferences in life. Tappan did not, however, directly transgress their civil rights, and he did little practical harm so far as his moral and religious impulses were concerned. Like many of his kind, he served democracy much more than he harmed it, and he belongs with the Progressives.

Has the moral element diminished in American life since the days of world-famous ministers and their religious-minded parishioners? Probably not much. A need for belief — in life, in society — is as apparent as ever and extends from the "Jesus Freaks" to the *New York Times* which, in its "Watergate" campaign, called for a new American ethic to implement its political goals.

Such books as the following reveal the search for a viable ethic: Fellowship of Reconciliation (United States), *Moral and Technical Implications of Peace on Earth* (1965), featuring essays by Daniel Berrigan and Kenneth E. Boulding, among others; Paul T. Menzel, ed., *Moral Argument and the War in Vietnam* (1971), by partisans ranging from Jean-Paul Sartre to Richard M. Nixon;

[†]Quoted in *ibid.*, p. 192.

Kenneth W. Thompson, *The Moral Issue in Statecraft: Twentieth Century Approaches and Problems* (1966); and Oliver A. Johnson, *Moral Knowledge* (1966).

Reinhold Niebuhr's *Moral Man and Immoral Society; A Study in Ethics and Politics* (1932) had an extraordinary influence among political "realists," helping, for example, to give philosophic direction to Arthur M. Schlesinger, Jr. Felix E. Oppenheim's *Moral Principles in Political Philosophy* (1968) had less, but repays reading. New efforts to face the question of morality in a shoreless universe include Bernard Gert's *The Moral Rules: A New Rational Foundation for Morality* (1970).

5. Women

Ultimately, it may seem wiser for would-be Progressives to recognize that women have always been a momentous factor in American life, and so recognized, rather than to imagine them as crawling out of dark caverns into light. Such compilations as Grace Greenwood's *Eminent Women of the Age; being narratives of the lives and deeds of the most prominent women of the age* (1868), a 628 page compilation employing male and female biographers; and Phebe Ann Hanaford's *Daughters of America, or Women of the Century* (1883), in 730 pages, are calculated to give a sense of scope to female achievement. The Edward T. James edited *Notable American Women 1607–1950* (1971), which took a dozen years to complete, suggests the dimensions of women's freely-acknowledged contribution, and by males as much as by females. Women were as progressive and unprogressive as their male counterparts, and for personal or political motives. The spinster Elizabeth Peabody founded kindergartens for the children she did not herself have; see Louise Hall Tharp's *The Peabody Sisters of Salem* (1950). Dorothea Dix's career, which could use further analysis — see Francis Tiffany's *Life of Dorothea Lynde Dix* (1891) — involved her needs as well as those of prison and asylum inmates. Clara Barton was as much a self-promoter as she was an *Angel of the Battlefield* (1956), as others beside the author Ishbel Ross termed her.

Maria Weston Chapman is immortal by reason of her declaration during the Boston antiabolitionist riot of 1835: "If this be the last outpost of freedom, then we might as well die here as anywhere." But Chapman was more a maverick than a reformer, and as a fanatical follower of William Lloyd Garrison rates more as a radical than a Progressive.

Most promising in the latter category were formidable women who emerged to fight for suffrage. They seemed radical in pre-Civil War reform days, but asked no more than the right to contribute to public consensus. Like Lucy Stone, they began with temperance and abolition, but gravitated toward the suffrage argument, producing such spokeswomen as Elizabeth Cady Stanton and Susan B. Anthony. Stanton, *et al.*, *The History of Woman*

Suffrage (1881–1922), in six massive volumes, tells much of their story in raw, undifferentiated materials, but needs to be qualified by Alice Stone Blackwell's *Lucy Stone* (1930), to whom the larger history was unfair. Eleanor Flexner's *Century of Struggle* (1959) is a reasonable overview of the subject. More knowledge of the background of women as social and political figures could have added a sense of proportion to more recent woman's rights developments, but intemperateness and forgetfulness are far from being un-American traits.[4]

6. Women as Progressives and Unprogressives

Women were individuals, perhaps more than they were self-consciously women. Rheta Childe Dorr's *A Woman of Fifty* (1924) was of interest, if only because she was more than fifty, though much more because she pioneered the study of the needs of women in an industrial age in her *What Eight Million Women Want* (1910). Mary A. Livermore's *The Story of My Life* (1899) was most useful, if only because Mrs. Livermore, temperance advocate, suffragist, and platform speaker, was beyond the vanities of age. Many women found as much sustenance in progressive stances toward life as in "unprogressive" ones. Hallie Q. Brown's *Homespun Heroines* (1926) told of a variety of Negro women, intelligent, activist, who honored womanhood as well as humanity without manifesting assertive, sensational qualities of any kind.

Many women, white as well as black, stirred little interest in later propagandists; but whether this somehow demeaned or minimized them is doubtful. It is quite likely that unspectacular personalities, not useful to propaganda campaigns by reason of good looks or exhibitionist talents, did much or more for the wide variety of females and their male admirers, than did some of the adventurous ones.

Ruth E. Finley's *The Lady of Godey's* (1931) describes the career of Mrs. Sarah Josepha Hale, best remembered as creator of "Mary Had a Little Lamb," but better remembered as editor (or editress, as she would have said) of the most successful of women's magazines of her time, *Godey's Ladies' Book*, and author (or authoress) of *Women's Record: or, Sketches of All Distinguished Women. . . .* The latter received three editions with revisions by 1873 and displayed a gamut of female talents and personalities instructive to peruse.

There are numerous biographies and compilations of Margaret Fuller's career. Two basic ones would be her own posthumous *Woman in the Nineteenth Century* (1845), published as by Margaret Fuller Ossoli, and Mason Wade's *Margaret Fuller, Whetstone of Genius* (1940). Julia Ward Howe's *Margaret Fuller* (1883) is of interest in its own right as being by a later proponent of woman's suffrage and self-expression.

Lydia Maria Child was among the greatest of all American women of her time: writer, editor, and abolitionist. At the same time she had no interest in "woman's rights," being totally dedicated to her husband David Lee Child. Child was a man of great integrity and courage, a pioneer in beet growing, and with no practical sagacity of any kind. See her *Letters of Lydia Maria Child, with a Biographical Introduction by John Greenleaf Whittier*. . . (1883).

James and Lucretia Mott were so much one that to think of them separately as male and female militants would be invidious. These distinguished Quakers were wholly committed to free speech and freedom. They had little regard for self-expression in twentieth-century terms. Lucretia, for example, criticized the use of music at reform meetings. But their work for peace, woman's suffrage, and abolition made them the admired of all progressive forces of their time and after; see Anna D. Hallowell, ed., *James and Lucretia Mott, Life and Letters* (1884). As austere as the Motts were the Grimké sisters, Angelina and Sarah Moore Grimké, daughters of one of the most distinguished of South Carolina families, who came North to give their testimony against slavery and so caused a national sensation. Gerda Lerner's *The Grimké Sisters* (1967) gives them their due as pioneers of public speech for women.

Jane Grey Swisshelm's *Half a Century* (1880) told of her career as early journalist, editor, and abolitionist in Pittsburgh and the Minnesota frontier. Mrs. Swisshelm also recounted the frustrations of her married life, which she rationalized with distaste for the freedom of choice and self-expression. This is detailed in Helen B. Woodward's story of *The Bold Women* (1953): women who could be said to run the gamut from progressive to radical. Yuri Suhl's *Ernestine L. Rose and the Battle for Human Rights* (1959) and D. C. Bloomer's *Life and Writings of Amelia Bloomer* (1895) more distinctly deal with strong enough minded women who saw no gain in cutting themselves off from the larger society of their time, but who spoke and wrote in ways which influenced its opinion. Bloomer, in addition, with her invention of the loose trousers under a short petticoat, put her impress on fashion as well as language.

7. Ethnics, Including Southerners and Indians

We are a nation of minorities; there is no one group in America which is not separated by characteristics or tradition from others. We work to overcome the more abrasive aspects of the problem this condition creates, some of us strenuously, some of us not at all. But we need better to understand the roots of our dilemmas, and their potential for good and ill. All reformers, for example, were not tolerant of others; Ray A. Billington's *The Protestant Crusade 1800–1860* (1938) saw that some worthy Evangelicals were malicious toward Catholics, though they were compassionate toward enslaved Negroes. Nor were Catholics, harassed by Protestant mobs, always taught kindness toward free Negroes by their own bitter experience; see John Tracy Ellis's *American Catholicism* (1956) for a judicious statement of the case. Not infrequently their attitude was that of John Mitchel, himself an Irish hero and a fugitive from harsh British rule in Ireland, but who despised Negroes as being properly slaves; his story is told in *John Mitchel*, by Louis J. Walsh (1934). See also Carl Wittke, *The Irish in America* (1956) and William V. Shannon, *The American Irish* (1963), as well as the lively *That Most Distressful Nation: The Taming of the American Irish (1972)* by Andrew M. Greeley.

Negro communities were necessarily tolerant of others, and essentially progressive in viewpoint, though also tolerant of rebels among them who were more bitter and separatist than Progressivism implied. James Forten, one of the great men of the early nineteenth century — his life is yet to be treated fully — urged constitutional guarantees for his fellow-Negro freemen. Yet the crisis condition which was the norm for all Negroes, whether free or slave, made them impatient with such stabilizing factors as law and order, patriotism, and nationalism, which true Progressives supported. Frederick Douglass's works, collected by Philip S. Foner (1950–1955), four volumes, are a monument to human courage and ingenuity, but lean toward the radical, rather than Progressive, tradition.

For writings on ante-Bellum Negroes which touch aspects of Progressivism, see Benjamin Quarles, *Black Abolitionists* (1969); Leon F. Litwack, *North of Slavery: The Negro in the Free States, 1790–1860* (1961); Charles H. Wesley, *Neglected History: Essays in Negro History by a College President* (1965); Carter G. Woodson, *The Mind of the Negro as Reflected by Letters Written during the Crisis, 1800–1860* (1926) and *Negro Orators and Their Orations* (1925); William C. Douglas, *Mr. Lincoln and the Negroes* (1963); William H. Pease, *Black Utopia: Negro Communal Experiments in America* (1964); Margaret Just Butcher, *The Negro in American Culture* (2nd ed., 1972).

Daniel A. Payne, bishop and builder of Wilberforce University in Ohio, was one of the greatest of his people, and his work bestrode the ante- and post-Civil War period; see his *Recollections of Seventy Years* (1888).

For an overview of Negro biography, see Carter G. Woodson and Charles H. Wesley, *The Negro in Our History* (1962 ed.).

Generally, ethnics in the pre-Civil War era tended toward radical or conservative attitudes as they struggled for a place in America. Abolitionists — mostly white, Protestant, and Anglo-Saxon in origin, and Whig — patronized the Negro. The Democrats under Andrew Jackson, made up of similar types but advocating more strongly separation of church and state, patronized the Irish, who repaid them with votes and bully boys at the Fire Department stations. See Herbert Asbury's *Ye Olde Fire Laddies* (1930). The Jackson political alliance, rude and opportunistic as it was, included more compromise, egalitarianism, and democratic opportunity than did the Whig groupings. The Whigs, however, could claim such idealists as Ralph Waldo Emerson, and such advocates of freedom as Governor William H. Seward of New York, later Secretary of State under President Lincoln, in politics.

Paradoxically, the Jackson alliance included the slaveholding class of the South.

It needs, however, to be noted that the South contributed its share to the growing progressive tradition, not only through its Jeffersonian and Jacksonian traditions, but through persons and tendencies which kept open its options for change. Clement Eaton's *Freedom of Thought in the Old South* (1940) argues that though the South had limitations on freedom, so did other sections, and that the South's history showed social achievement and promise. Also illuminating are Howard R. Floan, *The South in Northern Eyes, 1831–1861* (1958); William H. Nicholls, *Southern Tradition and Regional Progress* (1960); Lewis H. Blair (1834–1916), *The Prosperity of the South Dependent upon the Elevation of the Negro* (1889); Virginius Dabney, *Liberalism in the South* (1932); Wilma Dykeman, *Prophet of Plenty: The First Ninety Years of W. D. Weatherford* (1966); and Dykeman and James Stokely, *Seeds of Southern Change: Life of Will Alexander* (1962).

Other writings revealing the freedom and equality impulse in southern life include Isaac D. Seabrook (1855–1928), *Before and After: Or, the Relations of the Races at the South* (1967); and Charles E. Wynes, ed., *Forgotten Voices: Dissenting Southerners in an Age of Conformity* (1967).

Also helpful in understanding the complex southern people and their development are Charles Greer Sellers, Jr., ed., *The Southerner as American* (1960), composed of contemporary essays, and the well-written essays of Grady McWhiney, *Southerners and Other Americans* (1973).

Indians were a striking minority in that they had been made "immigrants" on their own land. Living separately, and subject to superior and exploitative forces, it was difficult for the numerous tribes to combine or build a progressive tradition. This therefore had to be done for them. Outstanding was Thomas L. McKenney, first superintendent of the Bureau of Indian Affairs (1824–1830), who negotiated Indian treaties, wrote of Indians in his *Memoirs, Official and Personal* (1846), and professed to be concerned for Indian welfare. Although skeptics saw McKenney as merely smoothing the road for the expulsion of Indians from tribal lands, he studied them and elucidated their points of view. Henry R. Schoolcraft (1793–1864) studied their ways and himself married a girl with Chippewa heritage. His promotion of Indian studies and his own numerous writings regarding them, such as *Notes on the Iroquois* (1847) and *Personal Memories of. . .Thirty Years with the Indian Tribes* (1851), were invaluable to Indian friends. (Both Schoolcraft and McKenney also published portraits of Indians which are priceless for what they preserve of earlier civilization.)

Most scholars of the progressive tradition prefer to honor Helen Hunt Jackson's "muckraking" in behalf of Indians, notably her *A Century of Dishonor* (1881) which surveys our betrayed treaties, and her novel *Ramona* (1884), a tale of treachery toward California Indians.

Studies of Indian-white relations include Georgiana C. Nammack, *Fraud, Politics, and the Dispossession of the Indians: The Iroquois Land Frontier in the Colonial Period* (1969); Jacob P. Dunn, Jr., *Massacres of the Mountains, a History of the Indian Wars of the Far West 1815–1875* (1886), which treats Indians as fighters; Loring Benson Priest, *Uncle Sam's Stepchildren: The Reformation of United States Indian Policy, 1865–1887* (1942); Robert W. Mardock, *The Reformer and the American Indian* (1971).

Francis P. Prucha, ed., in *Americanizing the American Indians* (1973), treats the "Friends of the Indians" who in the period 1880–1900 sought to assimilate them into the general population. They failed, and Prucha sees this as proper, since the "Friends" had not taken Indian preferences into account.[5]

Elements of Progressivism could be identified in all ethnic groups, but became significant as they reached *beyond* particular groups and influenced the larger society. For an examination of twenty-five different social ingredients, see Jack F. Kinton's *American Ethnic Groups and the Revival of Cultural Pluralism: A Sourcebook for the 1970's* (2nd ed., 1973). See also Theodore L. Gross, ed., *A Nation of Nations: Ethnic Literature in America* (1971) and Robert E. Park, *The Immigrant Press and Its Control* (1922), showing the relationship between immigrants' communication and the larger social purposes which muckrakers and others proposed.[6]

8. Gentility

This factor in American life seemed to become a victim of the popular enthusiasms which Progressivism encouraged, and to some extent it was. The Progressive novelist David Graham Phillips said he had given up use of "lady" and "gentleman" because of the company into which they had fallen. Theodore Roosevelt believed his genteel class had resigned from public service, but that he was determined to be socially effective. Despite his "strenuous" approach he can be counted as partisan to ladies and gentlemen and as one who worked for their traditional values. The high point of Progressivism was dominated by one who, despite his homely anecdotes and wit was totally a gentleman: Dr. Woodrow Wilson of Princeton University.

The genteel reformers looked forward to the rule of the "best," and they are scorned for that reason by John G. Sproat, in his *"The Best Men": Liberal Reformers in the Gilded Age* (1968). Nevertheless, gentility produced such notables as Henry Adams, Dorman B. Eaton, and E. L. Godkin. Adams was a critic of hard-driving and unscrupulous railroad tycoons, Eaton was of the foremost founders of the American civil service, and E. L. Godkin created in the New York *Nation* a keen intellectual publication for assessing national events.

Gentility produced one of the greatest of all reformers of the time, Josephine Shaw Lowell, young widow of the Civil War hero Charles Russell Lowell, who dedicated herself to work for the poor and delinquent, especially women. Over the years she all but modernized social work with her reports and organizing abilities, herself growing from concern for purposeful giving and rehabilitation techniques to an understanding that industrial-labor relations required drastic overhauling; see her *Public Relief and Preventive Charity* (1884), as compared to her *Industrial Arbitration and Conciliation: Some Chapters from the Industrial History of the Past Thirty Years* (1893). See also Frank Dekker Watson's *The Charity Organization Movement in the United States: A Study in American Philanthropy* (1922). Mrs. Lowell profoundly influenced the workings of this organization. See also William Rhinelander Stewart, ed., *The Philanthropic Work of Josephine Shaw Lowell* (1911), which collected her major papers, and *In Memoriam: Josephine Shaw Lowell* (1906).

Others contributed notably to closing the gap of misunderstanding between the genteel and the poor: a necessary preliminary before further work could be undertaken. A broad survey of developments is included in Robert M. Bremner's *From the Depths: The Discovery of Poverty in the United States* (1956). Jane Addams, founder of the Hull-House Settlement in Chicago contributed with six others to a valuable symposium, *Philanthropy and Social Progress* (1893). Their work led to new stages of inquiry in such a career as Mary E. Richmond's, who learned to deal with family and group predicaments, and then with those of individuals. See Richmond's *The Good Neighbor in the Modern City* (1907) and her later *What Is Social Case Work* (1922), the latter book prepared for the Russell Sage Foundation.

A typical genteel reformer of substance and achievement was the editor Richard Watson Gilder, whose daughter Rosamond edited his *Letters* (1916). Gilder interested himself in the poor, in their housing, and in civil service (1896–1900), all of which served New York City well.

The genteel reformers were stronger as critics of democracy than as augmenters of democracy. But to the extent that democracy needed criticism and curbs, they served it. They were balanced among Progressives by such others as Robert M. La Follette of Wisconsin and William Jennings Bryan of Nebraska, who made no fetish of elite leadership. But together they emphasized public service, moral leadership, and patriotism for newer democracy-inspired approaches.

Ari Hoogenboom, in *Outlawing the Spoils* (1961), surveys the genteel fight for civil service, giving a scholarly dimension to the account by one of the participants, William Dudley Foulke's *Fighting the Spoilsmen* (1919). See also Ari and Olive Hoogenboom, eds., *The Gilded Age* (1967). Allan Nevins in *Abram S. Hewitt: With Some Account of Peter Cooper* (1935), treats another outstanding genteel reformer, as does Gerald Kurland, author of *Seth Low* (1971), a president of Columbia University and mayor of New York who furnishes a transition from gentility to Progressivism.

The fight for "clean" city government was a genteel fight for the most part, and passed on directly to the Progressives. It was satirized, as in Sproat's *"The Best Men,"* mentioned before, as sanctimonious, giving the workers nothing when they needed help for jobs, for evading the law, and for cheating at the polls. Such help the political bosses provided. Harold Zink, *City Bosses in the United States* (1930) describes the city political machine and its functioning. Zane L. Miller, in *Boss Cox's Cincinnati: Urban Politics in the Progressive Era* (1968), describes one such organization. William L. Riordan's *Plunkitt of Tammany Hall* (1905) is a classic statement by a city machine politician of his "philosophy" and actions. Seymour J. Mandelbaum's *Boss Tweed's New York* (1964) all but applauds "Boss" William Marcy Tweed's "services" to New York, though they were steeped in personal and group fraud; compare Alexander B. Callow, Jr.'s *The Tweed Ring* (1966). It was the mission of the genteel reformers and their progressive successors to expose the corrupt base of machine politics so that at least they would become more modern and efficient.

William H. Tolman, in *Municipal Reform Movements in the United States* (1895), gives a sense of the causes and approaches clarified by the genteel reformers. Compare with Clifford W. Patton's retrospective *The Battle for Municipal Reform 1875–1900* (1940).

Numerous aspects of American life which involved the educated and refined were positively affected by them. One important career in the field is treated in Benjamin G. Rader's *The Academic Mind and Reform: The Influence of Richard T. Ely in American Life* (1966). Ely was an educator who wrote of the rights and needs of labor, and who fought effectively for academic freedom.

One of the significant charges against gentility was that it was a repressive force with respect to human and sexual relations. In fact, the attitudes it engrossed were more complex than is ordinarily realized, and involved idealism at least as much as an evasion of human feelings. Nevertheless, the latter appears in a barrage of criticism to be found in such works as John Tomsich, *A Genteel Endeavor: American Culture and Politics in the Gilded Age* (1971); Stow Persons, *The Decline of American Gentility* (1973); and, more specifically, Peter Schrag, *The Decline of the WASP* (1971).

David J. Pivar, *Purity Crusade, Sexual Morality and Social Control 1868–1900* (1973) is limited by its failure to understand that a species of social control over this combustible factor in life was necessary to public information and aid to troubled and sick individuals. That the issue was distorted by bigots and others does not deny this fact. Those who made a heroine of Victoria C. Woodhull, "free lover" and demagogue, did not sufficiently appreciate that her public antics and patent unscrupulousness hurt their cause. See Johanna Johnston, *Mrs. Satan: The Incredible Saga of Victoria C. Woodhull* (1967) and M. M. Marberry, *Vicky* (1967), another version of the Woodhull story.

At least some of Thorstein Veblen's life and work indirectly is critical of gentility. It is also, however, critical of other traditions. Veblen was a maverick, whose independence and private attitudes served several traditions, including Progressivism; see Joseph Dorfman's classic *Thorstein Veblen and His America* (1934), and also the Dorfman edited *Essays, Reviews and Reports: Previously Uncollected Writings of Thorstein Veblen* (1973).

9. Christian Socialism and Associated Reforms

Not unrelated to gentility, though separated from it was the role of the so-called Christian Socialists, to whom a church militant, a church concerned for temporal sorrows was important. They deplored violence in labor disputes, urged mediation, but above all called on the public to act as they believed Christ would have acted in social crises. An inadequately used masterwork of the time is W. D. P. Bliss's *Encyclopedia of Social Reform* (1897, 1908, 1909–1910 editions), which contains masses of information explaining the goals of Christian Socialists. See also Bliss's *Handbook of Socialism* (1895). Although emphasizing spirituality over economics, the Christian Socialists were a half-way house for both post-Civil War reformers and socialists. Reverend George D. Herron made a sensation in the 1890s as a Christian Socialist and in the next decade became a Socialist. John R. Commons was an academic who wrote, edited, or directed important works on labor and immigration; his autobiographical *Myself* (1934) expresses his humanism as well as his contributions. See James Dombrowski, *The Early Days of Christian Socialism in America* (1936); Charles Howard Hopkins, *The Rise of the Social Gospel in American Protestantism, 1865–1915* (1940); Henry F. May, *Protestant Churches and Industrial America* (1949).

Distinguished reformers had the Christian Socialist's approach without their make-shift solutions. Henry George was not only the creator of the Single Tax concept, with its effect on all budgets, city, state, and national; he was also a keen critic of all social inequities. His run for mayor of New York in 1886 and again in 1897 was one of many such challenges which prevented crime overlords and their aides from solidifying power. His son Henry George, Jr.'s biography of him (1904) still repays reading. Like George, and the Christian Socialists, Edward Bellamy also saw no difference between his economic solutions to poverty and oppression and human and religious feelings. Arthur E. Morgan's *Edward Bellamy* (1944) traces the roots of the ideas which made Bellamy's *Looking Backward* (1888), a work of fiction, one of the reform sensations of his time and after.

Such figures not only contributed reform ideas to the gathering Progressive program; they furnished inspiration to hundreds of others who went on to create programs of their own. George was especially fortunate in his disciples, who included Tom L. Johnson of Cleveland. Johnson won acclaim as the best mayor in the country, thanks to his broad program for serving the whole city and to the banner corps of remarkable aides who served him in his work.

Johnson, George, Bliss, and numerous others grappled with the problem of how to preserve regard for law and order, while not passing by human conditions which required drastic change. They did not always succeed in their aim, but they built toward better social structures and achieved some palpable results. The methods which they refined, though no doubt needing modern implementation, can still serve responsible students of human nature and human circumstances — still serve a society which cannot have enough agencies and ideas for mediating its disputes.

For a sense of the turbulence caused among religious reformers by the Darwinian hypothesis see George Daniels, ed., *Darwinism Comes to America* (1968) and R. J. Wilson, ed., *Darwinism and the American Intellectual* (1967). See also Paul A. Carter, *The Spiritual Crisis of the Gilded Age* (1971) and Orvin Larson, *American Infidel: Robert G. Ingersoll* (1962).

Washington Gladden was one of the most esteemed of Christian Socialists; see Jacob H. Dorn, *Washington Gladden, Prophet of the Social Gospel* (1968). Gladden's own *Recollections* (1909) reflects the tone of genteel hopes of social cooperation, as does his *Tools and the Man: Property and Industry under the Christian Law* (1893).

Audiovisual Aids

1. *America,* questions the "American dream", MAGNUM; *Roger Williams — Founder of Rhode Island,* EBEC; *Social Class in America,* MAGNUM.
2. *The Jackson Years — the New Americans* and *The Jackson Years — Toward Civil War,* AZRELA; *Andrew Jackson at the Hermitage,* CORF.
3. *Progress* and *The Meaning of Democracy,* NET; *Social Reform Movements,* EAV.
4. *Women on the March,* NFBC; *American Woman in the 20th Century,* WOLPER; *Susan B. Anthony,* EBEC.
5. *End of the Trail: The American Plains Indian,* TFC; *Trail of Tears,* NET; *Due Process of Law Denied,* TFC, an excerpt for classroom use of the feature-length *The Ox Bow Incident,* FOX.
6. *Immigration in American History,* CORF; *America — the Melting Pot,* HEARST; *Island Called Ellis,* MGHF; *Immigration in the 19th Century* and *Immigration in the 20th Century,* WOLPER.

11

Progressivism

1. Background and Bibliography

So complex a development as Progressivism, which involved social adjustments as well as pragmatic needs, can use broad and imaginative materials for full comprehension. Seymour Drescher's *Tocqueville and Beaumont on Social Reform* (1968), dealing as it does with poverty and industry, crime and reformation, slavery, and protest voices, is evocative, enabling the reader to contrast twentieth-century conditions with those the French visitors observed in Jackson's time. James Bryce's equally classic *The American Commonwealth* (1888) similarly stirs the mind to fresh interpretations of old materials. Arthur E. Morgan's *Nowhere was Somewhere: How History Makes Utopias and How Utopias Make History* (1946) is extraordinary in finding relations between "utopias" and practical affairs, and reminds us that no movement advances which does not dream of improvements. Charles Albro Barker's *Henry George* (1955) loses its subject in compendiousness, but can speak to many questions of reader concern, properly thumbed. Louis Filler, *A Dictionary of American Social Reform* (1963; new printing 1969) covers overall reform ground, while Thomas H. Greer, *American Social Reform Movements: Their Pattern since 1865* (1949) suggests one of many patterns.[1]

Filler's *Appointment at Armageddon: Muckraking and Progressivism in the American Tradition* (1976) seeks the roots of movements which have appeared under different names from the first crystallizations of American social relations. In its reassessment of muckraking and Progressivism in their classic era it offers wholly new materials, as well as takes into account previous treatments.

Several brief bibliographies are helpful; see George E. Mowry, *The Progressive Movement* (1958), and Arthur S. Link and William M. Leary, Jr., *The Progressive Era and the Great War* (1969); the latter pamphlet gives no assessments, but lists more items than Mowry. Filler, *Crusaders for American Liberalism*, in 1964 and following editions, includes an essay, "Toward a Bibliography of Muckraking" which discusses a variety of themes and books intended to define this important aspect of Progressivism. (For further discussion of this subject, *see* Chapter II-15.)

Mark Sullivan's *Our Times, 1900-1925* (1927-1935) is a trap by a master journalist calculated to draw readers into involvement with all the major figures of the era. It furnishes an antidote to the numerous "theses" concocted by young doctoral candidates who are tempted to offer magisterial judgments beyond their limited sources. Sullivan's tale is mainly about people, whom he brings vividly to life.

Robert H. Wiebe's *The Search for Order, 1877-1920* (1967) exemplifies the specialized thesis approach to the turbulent events binding Populism and Progressivism. Certainly bitter enemies in labor and capital required surcease from struggle, and worked from opposite ends to attain it. However, a broader approach recognizes that social components in society had goals beyond those of security, and fought, and in some cases died for them, as later references will indicate.

Several general works won esteem as efforts to grasp Progressivism whole. Eric F. Goldman, in *Rendezvous with Destiny* (1952), made little distinction between Muckraker-Progressives and, for example, Herbert Croly, who pointedly disapproved of the muckrakers as sentimentalists who believed in "the people." Richard Hofstadter's influential *The Age of Reform* (1955) was critical of the reformers as having too limited objectives, and concentering on old native stock rather than on the children of the "new immigration." Although Hofstadter's work was in secondary sources, readers found his thesis stimulating. Mowry's *The Era of Theodore Roosevelt 1900-1912* (1958) and Link's *Woodrow Wilson and the Progressive Era* (1954) cover political aspects of the time. Ray Ginger's *Age of Excess* (1965) is opinionated, but read along with more temperate writings, has challenging ideas.

John Chamberlain's *Farewell to Reform* (1932) is a curiosity, having been issued as a "left wing" survey of the Populist-Progressive period, impatient with its democratic goals, eager to get on with revolutionary perspectives. In due course, its author turned "right wing," but does not seem to have struggled to put his disparate views into one framework; see Filler, "John Chamberlain and American Liberalism," *Colorado Quarterly*, Autumn, 1957.[2]

2. Works for Orientation

A number of writings in the Progressive time and after sought to grasp its meaning: to perceive differences between the old time and the new, as well as the time which succeeded the heyday of Progressivism.

Edward L. Youmans believed fervently in popular education and science as capable of transforming human life. He founded the *Popular Science Monthly* as a means for achieving this end. His *The Culture Demanded by Modern Life: A Series of Addresses and Arguments on the Claims of Scientific Education* (1867) was a prophesy of what became one of the goals of Progressivism and its cultural adjunct, muckraking. William James also linked his investigations in psychology to public need, as spelled out in his *The Will to Believe, and Other Essays in Popular Philosophy* (1897).

Overall views of the intellectual conditions in which the Progressive attitude was nurtured include Merle Curti, *The Social Ideas of American Educators*

(1934) which includes discussions of William James and John Dewey; Morton G. White, *Social Thought in America: The Revolt against Formalism* (1949). An important book is W. Jett Lauck, *Political and Industrial Democracy 1776–1926* (1926) which emphasized efforts to curb competition in favor of cooperative relations between labor and industry.

Two works by historians during the Progressive era help show its relationship to the academic scene: Paul L. Haworth, *America in Ferment* (1915), and Charles A. Beard, *Contemporary American History, 1877–1913* (1914). An analysis of their viewpoint, not wholly sympathetic, can be found in Richard Hofstadter's *The Progressive Historians* (1968). See also David W. Noble's *The Paradox of Progressive Thought* (1958), which sees Progressives as following contradictory tenets, and Henry Steele Commager's *The American Mind* (1950) which is more tolerant of their alleged confusions.

John Dewey was far ahead of all others as the philosopher of Progressivism. His pragmatic tenets, his emphasis on action linked to goals, exactly defined the progressive spirit. Serving as inspirations were such books of his as *Moral Principles in Education* (1909), *Democracy and Education* (1916), and *Schools of Tomorrow* (1915), the latter written with Evelyn Dewey. William Wirt of the Gary, Indiana school system seemed to personify the Deweyan tenets; see Wirt's *Newer Ideals in Education* (1912) and Randolph Bourne's *The Gary Schools* (1916). *Characters and Events, Popular Essays in Social and Political Philosophy* (2 vols., 1929), edited by Joseph Ratner, offers a selection of Dewey's essays and shows the growth of his thought.

Also vital to progressive unfoldings was Thorstein Veblen, whose *The Theory of the Leisure Class: An Economic Study of Institutions* (1899) struck a forceful blow against nineteenth-century moral and intellectual presumptions. Veblen, as already noted, was not so much a Progressive as he was an outsider whose alien status showed him deficiencies in the social pattern requiring adjustment. In addition to Joseph Dorfman's masterly *Thorstein Veblen and His America* (1934), see David Riesman's *Thorstein Veblen* (1953) which provides more modern insights.

Modern appraisals of the Progressive era have not yet fully come to grips with one another, and have thus reflected the confusion which contemporary Americans feel on the subject. A number of views help perspective. Daniel Levine's *Varieties of Reform Thought* (1964) finds different principles interested well-known leaders of the earlier time. Oscar Cargill's *Intellectual America* (1941) focuses as few studies have on the cultural and literary aspects of the time.

Harold U. Faulkner, a well-esteemed historian of the era, in his *The Decline of Laissez-Faire, 1897–1917* (1951), sees the problem of interpretations in the changing social pattern as does, in more popular vein, Frederick Lewis Allen in *The Big Change: America Transforms Itself 1900–1950* (1952); see also Lloyd R. Morris's *Postscript to Yesterday* (1947) and his *Not So Long Ago* (1949).

Several writings directly challenged the validity of progressive thought and action. Albert C. Ganley's *The Progressive Movement, Traditional Reform* (1964) struck a note for those impatient for new social revelations. The accusation that Progressives thought themselves modern but were in fact looking back nostalgically to what they imagined had been a better time, was well known to the Progressives themselves and angered them. As one of them, Brand Whitlock, put it in a bitter comment on John Chamberlain's *Farewell to Reform* (1932), which treated Progressives in a derogatory vein:

> It seems to me that Chamberlain makes a straw man for the pleasure of knocking him down and putting him out. In those days Tom Johnson of Cleveland and Newton Baker and I and a lot of others were engaged in a struggle to bring about better conditions in the State of Ohio, and we weren't such damn fools as Chamberlain seems to think us. We had no idea of restoring agrarian democracy, and we were perfectly aware of the fact that industrialism had come and had come to stay. We were chiefly fighting local political machines, for in all our cities the Republican machines and the Democratic machines were working together and fooling all of the people all the time. And we did succeed in breaking them up, at least temporarily, and in amending the Constitution of the State, so as to provide home rule and non-partisan government for the cities. And incidentally we did accomplish a few other things.*

Carl Resek's *The Progressives* (1967) provides a useful spectrum of the era's achievements, from the literary revaluations (many controversial) in Vernon L. Parrington's *Main Currents in American Thought*, (3 vols., 1927–1930) to the work of the lawyer Roger Baldwin for the American Civil Liberties Union. Resek's book includes the labors of Margaret Sanger whose *My Fight for Birth Control* (1931) memorialized one of the brave battles of the 1910s and after. *The Progressive Era: Liberal Renaissance or Liberal Failure?* (1965), edited by Arthur Mann, asks one of the most momentous questions of all regarding the era, but no more than opens the question it asks.

Harold U. Faulkner's *The Quest for Social Justice, 1898–1914* (1931) and his later *Politics, Reform, and Expansion 1890–1900* (1958) are well researched. Although Faulkner's cultural insights — so central to muckraking — were limited, they can be supplemented by reference to works more deeply concerned for publications and writers.

The great work in the field of magazines was Frank L. Mott's *A History of American Magazines* (4 vols., 1930–1957); also distinguished was Mott's *American Journalism: A History, 1690–1960* (3rd ed., 1962). See also his posthumous volume five (1968) which includes sections about such muckraking magazines as *McClure's*. Mott was partial to the "smiling" aspects of American life, and thus not wholly fair or even accurate respecting them. His bibliographical work, however, was strictly dependable and his point of view, once perceived,

---

*Quoted in introduction by Filler to *Forty Years of It*, by Brand Whitlock (Cleveland, 1970), p. ix.

did little harm. For a quick overview, see Robert A. Rutland's *The News-mongers: Journalism in the Life of the Nation 1690–1972* (1973).

Christopher Lasch, in *The New Radicalism in America 1889–1963* (1965) was highly tendentious, too firmly pinpointing reformers as "intellectuals" to accord with their actual lives. The book, however, raised the question of the role of thinkers and writers in America.

3. Theodore Roosevelt

No study of Progressivism can fail to give a primary place to Roosevelt and, as will be seen, to Woodrow Wilson. Indeed, they will ultimately gain by being seen together. The task of the present era is to compare their past reputations with their more recent ones, for a working assessment. Matthew Josephson, in *The President Makers, 1896–1919* (1940), though generally unsympathetic to his topic, provides a context in which assessments can be qualified. Roosevelt suffered a severe loss in prestige thanks to his uncompromising nationalism, which was treated cynically in the 1920s and beyond. But readers of his *Autobiography* (1913) are likely to be struck by the vigor and many-sidedness which impressed his generation. Elting E. Morison and John M. Blum, eds., *The Letters of Theodore Roosevelt* (8 vols., 1951–1954) is formidable in the scope the work reveals of his activities and sharp handling of affairs. Henry F. Pringle's *Theodore Roosevelt* (1931) deserves to be read at length to appreciate how far Roosevelt's reputation has fallen. But Hermann Hagedorn's *The Roosevelt Family of Sagamore Hill* (1954), in heavily informed pages, catches the warmth and humanity of its subject as Pringle cannot.

Curiously, Pringle, having dethroned Roosevelt, proceeded to attempt to raise William Howard Taft to first-class stature in his *Life and Times* of Roosevelt's successor (1939). It seems unlikely that Pringle's version of the record can change their relative positions; it has failed to do so thus far.

Large modern efforts to view Roosevelt as an inevitable force in American society have helped to keep his image fluid and alive. George E. Mowry's *Theodore Roosevelt and the Progressive Movement* (1946) showed him as responsive to the premises of his age. William H. Harbaugh's *Power and Responsibility: The Life and Times of Theodore Roosevelt* (1961) saw the times in broader terms. Carleton Putnam's first volume of *Theodore Roosevelt, a Biography* (1958) — with more volumes promised — is remarkable in that it accepts Roosevelt's view of his class and kind as quite properly ruling the nation. Putnam's "racist" views of Roosevelt contrast with books which oppose that principle.

Roosevelt has distinctly lost prestige in connection with the so-called Brownsville (Texas) incident involving a shootout allegedly by Negro troops, for which they were dishonored by action of the President for failing to produce the culprits among them. Recent Army decisions reversing the more than sixty-year old event place Roosevelt in an invidious light; see the dramatically told *The Brownsville Raid* (1970) by John D. Weaver and Ann J. Lane's *The Brownsville Affair, National Crisis and Black Reaction* (1971).

Roosevelt's *Works* (20 vols., 1926) merit consultation on all issues which are later discussed. In general it will be seen that his effort to find a central position while asserting the authority of the President, though it harmed his prestige with elements of the "right" and the "left," suggests an attempt at balance which could be approved in principle.

On several issues his position has patently deteriorated. His aggressive faith in American expansionism, his notorious boast that he "took" the Panama Canal, his sending of the American fleet around the world in an exhibition of strength — all of these and more have curbed enthusiasm for Roosevelt and Progressivism. Such books as the following help spell out Roosevelt's ambitions and diplomacy: Howard K. Beale, *Theodore Roosevelt and the Rise of America to World Power* (1956); Tyler Dennett, *Roosevelt and the Russo-Japanese War* (1925); Robert A. Hart, *The Great White Fleet: Its Voyage around the World, 1907–1909* (1965); Dwight C. Miner, *The Fight for the Panama Route* (1940); Thomas A. Bailey, *Theodore Roosevelt and the Japanese-American Crises* (1934); Raymond A. Esthus, *Theodore Roosevelt and Japan* (1966). The milieu in which he worked is made more evident through Thomas A. Bailey's *The Man in the Street: The Impact of American Public Opinion on Foreign Policy* (1948) and Roger Daniels's *The Politics of Prejudice: The Anti-Japanese Movement in California and the Struggle for Japanese Exclusion* (1962). Contrast between the progressive position and that of a distinguished figure on the "right" is furnished in Richard W. Leopold's *Elihu Root and the Conservative Tradition* (1954). No simple formula suffices for Roosevelt's imperialism. He adjudicated the Russo-Japanese War, but was the "aggressor" in Cuba, Colombia, and elsewhere, and can be sympathetically or coldly interpreted in both areas and roles. A summary work is David H. Burton's *Theodore Roosevelt, Confident Imperialist* (1968).

Raymond A. Esthus's *Theodore Roosevelt and the International Rivalries* (1970) is especially useful because it enables the reader to judge Roosevelt relative to what other nations' leaders were doing. Roosevelt's policies are too often assessed against abstract ideals.[3]

4. Imperialism and Anti-Imperialism

It needs now to be recognized better than it has been that there were numerous American leaders proud of their Anglo-Saxon heritage and able to impart its riches in culture and traditions to newer immigrants without necessarily depriving them of their own. Imperialism has been seen invidiously, thanks to the deadly warnings implicit in the atom bomb; but it scarcely aids perspective not to accept the inevitable aspects of power, as exercised by Darwinians and imperialists. And it harms perspective to ignore the long and traditionalized labors of American peace advocates and anti-imperialists. Rubin F. Weston's *Racism in U. S. Imperialism* (1972) is a useful book, spelling out "the influence of racial assumptions on American Foreign Policy, 1893-1946." It even notes racialism in anti-imperialist attitudes, such as may be found in David Starr Jordan's *Imperial Democracy* (1899). Its limitation is that it does not to any extent probe the "racism" in Haitians, Cubans, Filipinos and others which would have made wholehearted rapport between Americans and others difficult. The uses and abuses of patriotism also merit attention as a factor in adequate analysis of imperialism; see John J. Pullen, *Patriotism in America: A Study of Changing Devotions, 1770-1970* (1971).

The topic of imperialism has been a blight on Progressivism and its accomplishments. This was mainly because events unforeseen and unforeseeable by inhabitants of the 1890s materialized and gave different — and complex — proportions to social and world events.

In 1890 the United States seemed separated from other nations by two vast oceans and two unthreatening nations to its south and north. Americans had a sense of possessing a democratic heritage unprecedented in history. They boasted that their slaves had eaten better than "free men" elsewhere. Their faith in their "manifest destiny" to take over the entire mainland of what became continental America, and at the expense of the relatively few and sparse Indian tribes, projected itself overseas in the minds of Chinese and South American Yankee traders. A major argument for imperialism was the fact that if Americans did not enter into the race for foreign markets, other nations would preempt all such opportunities.

The slight attention given the firm and continuous anti-imperialist tradition suggests weaknesses in modern pacifist and anti-American viewpoints. Anti-imperialism had taken the form of opposing war with Indian tribes, with Mexico, with Spain over Cuba (war had threatened in 1872), and with Chile in 1890; see Frederick B. Pike, *Chile and the United States, 1880-1962* (1963). Anti-imperialists had protested the American troop seizure of Hawaii in 1893, and had been joined in their strictures by then-President Grover Cleveland.

The anti-imperialist tradition continued during the second Cuban crisis which led to the Spanish-American War, and the subsequent Philippine War, and it continued as a peace crusade through the Progressive era. Its relative weakness was a comment on the spirit not only of the outspoken imperialists, but also of the era's pacifists. Walter Millis's *The Martial Spirit* (1931) was a bitter review of American foreign policy leading to and involving the Spanish-American War. Millis later continued his tale of American belligerency in *The Road to War* (1935), into what he clearly saw as the catastrophe of American intervention in World War I. It was, however, a remarkable fact that Millis later concluded that American participation in World War II was justifiable. Following the war he became a military analyst.

William D. Puleston in *Mahan, the Life and Work of Captain Alfred Thayer Mahan, U.S.N.* (1939) discusses one of the greatest of American imperialists, whose cause was a great Navy, without which overseas expansion was then an impossibility. Julius W. Pratt's *Expansionists of 1898* (1936) discusses the results of Mahan's and others' propaganda. Mahan had no interest in progressivist tenets, but Theodore Roosevelt, inseparable from Progressivism, was, as has been seen, at one with Mahan and others on America's need to show strength abroad or resign her greatness. See Gordon C. O'Gara's *Theodore Roosevelt and the Rise of the Modern Navy* (1943), and Chapter II-5.

Albert J. Beveridge, who fought for pure food and anti-child labor laws also believed in America's duty to show leadership and domination abroad; see Claude G. Bowers's *Beveridge and the Progressive Era* (1932). See also Beveridge, *The Russian Advance* (1903).

Remarkable in this connection was the attitude of the general public as compared with that of American commercial interests. In general business-men (as Roosevelt bitterly observed) opposed war. The military weakness of Spain was not realized, and war was feared as an adventure which could be catastrophic. Mark Hanna was opposed to war and could not stop war, though the Democratic press raged at him as having "bought" Indiana's votes for McKinley during the 1896 election. The public approved the decision for war, and elements of it gladly volunteered; the war of 1898 was wholly manned by volunteer troops.

A cliché of the 1930s had it that William Randolph Hearst "made" the war, but it is evident that no one was forced to read his papers. The *New York Post* opposed the war, but was patronized by fewer readers. Marcus M. Wilkerson's *Public Opinion and the Spanish-American War* (1932) and Joseph E. Wisan's *The Cuban Crisis as Reflected in the New York Press* (1934) are correctives to idle historical rumors.

Imperialism was defended philosophically as well as materially. Josiah Strong, in *Our Country* (1885), preached a patriotic and religious message to ready readers. See also Strong's *Expansion under New World Conditions* (1900). Albert R. Carman, in *Ethics of Imperialism* (1905), sought justification for imperialism in survival and altruistic tenets. But Oswald Garrison Villard's *Fighting Years* (1939) — a curious title for a pacifist's autobiography — is one influential liberal journalist's story of his efforts to impart sad and ugly facts to Americans. William B. Hixon, Jr.'s *Moorfield Storey and the Abolitionist Tradition* (1972) contributes importantly to the anti-imperialist saga. Storey became a founder of the National Association for the Advancement of Colored People. Warren F. Kuehl's *Hamilton Holt* (1960) contributes further to the tale, though Holt's major cause was peace.

It seems clear that Americans mixed social generosity with a belief that their presence brought progress to the nations they brought into their sphere. The historian Allan Nevins told the present writer that the American victory over yellow fever in itself justified the United States assault on Spanish Cuba. The medical triumph was certainly a memorable event which ought never to be forgotten. Whether imperialism would ever recapture any of the glory which it once claimed by simple arts of war and production of heroes was uncertain in 1976. What was certain was that, for better or worse, imperialism and Progressivism were related.

Both may be traced before the events of the 1890s, as in David M. Pletcher, *The Awkward Years: American Foreign Relations under Garfield and Arthur* (1962). Events of the later decade are unfolded in David F. Healy, *United States Expansionism* (1970) and H. Wayne Morgan, *America's Road to Empire* (1965). Jaundiced views of American policy are contained in William Appleman Williams, *The Contours of American History* (1961) and James Weinstein and David W. Eakins, eds., *For a New America: Essays in History and Politics from Studies on the Left 1959-1967* (1970). Herbert Ershkowitz examines *The Attitude of Business toward American Foreign Policy 1900-1916* (1967).

The title of Philip S. Foner's book, *The Spanish-Cuban-American War and the Birth of American Imperialism, 1895-1902* (2 vols., 1972), furnishes a key to its contents. Garel A. Grunder and William E. Livezey's *The Philippines and the United States* (1951) is less tendentious in its premises. See also *American Imperialism and the Philippine Insurrection* (1969), edited by Henry F. Graff, which interestingly reproduces testimony before the United States Senate Committee on the Philippines in 1902.

A contemporary account by a noted journalist of the time reflects one aspect of popular opinion to which he catered, and which anti-imperialists had to resist: Murat Halstead, *Pictorial History of America's New Possessions the Isthmian Canals and the Problem of Expansion. . .Porto Rico, Cuba, Hawaii* [etc.]. . .*Giving the Story of the. . .Farmer Fathers, Who, with the Rifle, and the Axe, and the Plow, Moved West the Center of Population, and Made Necessary MORE LAND FOR THE PEOPLE. . .*(1898).

There is dramatic contrast between Halstead's florid narrative and that of one who became a leading muckraker, a constant friend of the Filipinos, and the biographer (with a Filipino associate) of one of their national heroes; see Charles Edward Russell and E. B. Rodriguez, *The Hero of the Filipinos, the Story of José Rizal, Poet, Patriot and Martyr* (1923).

Such works as Jerry Israel's *Progressives and the Open Door: America and China 1905-1921* (1971) need to multiply, so that we can hope to capture a full sense of the dimensions of Progressivism at home and abroad. This work not only summarizes the literature in the area, but offers a theory: that Americans, probably wrongly but with some sincere good intentions, tried to help build societies similar to their own abroad. The phenomenon of isolationism also merits investigation, and would profit from contrast with a study of a later period, Manfred Jonas's *Isolationism in America, 1935-1941* (1966). See also Selig Adler, *The Isolationist Impulse* (1957).[4]

5. The World Progressives Faced

It needs always to be recalled that "imperialism" is a word which has fallen from a once high estate. Ancient Romans were not ashamed of being imperialists; it was their pride and evidence of triumph. Disraeli did not arrange in secret for Great Britain to assume authority in India. He gave India to Queen Victoria to the accompaniment of rockets and cannon fired off around the British-dominated world.

No one now boasts of being an imperialist. And yet there are manifest efforts today, by major powers, to influence world affairs. It is evident that imperialism was not, in the 1890s, a uniform effort by advanced nations to crush primitive people, nor is anti-imperialism in the 1970s always a wholly philanthropic enterprise.

In short, it is necessary to understand the changing world in order accurately to assess the nations which compose it. Thus, the Boers of South Africa were, in the late 1890s, the heroes of anti-imperialism in their indubitably brave efforts to resist the efforts of British army units, which included then-young Winston Churchill, to foist British power upon the southern tip of Africa. Today, people around the world are critical of the Boers's descendents as being racists who are unwilling to grant certain human rights to descendents of the Negroes of their realm. The British, on the other hand, officially express their lack of sympathy with South Africa's apartheid policy.

Much of the future of Progressivism hinges on the breadth of vision which readers will bring to their reading of progressive writings. It is evident that the manner in which the progressive world is interpreted will contribute to final judgments.

Barbara Tuchman's *The Proud Tower: A Portrait of the World before the War 1890–1914* (1966) reflects the insights of the author's sensitive studies. Bernard Semmel's *Imperialism and Social Reform, English Imperial Thought 1895–1914* (1960) aids the comparative method necessary to appraising American deeds and dubieties of the time. See also William T. Stead's *The Americanization of the World* (1902). Stead was a prototypical English muckraker, who foresaw that America must become the major world power. He urged British union with the United States for mutual gain, which he saw as spiritual as well as material. John A. Hobson's *Imperialism: A Study* (1902) has the distinction of having influenced V. Lenin's own formulations.

Other overall studies include Milton Plesur's *America's Outward Thrust: Approaches to Foreign Affairs 1865–1890* (1971) which helps bridge the gap between our isolationist 1870s and 1880s and the more active era of the Nineties; Julius W. Pratt's *America's Colonial Experiment* (1950) which sees us positively as having governed and then given away power to nationalists; and

Edward McNall Burns's *The American Idea of Mission* (1957) which emphasizes philosophic approaches.

See also Milton Berman's *John Fiske, the Evolution of a Popularizer* (1961). We have already seen Fiske as a bugler for evolution and progress. These convictions made him a ready friend of imperialism.

Ernest R. May's *Imperial Democracy* (1961), like several other works mentioned earlier, helps us with descriptions of the attitudes of European and Asiatic statesmen. Walter La Feber's *The New Empire* (1963) emphasizes the economic factors which entered into our late 1890s imperialism.

Imperialists and anti-imperialists vied for public and governmental attention, and made points which sometimes met. Grover Cleveland, as President, in what seemed to be the interests of Hawaiian nationalism, denounced the arrogance of large nations when treating smaller ones without consideration. He grimly warned Great Britain against trying to force a land settlement on Venezuela. (Anti-imperialists interpreted the latter policy as an imperialist threat to resort to war, if United States "protected" nations were transgressed.) See Allan Nevins, ed., *Letters of Grover Cleveland, 1850–1908* (1933) which help readers make up their own minds on the meaning of these events. See also Sylvester K. Stephens, *American Expansion in Hawaii, 1852–1898* (1945).

Similarly, William James sought peace. Yet in his great essay, "A Moral Equivalent for War," first published in 1910, he praised militarism as the great preserver of our ideals of hardihood, and asserted that "life with no use for hardihood would be contemptible." See James, *Essays on Faith and Morals* (1943) for a sense of the complexity of James's thought.

Anti-imperialists with a faith in the American world destiny included Senator George F. Hoar, whose *Autobiography of Seventy Years* (2 vols., 1903) also told of his belief in the righteousness of the Civil War. His general view also applied to Carl Schurz, a German immigrant Republican who served in the Civil War and who became an outstanding American liberal and pre-Progressive; see his *Reminiscences,* edited by Frederic Bancroft and William A. Dunning (3 vols., 1908), and the Bancroft-edited *Speeches, Correspondence and Political Papers of Carl Schurz* (6 vols., 1913).

See also Archibald Colquhoun, *Greater America* (1904) and especially Professor Franklin H. Giddings, *Democracy and Empire* (1900). Both mix liberal stances with faith in the validity of expansion, and foreshadow the work of Herbert Croly (see Chapter II-23).

The overthrow by American troops of Filipino nationalists furnished favorite evidence to anti-imperialists who criticized the United States government and army policies. Murat Halstead's *Aguinaldo and His Captor: The Life Mysteries of Emilio Aguinaldo and Adventures and Achievements of General [Frederick] Funston* (1901) was an example of American journalism which assumed the virtues of American actions in the Philippine Islands. It bears mention that the Filipino national hero Aguinaldo himself later agreed that it was desirable for Americans to have established order in his native land; see General Emilio Aguinaldo and Vicente Abano Pacis, *A Second Look at America* (1957).

The Cuban War has been seen more disinterestedly than in Philip S. Foner's treatment (*see* Chapter II-4). See David F. Healy, *The United States in Cuba, 1898–1902* (1963). Frank Freidel's *The Splendid Little War* (1958) is a vivid account in words, photographs, and illustrations. Theodore Roosevelt's *The Rough Riders* (1899) was once appreciated as a classic account of the Cuban adventure by a major participant, and merits a modern rereading.

6. Rural and Urban Factors in Progressivism

Focusing accurately on the transition from Populism to Progressivism has been a major problem in the last several decades. Historians have been puzzled to decide whether either movement or both were more reactionary than truly progressive as they pored over religious attitudes of the past, political figures, and programs for meeting the needs of the poor and socially oppressed. Irvin G. Wyllie's *The Self-Made Man in America* (1954), for example, was intended to expose the hollowness of the American "myth." It may have done no more than retard understanding of the meaning of the self-made man in native ambitions and achievements.

Henry Nash Smith's *Virgin Land* (1950) overdid its analysis of the meaning of the frontier to Americans, but it did develop a method for interpreting their ambitions. A. Whitney Griswold's *Farming and Democracy* (1948) spoke knowledgeably to the question of whether the American farmer did or did not have something to contribute to progressive ideals.

The basic problem has been that the farmer and the city person have been unwarrantedly separated by academics as national components. In fact, both have had marked influence on the other, first when the farmer constituted a majority of the population and next when about the turn of the century, the shift to the city became unmistakable. Farmer ideals weighed heavily on the rising labor movement's dreams, and in turn, city prospects influenced the gathering "farm bloc": too small to win elections, but large enough to determine their results.

To note the interrelationship of rural and urban attitudes, compare Nathan Fine, *Labor and Farmer Parties in the United States 1828–1928* (1928), and Arthur Mann, *Yankee Reformers in the Urban Age* (1954). See also Ray Ginger, *Altgeld's America: The Lincoln Ideal versus Changing Realities* (1958). Not unrelated to those changing realities were religious inclinations which created some antagonisms between the heavily Protestant rural areas and the more mixed denizens of towns, but less than is often imagined; see William R. Hutchison, ed., *American Protestant Thought: The Liberal Era* (1968).

The problem is to see the changing times whole and to take partisan theses with a grain of salt. Margaret Leech's rich *In the Days of McKinley* (1959) is an antidote to tight, constricted, often prejudiced interpretations of the changing American countryside. Arthur Meier Schlesinger's masterly *The Rise of the City 1878-1898* (1933) puts its subject in balanced relief.

Populism proper will be considered in the section following this one. However, it may here be noted that Paul W. Glad's *McKinley, Bryan, and the People* (1964) paints a picture which is far from the stereotypes of gawky farmers and surly city folk. William Jennings Bryan's *The First Battle* (1897), though overly-optimistic, reveals him as speaking to the entire nation, rather than a limited constituency. Donald L. McMurry's *Coxey's Army: A Study of the Industrial Army Movement of 1894* (1929) describes the effects of the fierce economic collapse of 1893 upon all the sections of the nation, whether rural or urban.

Theodore Saloutos, ed., *Populism: Reaction or Reform?*(1968) speaks lucidly to the question of how to interpret the "farmer's" program for social and economic progress; the reader may judge how much it was a farmer's program and how much a contribution to national stability. *A Populist Reader* (1966), edited by George B. Tindall, gives a full-bodied account of the movement's divisions.

Certainly there were cities with problems distinctly their own. Stephen Smith's *The City that Was* (1911) is all but shocking in its account of the degradation suffered by elements of the city population, thanks to the greed and ignorance of their "boss" leaders. Although Reverend Charles H. Parkhurst's *Our Fight with Tammany* (1895) did not see deeply into the causes of urban malaise, it did reveal the elements of vice, municipal corruption, and inadequate police measures which Progressives were soon to take in hand.

A number of studies survey the rise of the city in large terms of process and necessity: Blake McKelvey, *The Urbanization of America, 1860-1915* (1963); Charles Glaab and A. Theodore Brown, *A History of Urban America* (1967), and Glaab, ed., *The American City: A Documentary History* (1963). Early in the twentieth century, it appeared that the future was with the city, and that its troubles no more than attended its inevitable growth and organization. Reverend Josiah Strong's *The Twentieth Century City* (1898) attacked the "materialism" engendered by urban conditions. Strong was to be made notorious by historians for his mixture of religion and imperialist goals. Nevertheless, his call for a *new patriotism* of civic good might deserve a second look in our own time.

Almont Lindsey's *The Pullman Strike* (1942) is illuminating because it took place in what was intended to have been a model town. Its failure to satisfy the workers who were supposed to have been grateful to its founder, the railroad magnate George F. Pullman, turned attention to basic principles of legitimate city growth. Henry David's *History of the Haymarket Affair* (1936) — the explosion of a bomb among police in 1886, as a result of a major strike in Chicago, for which four accused were hanged and others sentenced to prison — also highlighted urban troubles.

Efforts to improve conditions were constant, but goals were harder to establish. Thus, Mark Hanna, Cleveland industrialist and Republican party leader, premised a rough and tough world in which the strongest survived. Many who agreed with him were not, however, willing to go so far as Hanna in letting the cities proliferate as they would. They respected reform and reformers, though uncertain how far they were willing to have their personal prerogatives curbed. Interesting as being not by a dedicated reformer but by a generous-minded urbanite is "Mul" [William H. Muldoon], *Mark Hanna's "Moral Cranks" and — Others. A Study of To-day* (1900). "Mul" wrote for the *Brooklyn Eagle*, and in his book defended Christian Socialists and municipal reformers of the 1890s who were seeking to organize movements for controlling the poor services and waste which attended the rule of the political machines.

The modernization of the city was one of the great achievements of 1900s Progressivism, but several works may be mentioned here to indicate aspects of the field. Edward W. Bemis, who had been a professor at the University of Chicago and was courageously interested in reform — for which he was deprived of his position — edited a work on *Municipal Monopolies* (1899), in which he argued for municipal ownership of public utilities. Tom L. Johnson stopped manipulating public franchises through special influence and bribes to become the progressive mayor of Cleveland; see Elizabeth J. Hauser, ed., *My Story*, by Tom Johnson (1911). Frederic C. Howe became famous as a Progressive and student of urban configurations and plans for dealing adequately with them, as in his *The Modern City and Its Problems* (1915). For an example of the ebb and flow of reform — a process which all Progressives faced — see Jean L. Stinchcombe, *City Politics in Toledo* (1968).

In time the city expanded and then accreted new problems which threatened its very existence. The beginnings of this process may be observed in such a study as Samuel B. Warner, Jr.'s *Streetcar Suburbs: The Process of Growth in Boston, 1870–1900* (1962). See also Robert L. Branyan and Lawrence H. Larsen, eds., *Urban Crisis in Modern America* (1971).

7. From Populism to Progressivism

Movements rarely arise from nowhere, and when occasionally they do, they hasten as best they can to establish their legitimate descent from some preferred ancestry. Populism has no such problem in a land which was wholly agricultural at its inception. A number of books readily underscore this fact from various standpoints; see, for example, H. C. Hubbart, *The Older Middle West, 1840–1880* (1934), which treats of a region identified somewhat inaccurately with the farmers' complaints; William Bennett Bizzell, *The Green Rising, an Historical Survey of Agrarianism* (1926); Fred A. Shannon, *The Farmer's Last Frontier, 1860–1897* (1945); and Russel B. Nye, *Midwestern Progressive Politics: A Historical Study of Its Origins and Development 1870–1950* (1951).

Carleton Beals's *The Great Revolt and Its Leaders: The History of Popular American Uprisings in the 1890's* (1968) is not the most sophisticated history, but does help us to grasp what persons with no professional equipment, but respectful of the past, perceive in the old upheavals. More doubtful is Simon Lazarus's amateur *The Genteel Populists* (1974), which tries to find relations between Populism and the recent Senator George McGovern partisans, with little profit.

Despite a "new Populism" then, which sadly knows too little of the old, there are numerous substantial books to guide us into its fold. John D. Hicks's *The Populist Revolt* (1931) is the recognized classic in the field, though as in other related areas, it is not whole in respect to Populism's vital cultural aspect. Ralph L. Rusk's *The Literature of the Middle Western Frontier* (1926) repays study in this connection. Hamlin Garland's "populist" fiction wants understanding, especially the contrast between his "veritistic," as he would have termed it, *Main-Traveled Roads* (1891) and his popular as well as Populist *A Son of the Middle Border* (1919). The realistic (and pessimistic) *The Story of a Country Town* (1883) by E. W. Howe also bears on how the nascent Populist thought and felt, and helps combat naive and uniformed impressions of the farmer as a bumpkin and a fool. Fools there were in the country as elsewhere, but at the hard center of rural thought were strong impulses toward survival and adjustment, adding up to a process of modernization from the past to the present.

Solon J. Buck's *The Granger Movement* (1913) and *The Agrarian Crusade* (1921) are basic works. Fred E. Haynes's *Third Party Movements since the Civil War* (1916) traces tendencies which finally brought on the milestone election year of 1912. George H. Knoles's *The Presidential Campaign and Election of 1892* (1942) sets the stage for the Populist showdown of 1896.

Haynes's *James Baird Weaver* (1919) is significant as discussing the Greenback Labor candidate of 1880 as well as the People's party candidate of 1892. (See also Ellis B. Usher, *The Greenback Movement of 1875–1884 and Wisconsin's Part in It* [1911].) Why this tried Populist dropped so deeply into the shadows of William Jennings Bryan in that later year helps explain the differences between the older agrarianism and the emerging Progressivism. The difference is further explicated by Theodore Saloutos and John D. Hicks, in their *Agricultural Discontent in the Middle West, 1900–1939* (1951).

Martin Ridge's *Ignatius Donnelly: The Portrait of a Politician* (1962) traces the early career of a profoundly interesting Populist personality. Donnelly is best known as author of the famous Preamble to the People's Party Platform of 1892. But his own development from Democratic party regular to articulator of Populist dreams, and his best-selling fiction, notably *Caesar's Column* (1891), which seems to foretell an American dictatorship, merit thoughtful analysis for their unconscious expectations.

Significant highlights of this period include Donald L. McMurry's *Coxey's Army* (1929), already noted, which discusses a spectacular effort of the time to apprise the Washington Administration of popular feeling: a first which would be later emulated by suffragists, unemployed veterans, and peace advocates who would further test the will of administrators to resist popular pressure. See also Charles Hoffman's *The Depression of the Nineties* (1970) which sees the era as a time of "intense dislocation" in the advancing capitalist economy.

An enduring work is Harry Barnard, *Eagle Forgotten: The Life of John P. Altgeld* (1938) which deals with the hero-governor of Illinois.

The individual states require directed attention; we need from time to time to remind ourselves that no state, whatever its size, has more than two senators in Washington. Paul R. Fossum, in *The Agrarian Movement in North Dakota* (1925), and Alex H. Arnett, in *The Populist Movement in Georgia* (1922), tell of two disparate states which not only affected the course of Populism, but of its successor Progressivism. C. Vann Woodward, in *Tom Watson, Agrarian Rebel* (1938), tells the tragic story of a young Georgian idealist who ended his career as the most vicious of demagogues and yet continued to bewilder liberals by his denunciations of war and profiteer capitalists.

The Populists were given a bad name in recent years by various academics, as in Richard Hofstadter's influential *The Age of Reform* (1955), being charged with Negrophobe tendencies, anti-Semitism, mean-mindedness, and sentimental longings for the illusory past, among other things. Some new studies have helped put a number of these issues into perspective; see Robert F. Durden, *The Climax of Populism: The Election of 1896* (1965); Walter T. K. Nugent, *The Tolerant Populists: Kansas Populism and Nativism* (1963); Norman Pollack, *The Populist Response to Industrial America* (1962); and Stanley B. Parsons, *The Populist Context: Rural versus Urban Power on a Great Plains Frontier* (1973).

William Jennings Bryan has long been patronized as an emotional ranter who lacked brain power. Paolo E. Coletta, in *William Jennings Bryan, Political Evangelist, 1860–1908* (1964) and *William Jennings Bryan, Progressive Politician and Moral Statesman, 1909–1915* (1969), has determinedly brought him into the time-picture and, to a degree, rehabilitated him as a true adjunct of Progressivism.[5]

8. Muckraking

There were scandals and exposures of public betrayal early in the Republic, but the bitter charges of Federalists and Jeffersonians were too evidently partisan to rate as durable information. Recognizable muckraking — as it came to be called in the Progressive era — had its start in the labors of the redoubtable Anne Newport Royall, who kept a sharp eye on Washington politicians in her paper *Paul Pry* (1831–1836) and its successor *The Huntress* (1836–1854). Mrs. Royall's career is recounted most recently in the introduction to her reprinted *Letters from Alabama 1817–1822*, edited by Lucille Griffith (1969). See also Bessie Rowland James, *Anne Royall's U.S.A.* (1972). William Lyon Mackenzie's muckraking career has been lost between his famous Canadian adventure in revolution in 1837 and his publication in 1845 of the inner workings of the Martin Van Buren New York political machine, in Mackenzie's *Lives and Opinions of Benjamin Franklin Butler. . Jesse Hoyt. . .and Their Friends*, a lurid work of detail and exegesis, reminiscent of Watergate, but with none of its effects.

There was no lack of sensational journalism, which was also to become characteristic of some later muckraking, though far from all. The 1830s and 1840s saw the rise of the "penny press," newspapers sold for a penny: popular journalism which mixed scandal with enterprising investigations and which was the precursor of the "yellow," highly colored journalism of the later part of the century. James L. Crouthamel's *James Watson Webb* (1969) tells the career of the editor of the New York *Courier and Enquirer*, and details the newspaper quarrels and competition which inspired such other famous papers as the New York *Sun* and the New York *Herald*, as well as such other ones as the Chicago *Tribune*, so highly important in seeking and attaining the Republican nomination for President of Abraham Lincoln in 1860.

Most successful among editors and publications was Horace Greeley and his New York *Tribune*, which became the forum of the North, as the nation's sections divided on the slavery and free soil issues. Such treatments as Glyndon G. Van Deusen's *Horace Greeley* (1953) underscore Greeley's importance in the politics and journalism of his time. See also Francis Brown's *Raymond of the Times* (1951) and Oliver Carlson's *The Man Who Made News: James Gordon Bennett* (1942). Bernard Weisberger's *The American Newspaper Man* (1961) is a brief treatment which shows transitions in journalism over the years. Charles F. Wingate, ed., *Views and Interviews on Journalism* (1875) reports the major editors of its time including David G. Croly, the father of Herbert Croly (*see* Chapter II-24), his mother Mrs. Jennie C. Croly, pioneer woman journalist, Bennett, and many others.

Journalism reflected a growing and turbulent nation in post-Civil War decades, as seen in two histories, sections apart: Louis M. Lyons, *Newspaper Story: One Hundred Years of the Boston Globe* (1971) and Thomas H. Baker, *Memphis Commercial Appeal* (1972). The history of the New York *Sun* illustrated the fact that old, popular papers tended to become conservative over the years; see Frank M. O'Brien, *The Story of the Sun* (1918) and Charles J. Rosebault, *When Dana Was the Sun* (1931). Journalism, however, continued to produce new master journalists who studied the people's wants and success-fully met them, as told, for example, in Negley D. Cochran's *E. W. Scripps* (1933) and Gilson Gardner's *Lusty Scripps: The Life of E. W. Scripps* (1932); Mrs. Fremont Older's *William Randolph Hearst* (1936), one of a number of studies of this controversial figure, and W. A. Swanberg's *Pulitzer* (1967). Such owners of newspapers activated an entire generation of ambitious newspapermen who went on to create much as literary mediators which gave similar purposes to readers and politicians. Oliver Knight, ed., *I Protest; Selected Disquisitions of E. W. Scripps* (1966) is a valuable collection of this great publisher's views. Scripps was the founder of the Scripps newspaper chain.

We have already remarked Hearst's controversial career (*see* Chapter I-2). Joseph Pulitzer's was in some ways as formidable, and more patently useful to society. See Don C. Seitz's affectionate *Joseph Pulitzer: His Life and Letters* (1924); three books by Pulitzer's last city editor, James Wyman Barrett, *The End of the World* (1931), *The World, the Flesh and the Messers Pulitzer* (1931), and the more detailed *Joseph Pullitzer and His World* (1941). John L. Heaton, comp., *Frank I. Cobb* [of the *World*]: *A Leader in Liberalism* (1924) memorializes one of the most respected of the era's journalists.

Oswald Garrison Villard's *Some Newspapers and Newspapermen* (1923) contributed post-Progressive assessments. Evelyn Wells's *Fremont Older* (1936) wrote of the most famous journalist of the West Coast, editor of the *San Francisco Bulletin*; compare with Older's *My Own Story* (1926).

The *New York Times* was fated to become the most influential newspaper of the coming decades. Although it no more than vied with other papers in the Progressive era, the source of its staying power warrants understanding. See Elmer Davis's *History of the New York Times 1851-1921* (1951) and Meyer Berger's *The Story of the New York Times, 1851-1951* (1951). Gay Talese's *The Kingdom and the Power* (1969) is a brilliant, personalized account. Herman H. Dinsmore, *All the News that Fits* (1969) is a bitter, disillusioned examination of the *Times's* news and editorial policies by a former *Times* employee.

Also requiring notice were the literary trends of the times, for the best of the new journalists developed style and an imaginative sense of drama which gave edge to their most famous writings. Somewhere between Victoria and Robert Case's *We Called It Culture* (1948), a study in literary refinement and the sterner discipline of Charles C. Walcutt's *American Literary Naturalism* (1956), which notes romantic but also harsh detail in the new, hardhitting journalism, muckraking was born.

An important prototypical muckraking fiction-writer was John W. DeForest (1826-1906), who aspired to be a great novelist and was at least a pioneer in realism in his *Miss Ravenal's Conversion from Secession to Loyalty* (1867). DeForest served with honor in the Civil War, and his *A Volunteer's Adventures* (1946), which collects his Civil War letters and articles, is a permanent item in the literature. DeForest's *Honest John Vane* (1875) and *Playing the Mischief* (1875) are political novels set in the sordid atmosphere of the Grant administrations, and though they do not wholly succeed as literature, they did help chart ways for later Progressives.

One assured literary classic among writings by the journalist-storytellers is Finley Peter Dunne, creator of Mr. Dooley, a sagacious saloonkeeper; see Elmer Ellis, *Mr. Dooley's America* (1941), and Louis Filler, ed., *The World of Mr. Dooley* (1962).

A precursor of muckraking was W. T. Stead, who seized public attention in both England and America with his emotional exposures of moral delinquency. Stead also helped General William Booth, founder of the Salvation Army, to prepare his milestone work in social reform, *In Darkest England and the Way Out* (1890). See also Frederic Whyte's *Life of W. T. Stead* (1925). Another precursor was Henry Demarest Lloyd in the United States. Lloyd's *Wealth against Commonwealth* (1894) boldly challenged the Standard Oil Company as operating against the public interest; a biography of Lloyd by Caro Lloyd appeared in 1912.

Although there was much newspaper muckraking in the 1890s — magazines were then thought to have more dignified or entertainment functions — much of it was weakened by partisanship and careless research. The breadth and limitations of newspaper muckraking are yet to be fully spelled out. A major criticism of their basic mission has recently been developed not only by cynical politicians but by academics. They have argued that the city machines which were run on bribes and self-interested understandings actually helped the poor as reformers would not. To be sure, the politicians exacted a price. They made private fortunes from the city's wealth. They gave away municipal contracts, municipal resources. But it was a price the poor willingly paid for a drink, a bribe for voting falsely at the polls, for a temporary job during layoffs.

How then could reformers and their journalistic friends compete against the machine? Criminal alliances weakened. Conniving politicians fell out and exposed each other's frauds. "Reform waves" attracted interested citizens and attractive leaders. Muckraking achieved its place in history by bringing together an unusual corps of talented and earnest writers who persuaded readers that they were discussing not petty or personal matters, but events which affected the entire nation. In effect, readers were made aware that social crises far away affected them directly or indirectly, and were fascinating and educational in their own right.

9. Journalists

The tale of journalists and their relationship to the popularization of literature and the literature of exposure is lengthy and picturesque. Charles Edward Russell's *These Shifting Scenes* (1914) gave some sense of its romance and excitement in such chapters as "Old Days with the Tramp Printers" —

inside stories of the nominations for President of William Henry Harrison and Grover Cleveland — and "Tales of a City Room Caliph." The chapter called "The Art of Reporting" underscored the determination of some of the reporters to write memorable prose and fiction.

The newspapers gave a living to such genuine artists as Lafcadio Hearn, the exotic writer who was born of Irish-Greek parents in the Ionian Islands, and who was raised in Ireland, England, and France before coming to America while still a young man. He wrote individualistic prose for Cincinnati and New Orleans newspapers, his sense of color being accentuated by the fact that he was half-blind and of complex spirit. He ended as Koizsimi Yakumo, a Japanese citizen and teacher whose accounts of Japan influenced American opinion of the Japanese. The newspapers also employed Stephen Crane, who continued to act as a reporter even after the success of his *The Red Badge of Courage* (1895).

The most famous of the journalists was Richard Harding Davis, handsome, competent, the original of the Gibson Man who courted the resplendent Gibson Girl. Davis was the son of Rebecca Harding Davis, whose 1861 *Atlantic Monthly* article, "Life in the Iron Mills," and other pieces pioneered realism. Davis himself was superficial in many ways, but his *Cuba in War Time* (1898) included accurate accounts of American actions there, and he inspired superior work by Crane, Jack London, and others. See Gerald Langford, *The Richard Harding Davis Years* (1961).

William Salisbury's *The Career of a Journalist* (1908), in its frank and intelligent account, distinguished accuracy from the sensationalism and opportunism which muckrakers had to overcome to produce their enduring work. James Creelman was one of the best esteemed of newspapermen of his time, and his *On the Great Highway* (1901) similarly throws light on the craft of the journalism of the time.

Ambrose Bierce was, if anything, an antimuckraker, pouring the acid of his contempt on do-gooders as he saw them. But in the sharpness of his epigrams, the precision of his prose, and in his antireform prejudices, he produced a species of reform writing which helped keep the craft of journalism up to the mark; see his *Letters*, edited by Bertha C. Page (1922).

10. The Magazines

The magazines became vehicles for the muckraker's message. Peter Lyon's *Success Story: The Life and Times of S. S. McClure* (1963) tells of the publication which became symbolic of the movement. *McClure's Magazine* is also treated in Ida M. Tarbell's autobiographical *All in the Day's Work* (1939) and other memoirs. Theodore P. Greene's *America's Heroes* (1970) interestingly assesses popular attitudes toward success, as reflected in the magazines.

John Tebbel's *The American Magazine: A Compact History* (1969) provides an adequate survey of the field for working purposes, and his *George Horace Lorimer and the Saturday Evening Post* (1948) breaks ground for this greatest of all magazine successes, though it needs to be further explored. *The Americanization of Edward Bok* (1921) tells of a comparable success, that of the *Ladies' Home Journal*. Madeleine B. Stern's *Queen of Publishers' Row* (1965) tells the extraordinary tale of Mrs. Frank Leslie, who began as an adventuress and ended as a woman of wealth and influence. Although she was no reformer in a true sense, her very success as a woman influenced attitudes and events which contributed to change. On another level, Alan Pendleton Grimes's *The Political Liberalism of the New York Nation, 1865–1932* (1953) shows the magazine's changes of policy from E. L. Godkin, the tight-minded prophet of Free Trade, through the conservative humanist Paul Elmer More, and Oswald Garrison Villard. Of special interest is chapter four: "Progressivism: The Union of Politics and Economics."

11. Muckrakers

Muckrakers were varied. Anyone looking for drama in Tarbell's *History of the Standard Oil Company* (1904) would be bound to be disappointed, for it was written with utmost sobriety. Its outstanding feature was care in research and clarity of expression. One of the highpoints of muckraking, however, was fiction: Upon Sinclair's *The Jungle* (1905) which shocked readers with its revelations of tainted meat. Lincoln Steffens's series on *The Shame of the Cities* (1904) made him famous not only because of his revelations of municipal corruption, but because he seemed to have a scientific method for weighing its meaning.

The leader of the muckrakers was Charles Edward Russell, whose autobiography *Bare Hands and Stone Walls* (1933) covers his career from Populism through Progressivism. Lincoln Steffen's *Autobiography* (1931) is the most distinguished of muckrakers' memoirs. However, there are others which amply repay reading. Brand Whitlock was an anti-capital punishment reformer, progressive mayor of Toledo, and later the great American ambassador to Belgium. His *Forty Years of It* (1914) is written with art and understanding. Ray Stannard Baker's *American Chronicle* (1945); William Allen White's *Autobiography* (1946); *Progressive Men, Women and Movements of the Past Twenty-five Years,* by the editor of the reformist *Arena,* B. O. Flower (1914); Josiah Flynt (Willard's) *My Life* (1908), by the tragic figure who accidentally began municipal muckraking by writing of the nether world he knew too well; Mark Sullivan's *The Education of an American* (1938); Norman Hapgood's *The Changing Years* (1930), by the editor of the muckraking *Collier's Magazine*; and his brother Hutchins Hapgood's *A Victorian in the Modern World* (1939); Rheta Childe Dorr's *A Woman of Fifty* (1924), by a muckraker in behalf of women's rights — such are a few of the available accounts touching upon personalities and publications.

Will Irwin was one of the best-known of progressive journalists, and his *The Making of a Reporter* (1942) says much of the craft his better-known muckraking associates pursued. Irwin studied the newspapers during the Progressive period and after. His *Propaganda and the News* (1936) gives perspective on the changes they experienced.

The muckrakers merit more individual study than they have received. Justin Kaplan's *Lincoln Steffens: A Biography* (1974), though conscientious, fails to dig deeply into the subject. Walter Johnson, ed., *Selected Letters of William Allen White 1899–1943* (1947) and White's own *Autobiography* (1946) are more evocative than Johnson's *William Allen White's America* (1947). The availability of Ray Stannard Baker's papers encouraged the ready production of two different attempts at biography, Robert C. Bannister, Jr.'s *Ray Stannard Baker: The Mind and Thought of a Progressive* (1966) and John E. Semouche's *Ray Stannard Baker: A Quest for Democracy in Modern America 1870–1918* (1969). Jack Tager's *The Intellectual as Urban Reformer: Brand Whitlock and the Progressive Movement* (1968) is unpretentious but informative. Yet more needs doing. (*See* Chapter II-15).

Filler, *The Unknown Edwin Markham* (1966) involves among other things Markham's little-recognized services to reform, notably as author of an outstanding series on child labor. McClure's own *My Autobiography* (1914) is a folk-classic; it is not widely realized that it was written with the aid of his genius-editor Willa Cather. Andy Logan's *The Man Who Robbed the Robber Barons* (1965) deals with Colonel William d'Alton Mann, once a hero of Gettysburg, during the Progressive era the blackmailing owner of *Town Topics* in New York. Mann actually employed talented writers. Overall, however, he contributes more to the connotation of muckraking as shoddy sensationalism than to that of social contribution.

Filler, *Crusaders for American Liberalism* (1939 and subsequent editions) displays the muckraker's collective story. See also, David M. Chalmers, *The Social and Political Ideas of the Muckrakers* (1964), and his *The Muckrake Years* (1974), a collection of documents, with an essay on the subject. John M. Harrison and Harry Stein, ed., *Muckraking, Past, Present, and Future* (1974), is a volume of essays drawn from a conference on the subject. Arthur and Lila Weinberg, eds., *The Muckrakers* (1961) reprints a selection of articles by outstanding journalists of exposure.

Thomas W. Lawson, a multimillionaire speculator, turned on his associates in *Frenzied Finance* (1905), which exploded in *Everybody's Magazine* with remarkable effect. Although *Crusaders for American Liberalism* dealt with it many years ago, there have been no additions to its materials, by friends or foes. However, I add to the information myself in *Appointment at Armageddon* (*see* Chapter II-1).

The muckrakers were more numerous than the above may suggest. Many social activists contributed to their work, as in the case of "the kid's judge," Ben B. Lindsey, who with the aid of the journalist Harvey J. O'Higgins — Lindsey always required such cooperation — indicted the schemes of Colorado corporations in *The Beast*, originally published in 1910, reissued in 1970 with an introduction by Charles E. Larsen. Some muckrakers exhibited power as writers; see, for example, James Hopper's *"9009"* (1909), a tale of prison injustice which inspired actual prison reform. See also Jack London's *The People of the Abyss* (1903), elsewhere noted. There are many other such works inspired by the best muckraking assumptions that the truth would make one free.[6]

12. The Literary Factor and Upton Sinclair

One of the most vital facts about muckraking — one which merits emphasis — was that it involved not only information about trouble spots in the American social fabric, but ways to present the information in memorable form. Muckrakers concerned themselves with individuals as well as group situations. They stirred readers with tales of injustice which became a species of folklore: the insidious smile of an anti-social industrialist, the trials of a city waif, the brazen thefts of a city boss. Intimate tales of vice rings, insurance frauds, the cynical handling of food could be couched in ways which upset readers and made them think of ways to curb such infamies.

Such work required investigators, but investigators with a creative sense of people and social values. At the height of muckraking exposure it was often difficult to tell where exposure ended and artistic presentation began. It was no accident that muckraking was called "the literature of exposure."

The Social Revolt: American Literature from 1888 to 1914 (1933), edited by Oscar Cargill, captures some sense of the effort expended by writers of merit to speak artistically to the question of society's problems. Joseph L. Blotner's *The Political Novel* (1955) is limited in scope and insight, but suggests possibilities for further study. Hamlin Garland's best tales belong to the literature of Populism rather than Progressivism. Frank Norris, dying in 1902, was not required to assess the values of the Progressive era. Various notable writers contributed, though not consistently, to social understandings. This would be true of Jack London, and of the Edith Wharton of *The House of Mirth* (1905).

One of the most highly touted "socialist" novels was written by Ernest Poole, who capped a sound career as journalist and writer on social questions with *The Harbor* (1915). It won universal acclaim for its solid texture and character portrayals. *The Harbor* has since been ignored by literary criticism, but its value can be reconsidered in Truman Frederick Keefer's *Ernest Poole* (1966). See also Poole's *The Bridge: My Own Story* (1940).

A curious item, revealing potentialities in the literature of Progressivism still to be explored, is Abe C. Ravitz's *Clarence Darrow and the American Literary Tradition* (1962) which treats the famous attorney in terms of his literary philosophy and writings. It places him in the realistic school, and requests appreciation especially for his 1904 novel, *Farmington*, which includes Darrow's memories of his Ohio boyhood. Too low-keyed for attention by any but the most thoughtful and those willing to read outside of established patterns, the question of Darrow as a literary personage raises questions about some of his contemporaries as well.

The two most formidable muckraker-novelists of the Progressive era were Upton Sinclair and David Graham Phillips. Although Sinclair was un-equivocally in the public eye for some forty years and a legend the remainder of his long life, the years brought him no literary assessment of any kind. His *The Jungle* (1906) was as unshakable in the public consciousness as Harriet Beecher Stowe's *Uncle Tom's Cabin*, but elicited even less cultural response despite the fact that Sinclair was one of the best-known American writers throughout the world, his work appearing in numerous translations, from the French to the Chinese.

Although it is not here possible to undertake an investigation into the merits or demerits of Sinclair's writings, it is possible to indicate the categories they cover and several of the works immediately relevant to muckraking and Progressivism.

Sinclair engaged in polemics all his life. He quoted from his own correspondence and memories at formidable length; Ronald Gottesman, *Upton Sinclair, an Annotated Checklist* (1973) comprises 544 pages of closely-knit bibliography. Sinclair's *American Outpost: A Book of Reminiscences* (1932), his *My Lifetime in Letters* (1960) — composed of letters from famous correspondents — and his *Autobiography* (1962) contribute to understanding of American hopes for social betterment.

The Journal of Arthur Stirling (1903) was on the surface very different from the work with which he became identified. It was the cry of a poet, unheard in a materialistic world. The poet was Sinclair himself — not an original poet, but a most original individual, born in the South, raised in the North, and with a curious objectivity about America's virtues and vices.

As a socialist he wrote *The Jungle*, depicting a world of suffering and uncivil industry based on false human values. Sinclair's dream of a better existence obscured from him the depths of tragedy which a Theodore Dreiser was able to perceive. But Sinclair's vision had its own logic. It comported with the positive side of American enterprise, one which was cooperative, experimental, yea-saying.

The Industrial Republic (1907) gave a happy picture of the socialist American commonwealth due to arrive, Sinclair thought, by 1912. *Good Health and How We Won It* (1909), written with Michael Williams, contained many useful suggestions for rational living. *Samuel the Seeker* (1909) contained thin characterizations, but in the spirit of Voltaire, who was also famous for his wit and inquiry, rather than the novelist's depth.

Love's Pilgrimage (1911) was one of Sinclair's best novels, and recounted the story of his own odyssey in romance and marriage with irony and insight.

In 1918 Sinclair issued the first of what his only biographer Floyd Dell, in his *Upton Sinclair* (1927) called "the great pamphlets." *The Profits of Religion* (1918), *The Brass Check* (1919) — a study of contemporary journalism — *The Goose-Step: A Study of American Education* (1923), and *The Goslings* (1924) saw American affairs in jaundiced terms. Sinclair's limited view of human nature did not, however, keep him from perceiving the mercenary vein in public service enterprises. The same could be said of his *Mammonart* (1925), his long view of the masters writers served, and his study of contemporary authors, *Money Writes!* (1927).

Jimmie Higgins (1919) — the name given to rank and file socialist workers — and *100%: The Story of a Patriot* (1920) commemorated a worthy and unworthy person in fiction; *100%* was the bigoted view of American patriotism which crushed dissent during World War I. Sinclair wrote several plays, of which the best by far was *Singing Jailbirds* (1924) which utilized expressionist methods successfully to portray the persecution of radicals with sad accuracy.

Sinclair usually maintained an ironic approach to his unsympathetic characters in fiction. He was a kind man who saw many of them as manipulated by economic factors in their upbringing and life. *Oil!* (1927) was precise in depicting the exploitation of an industry with means which would contribute to the coming depression. *Boston* (2 vols., 1928) treated the Sacco-Vanzetti saga as one of martyrdom to police and capitalist cruelty. It caused a furor by being banned in Boston proper. Sinclair later had reason to repent of aspects of his account, having been convinced that Sacco, at least, had indeed been involved in the crime for which he was executed.

The Wet Parade (1931), a novel, defended prohibition. More profitable was *The Cup of Fury* (1956), Sinclair's brief prose account of the many friends he had had who, he thought, had died or been driven toward death by dedication to liquor. *Upton Sinclair Presents William Fox* (1933) revealed another clear limitation in Sinclair's thinking. He saw the motion picture magnate, Fox, as having been robbed of his holdings in cinema by cunning conspirators. Yet Fox had himself been a freebooting capitalist. Sinclair's muckraking here no more than exposed aspects of warfare which attended free enterprise, and it surprised no one.

An approach to these and numerous other plays, stories, and even poems (Sinclair had published the poems of his late wife) could be sought in *An Upton Sinclair Anthology* (1934), edited by I. O. Evans. I do not here include Sinclair's "Lanny Budd" series of novels, since they constitute a special problem in literature and changing times remote from problems of Progressivism.

13. The Challenge of David Graham Phillips

Phillips was the fictional meteor of the 1900s, publishing his first novel in 1901, and his eighteenth in 1911 when he was assassinated by a paranoid musician of good family who imagined Phillips had maligned his people in a novel. Thereafter, Phillips's fiction continued posthumously to appear until 1915 when his *Susan Lenox: Her Fall and Rise* began serialization and, as a book, became a test case in obscenity, being prosecuted by the Society for the Prevention of Vice.

The publisher obligingly cut a hundred pages from the text, but it in any event lost the public's interest. Oddly, since it was not issued in reprint form, it became less available than some of Phillips's novels which were, and which persisted in what Ludwig Lewisohn called an underground through the 1920s. By 1930 Phillips's reputation was completely down, and was given the *coup de grace* by the publication the next year of an essay by Granville Hicks, then a Communist, "David Graham Phillips: Journalist," which satisfied the literary establishment that Phillips had been thoroughly separated from its professional concerns; see Filler, "The Reputation of David Graham Phillips," *Antioch Review*, Winter, 1951.

The basic reason for Phillips's decline had been the rise of Theodore Dreiser, whose pessimistic erotic version of American reality had seemed, in post-Progressive days, to make more sense than Phillips's fighting, optimistic view that man was not a fallen angel but a rising animal. The curiosity here was that an article could as readily have been written entitled "Theodore Dreiser: Journalist," for Dreiser's and Phillips's careers had in some measure paralleled one another.

In the post-World War II era Dreiser's reputation declined also, though he continued to receive lip-service. An article by the influential critic Lionel Trilling spelled out the indictment of Dreiser as an insensitive, myopic scribbler who, even in the hands of a defender, was over-sentimental, merely documentary, and whose work rested on a "faulty base of capitalism and eroticism"; compare Alfred Kazin and Charles Shapiro, eds., *The Stature of Theodore Dreiser* (1955) and Charles Shapiro, *Theodore Dreiser: Our Bitter Patriot* (1962). The subject is reviewed in Filler, "A Tale of Two Authors: Theodore Dreiser and David Graham Phillips",in Ray B. Browne and others, *New Voices in American Studies* (1966).

The most confusing aspect of the Phillips subject is his reputation as a muckraking novelist. When one considers that he ended by writing twenty-four novels, that his most famous novel, *Susan Lenox*, had absorbed him through his entire progressive period till his death, and that the disparity between his first efforts — published when he was still a working journalist — and his last efforts is startling in details and subject, it becomes clear that clichés have ossified until they serve no purpose but to retard understanding.

Phillips was in fact a muckraker — the original author whom Theodore Roosevelt had designated a muckraker — and he wrote articles during the time of muckraking which were clearly in that genre. His "Treason of the Senate" series for *Cosmopolitan* in 1906 was a highpoint in the entire era; the articles were finally published in book form in 1964; see G. E. Mowry and J. A. Grenier, eds., *The Treason of the Senate*.

But by 1906 Phillips had established himself as a novelist, and more and more firmly refused to write in the muckraking genre. His first major success, *The Plum Tree* (1905), had freed him to publish novels which grew increasingly deep and carefully prepared, as he insisted that the one topic demanding attention was man-woman relations. At the time of his death he had turned more and more to considering what science was doing to human life; passages in his last fiction reflect that concern.

With Phillips and Dreiser both securely in history, they can more disinterestedly be reviewed for what they have to offer a new generation. A brief list of Phillips's most challenging books aside from *Susan Lenox* would include: *Light Fingered Gentry* (1907), *Old Wives for New* (1908), *The Hungry Heart* (1909), *The Husband's Story* (1910), *The Grain of Dust* (1911), *The Price She Paid* (1912). These works range from the clearly contemporaneous, with muckraking overtones, to the last which are totally absorbed in the problem of finding a place in the world as man or woman.

14. Work that Needs To Be Done

The muckraking generation was matter of fact about its place in American annals, too busy living to be interested in future researchers, and it did little about ensuring that its story would be adequately told. Remarkably few caches of muckraking materials exist. Yet it reflects upon researchers, among others, that none has yet been able to make extensive use of Charles Edward Russell's fine files of material in the manuscript division of the Library of Congress. Lincoln Steffens's two volumes of published letters are most valuable. (More of his letters are yet to be published.) But enough about uncollected muckrakers could be gathered from the checklist of holdings in libraries, *American Literary Manuscripts* (1960), compiled by the American Literature Group of the Modern Language Association, to break ground for further varied and enlightening compilations.

David Graham Phillips scrawled to associates and publishers hard-to-read notes of considerable interest, but he was unconcerned about aiding the future. Ben B. Hampton, who made *Hampton's* a vibrant muckraking publication, hurried on, once his magazine was destroyed, to become a motion-picture entrepreneur, and let his former reading public fend for itself. Alfred Henry Lewis was called a muckraker, though this ex-cowboy, author of the immortal "Wolfville" stories based on life in the Tombstone, Arizona of the 1880s, was too personal, too western in attitude to write with analytical control. And he left no papers.

David M. Chalmers, in *The Social and Political Ideas of the Muckrakers* (1964), set a good example by focusing on a number of the muckrakers. But more needs to be done with all of them, as personalities as well as pens, and especially the "sub-marginal" ones. (I have discussed this easy out for uninformed academics in my essay "Acorns into Oaks: Notes on the 'Marginal' and 'Sub-Marginal' in American History," which introduces *The Pantarch: A Biography of Stephen Pearl Andrews*, by Madeleine B. Stern [1968].)

Burton J. Hendrick wrote powerfully of insurance during the muckraking era, and later won Pulitzer prizes. Yet nothing outside of Chalmers remains to commemorate his own thought and career. George Kibbe Turner was one of the most effective of McClure writers on urban vice, and wrote novels after the era passed; but his transition from fame to forgetfulness remains unexplored.

Christopher P. Connolly was one of the most highly esteemed of all muckrakers. A lawyer and investigator, he contributed understanding and communicative prose to such widely separated events as the assassination of ex-governor Frank Steunenberg of Idaho and the subsequent trial of labor leaders, and the murder trial of Leo Frank in the next decade. As late as 1938, Connolly reviewed the old war among the copper kings of Montana in *The Devil Learns to Vote*. But no survey of his long and worthy labors feeds our understanding.

John O'Hara Cosgrave, editor of *Everybody's*, who had in 1904–1906 done as much as anyone could to bring Tom Lawson's revelations to public attention, and Bailey Millard of *Cosmopolitan*, who had "discovered" Edwin Markham and sponsored David Graham Phillips's "The Treason of the Senate" — both editors had illuminating tales to tell of America's intellectual ways, but their stories are yet to be told.

Lincoln Steffens's *Upbuilders* (1909) recounted heartening stories of distinguished citizens. Of the five he portrayed only Ben B. Lindsey survives in recollection. Yet Everett Colby of New Jersey had been a reformer of intellect as well as integrity, and W. S. U'Ren of Oregon was known as the "father of the Initiative and Referendum": a democracy-giving device which made local and state government more flexible and open to reformers. U'Ren's career and others like his had much to offer a new time, and still have.

Finally, such writers as Jack London were well-known, but their relationship to Progressivism and even muckraking has yet to be substantially analyzed.

The story of the muckrakers was not properly a closed record. Much of it could be opened and added to, and with great profit to a new generation.

15. Progressive Issues

To get the full force of the era, we need to see it in the lives of some of the participants and their circumstances, as in Louis G. Geiger's *Joseph W. Folk of Missouri* (1953), Walton E. Bean's *Boss Ruef's San Francisco* (1952), and Lately Thomas's (Robert V. P. Steele) *A Debonair Scoundrel: An Episode in the Moral History of San Francisco* (1962). See also Dewey W. Grantham's *Hoke Smith and the Politics of the New South* (1958). Such books provide rounded accounts of conditions which confronted city and farm dwellers, explain why and how they became more receptive to the muckrakers' expositions, and tell how they were able to find leaders to implement them with action.

[Arthur Train] *Yankee Lawyer: The Autobiography of Ephraim Tutt* (1943) is here of interest because it is not by a spectacular Progressive, but by a then progressive-minded young lawyer, one of many who formed the seedbed of such sensational figures as Clarence Darrow, whose *The Story of My Life* (1932) studs the pages of classic Progressivism.

Carter Harrison, Jr., mayor of Chicago in the Progressive era, in *Stormy Years* (1935), his account of issues and campaigns, provides a picture against which later Chicago administrators can be set for contrast.

Although Theodore Roosevelt has been treated earlier (*see* Chapter II-3), a brief note deserves to be added to remind the reader that as President he broadened the personality he had developed as civil service reformer, author, and soldier, and both helped shape, and was shaped, by contemporary reformers. Harold F. Gosnell's *Boss Platt and His New York Machine* (1933) describes New York politics which Roosevelt, as governor, worked with and against. Harold Howland's *Theodore Roosevelt and His Times* (1921), written not long after Roosevelt's death, gives a sense of the long shadow he cast. John M. Blum's *The Republican Roosevelt* (1954) is a judicious summary of his political career. Morton Keller, ed., *Theodore Roosevelt: A Profile* (1967) seeks a rounded portrait of the subject by various authors who treat Roosevelt in his several phases as personality and public figure. Richard H. Collin, ed., *Theodore Roosevelt and Reform Politics* (1972) reprints a number of articles bearing on the subject.

Although some of the greatest progressive issues were national and involved the vast countryside, as in matters involving the country's resources, the city did tend to preempt much of the reform news, simply because of the conditions created by high concentrations of people, many of them "new immigrants" especially beset by novel and painful situations. Thus the deteriorated homes of discouraged farmers were depressing aesthetically, but not so dangerous to society as the overoccupied buildings of the city slums; see Roy Lubove, *The Progressives and the Slums: Tenement House Reform in New York City, 1890–1917* (1962). In this field, reformers built on the labors of Jacob A.

Riis, whose masterpiece, *How the Other Half Lives* (1890), had revealed onerous living circumstances to trouble the New York conscience.

For a view of the urban challenge, see A. L. Strauss, ed., *The American City* (1969) which uses documents and literary writings to reveal nineteenth-century roots. See also Ann Cook and others, eds., *City Life 1865–1900* (1973), a well-illustrated work.[7]

Samuel P. Orth, *The Boss and the Machine* (1919) is a sound chronicle of the challenge of political organizations which impeded the reformer. Melvin Holli, in *Reform in Detroit* (1969), writes of the famous Hazen S. Pingree, whose achievements gave hope to reformers. The problem of bosses may be weighed in Ralph G. Martin's *The Bosses* (1964) and Joel Arthur Tarr's *A Study in Boss Politics: William Lorimer of Chicago* (1971). Bosses were indeed of varied quality, as Nancy J. Weiss indicates in *Charles Francis Murphy 1858–1924: Respectability and Responsibility in Tammany Politics* (1968). The same may be said of Zane L. Miller's *Boss Cox's Cincinnati: Urban Politics in the Progressive Era* (1968) and J. Joseph Huthmacher's *Senator Robert F. Wagner and the Rise of Urban Liberalism* (1968). Furthermore, all the goals of reformers were not above question; as James B. Crooks wrote in *Politics & Progress: The Rise of Urban Progressivism in Baltimore 1895 to 1911* (1968): "In effect, progressive reforms were attempts to heal the social, political, and economic ills of urban society while maintaining the fundamentals of freedom, democracy, and capitalism" (p. 220). Nevertheless, reformers had no alternative but to press forward.

As indicated earlier, there is a constant need to put the invisible government of machine politics into perspective (*see* Chapter I-8). Doing so takes many forms. This requires seeing the city not only as a conglomerate of people striving to subsist in greatest comfort and satisfaction — the respectable majority — but also seeing city folk as seeking diversion, special favors, easy outlets of self-expression. It requires, in other words, a sense of the forces which tolerate and direct the vice of a metropolis.

Vice found an unusual historian: Herbert Asbury who was a descendant of Bishop Francis Asbury, a founder of Methodism. Herbert Asbury, a child of the cynical 1920s, wrote *Up from Methodism* (1926), and entertained himself and his readers by writing a series of highly informed, but informally told, accounts of vice in the nation. He despised prohibition, and set down his urbane contempt in a biography of the militant prohibitionist *Carry Nation* (1929) — not in any sense a Progressive; all her thoughts and deeds were constricted by old, unreviewed, fundamentalist notions — and in his *The Great Illusion* (1950), as he perceived the national effort to end the drinking of spirits by law.

Asbury's most famous book was *The Gangs of New York* (1928) which made it abundantly clear that the metropolis was not to become an oasis of saints. Asbury also wrote accounts of the vice rings, prostitutes, gangsters, traditions, and notorious thefts and killings of New Orleans, San Francisco, and Chicago:

works both entertaining and enlightening with respect to the potentials of human nature. *Sucker's Progress: An Informal History of Gambling in America* (1938) also made clear that such vice was not confined to degenerates or outlaws, but involved some of the most seemly names in society and politics.

City bosses and vice were far from separated. More separated were they both from forces which opposed them for good or specious reasons. See, for example, Blaine A. Brownell and Warren A. Stickle, eds., *Bosses and Reformers* (1973); Robert F. Wesser, *Charles Evans Hughes and Politics and Reform in New York, 1905–1910* (1967). Mortimer Smith's *William Jay Gaynor, Mayor of New York* (1951) and Lately Thomas's *The Mayor Who Mastered New York* [Gaynor] (1969) both discuss one who fought the Tammany machine. Jacob A. Friedman's *The Impeachment of the Governor* [of New York] William Sulzer (1939) discusses one who resisted the machine and was destroyed by it.

A curious book by one who administered the Democratic party in the time of Franklin D. Roosevelt is Edward Flynn's *You're the Boss* (1947) which argued that the voter ultimately calls the tune of the kind of administration he prefers. Oscar Handlin's *Al Smith and His America* (1958) is an argument for machine politics as producing positive results, though at what cost remains unanswered.

A vast literature surrounds Tammany Hall. M. R. Werner, *Tammany Hall* (1928), Jerome Mushkat, *Tammany: The Evolution of a Political Machine, 1798–1865* (1971), and Lorin Eisenstein and Elliott Rosenberg, *A Stripe of Tammany's Tiger* (1966) provide various data and approaches to this subject.

Lothrop Stoddard's *Master of Manhattan: The Life of Richard Croker* (1931) is interesting as being a critical review of this Tammany boss's corrupt career. However, Stoddard himself has been highly criticized for his own racist book, *The Rising Tide of Color* (1927). This places the reader in the position of having to judge between the boss, with his largely fraudulent tolerance of the poor and oppressed, whose votes he cherished, and the elitist Stoddard, scornful of public dishonesty, but without regard for those he arbitrarily deemed "inferior."

Harold C. Syrett, ed., *The Gentleman and the Tiger: The Autobiography of George B. McClellan, Jr.* (1956) deals with the son of the famous Civil War general, who fought the Tammany which had elected him mayor, and was then soundly trounced by the machine when he turned against it.

Cities other than New York have memorialized their bosses. Readers interested in Lincoln Steffens's pages on the Boston boss, Martin Lomasney, may compare them with Leslie Ainley's *Boston Mahatma: The Public Career of Martin Lomasney* (1949). His successor, James M. Curley, made a greater splash in the world. Reinhard H. Luthin's *American Demagogues: Twentieth Century* (1954) provides a succinct and authoritative account of this Boston phenomenon. Edwin O'Connor's best-selling novel, *The Last Hurrah* (1956), though not wholly based upon Curley as demagogue and the working man's best friend — according to O'Connor — brought Curley to national attention and inspired him to write his own apology, *I'd Do It Again* (1957): a self-serving and uncandid account. A striking work, undoubtedly subsidized by Curley, was intended to identify him with the 1932 victory of Franklin D. Roosevelt and perhaps gain him an ambassadorship, which, incidentally, did not materialize. James H. Guilfoyle's *On the Trail of the Forgotten Man* (1933) showed how intellectuals could be persuaded to ignore the patent skulduggery of politics, presumably in the interests of higher social goods.

Pennsylvania bossism is represented by the Philadelphia leader William S. Vare's *My Forty Years in Politics* (1933) and Robert Bowden's *Boies Penrose* (1937), and the Jersey City political apparatus by Dayton David McKean's *The Boss: The Hague Machine in Action* (1940). A remarkable work, George C. Rapport's *The Statesman and the Boss* [Frank Hague] (1961), traces relations, direct and indirect, between the high-minded Woodrow Wilson and the less than high-minded Boss Hague. Two works tracing the devices and traditions which defined Chicago politics, and which incubated their 1960s and 1970s master, Richard J. Daley, are Wayne Andrews's *Battle for Chicago* (1946) and Harold F. Gosnell's *Machine Politics: Chicago Model* (1968). For contrast see Joe Mathewson's *Up against Daley* (1974) which expressed the hopes of those who hungered to overthrow the Boss, as it turned out, without reason.

Reform never ended machine politics. It did force it to modernize. As such, reform in one — but only one — of its aspects was an efficiency movement. However, the idea of stream-lined municipal government did grow during the reform era, and is the subject of Leonard D. White's *The City Manager* (1927). See also John Porter East's *Council-Manager Government: The Political Thought of Its Founder, Richard Childs* (1965).

16. Settlement Houses and the Immigrants

Settlement houses were a major powerhouse of Progressivism, creating bonds between native Americans and the new immigrants, inspiring writers, union organizers, woman suffragists, and mentors of youth. The great name in American settlement houses was Jane Addams, whose *Twenty Years at Hull-House* [in Chicago] (1910) stirred and made creative numerous social workers and publicists. See also Daniel Levine, *Jane Addams and the Liberal Tradition* (1971) and John C. Farrell, *Beloved Lady: A History of Jane Addams' Ideas on Reform and Peace* (1967). Jane Addams's *The Second Twenty Years at Hull-House* (1930) reveals the deepened maturity of her life work. See also her *My Friend, Julia Lathrop* (1935).

Others had pioneered before Addams in furthering aspects of charity, social work, and the amelioration of evil conditions affecting men, women, and children. Robert H. Bremner's *From the Depths: The Discovery of Poverty in the*

United States (1956) and his *American Philanthropy* (1960) show the paths laid down by competent workers in the field to overcome American reluctance to (as they saw it) subsidize poverty and improvidence. See also Paul T. Ringenbach, *Tramps and Reformers 1873–1916; The Discovery of Unemployment in New York* (1973); Roy Lubove, *The Professional Altruist: The Emergence of Social Work as a Career, 1880–1930* (1965); and *Homer Folks, Pioneer in Social Welfare*, by Walter I. Trattner (1968).

The Settlement Idea, as Arthur C. Holden termed it (1922) was a focus for positive action, involving everything from teaching English to immigrants, sewing and child care to women, and the rights of workers before the law. Some later critics would protest that settlements taught Anglo-Saxon ideals at the expense of the immigrants' natural heritage; see, for example, Sam Bass Warner, Jr.'s bitter foreword to Robert A. Woods's and Albert J. Kennedy's distinguished pioneer work, *The Zone of Emergence: Observations of the Lower Middle and Upper Working Class Communities of Boston 1905–1914* (1962), published from a 1905–1914 manuscript. But settlements did act as an adjustment factor to immigrant groups which urgently needed one. We have no comparable agency today for our separated populations, even when they have long since been "Americanized."

Among the imposing figures in the settlement movement were Woods and Kennedy and their South End House in Boston which did much for the residents of the area, and for its numerous observers who carried their perceptions elsewhere to good effect. It is worth underscoring that these pioneers were realists. As they said in their *The Settlement Horizon: A National Estimate* (1922):

> Observation and experience. . .made it clear that workingmen are not greatly attracted by the motive nor satisfied with the fruits of merely honest government. They dream of a broadly and humanly serviceable city, powerful, generous, considerate. (P. 227)

Such imaginative understanding was especially valuable in view of the deep anti-immigrant feeling in the country; see John Higham's *Strangers in the Land: Patterns of American Nativism 1860–1925* (1955). See also David M. Chalmers's *Hooded Americanism; The First Century of the Ku Klux Klan, 1865–1965* (1965), affecting immigrants as well as Negroes. This is true also of Kenneth T. Jackson's *The Ku Klux Klan in the City 1915–1930* (1967). Donald E. Kinzer's *An Episode in Anti-Catholicism: The American Protective Association* (1964) of course affected one class of new citizens more than other classes.

A formidable Progressive in this field was Florence Kelley whose career as political lobbyist for reform measures is detailed in Josephine C. Goldmark's *Impatient Crusader* (1953) and in Dorothy Rose Blumberg's *Florence Kelley: The Making of a Social Pioneer* (1966). Lillian Wald told her own story in *The House on Henry Street* [New York] (1915) and in her *Windows on Henry Street* (1934).

Another outstanding figure is memorialized in Louise C. Wade's *Graham Taylor: Pioneer for Social Justice, 1851–1938* (1964). Taylor speaks for himself in *Pioneering on Social Frontiers* (1930) and *Chicago Commons through Forty Years* (1936).

See also Allen F. Davis, *Spearheads for Reform: The Social Settlements and the Progressive Movement, 1890–1914* (1967). Davis is also author of *American Heroine: The Life and Legend of Jane Addams* (1973).

The settlement idea drew together and activated some of the finest and most dedicated of progressive energies. They are celebrated in many volumes, such as Stanton Coit's *Neighborhood Guilds* (1891), a pioneer work, and Gregory Weinstein's *The Ardent Eighties: Reminiscences of an Interesting Decade* (1928)· which gives a sense of the high ideals protagonists carried with them.

One of the most important enthusiasts for settlement work was the educator Vida Scudder, whose *On Journey* (1937) tells much about her generation's social ambitions. It is all but invidious, however, to single out anyone among the settlement innovators. The following works depict only a few of the workers and publicists who helped create fighting chances for new Americans in their competitive new home.

Canon and Mrs. S. A. Barnett, *Towards Social Reform* (1909); Esther G. Barrows, *Neighbors All: A Settlement Notebook* (1929); Mary M. Simkhovitch, *Neighborhood: My Story of Greenwich House* (1938) and her *Here Is God's Plenty* (1949); Robert L. Duffus, *Lillian Wald, Neighbor and Crusader* (1938); Howard E. Wilson, *Mary McDowell: Neighbor* (1928); Mercedes M. Randall, *Improper Bostonian: Emile Green Balch* (1964); William H. Matthews, *Adventure in Giving* (1939); Charles Bernheimer, *Half a Century in Community Service* (1917); Mary W. Ovington, *The Walls Came Tumbling Down* (1947).

Several of numerous works require separate mention because of the specific activities they involve: E. T. Devine discussed *Misery and Its Causes* (1909) as a technical as well as humanistic matter. Alice Hamilton's memoirs involved *Exploring the Dangerous Trades* (1943). Robert Hunter, one of the "millionaire socialists," contributed to sociology as well as progressivism with his ground-breaking *Poverty* (1905). John Spargo, his socialist comrade, was lucid and effective in his *The Bitter Cry of the Children* (1908), one of the era's most famous titles.

Charles Zueblin's *A Decade of Civic Improvement* (1905) is useful as helping to distinguish the spirit of reform in the Progressive era from that which had made its beginnings in the 1890s.

Progressivism is written into the tale of accommodating strangers into the American pattern. Histories help to distinguish exploiters from friends; see, for example, George M. Stephenson, *A History of American Immigration* (1926) and Marcus Lee Hansen, *The Immigrant in American History* (1964). Edward G. Hartmann discusses a controversial subject in *The Movement to Americanize the Immigrant* (1948), raising the question of just what "Americanization" connoted. See also the more contemporaneous Edward Hale Bierstadt, *Aspects of Americanization* (1922).

Samuel P. Orth, in *Our Foreigners* (1921), discussed the several ethnic groups with his usual clarity and forthrightness. More recent volumes include Oscar Handlin, ed., *Immigration as a Factor in American History* (1959), J. Joseph Huthmacher, *A Nation of Newcomers: Ethnic Minority Groups in American History* (1967); and John M. Allswang, *A House for All Peoples: Chicago's Ethnic Groups and Their Politics, 1890-1936* (1971).

Progressives were unpretentious in dealing with immigrants, and they sought always to be helpful. Hamilton Holt, editor of the liberal *Independent*, collected a fascinating volume, *The Life Stories of Undistinguished Americans as Told by Themselves* (1906), the new Americans including a Polish sweatshop girl, a Greek peddler, and a Negro "peon" among others. John R. Commons, professor and student of labor, prepared a compact and dependable volume on *Races and Immigrants* (1907).

A remarkable work by a Rumanian Jew told of his growth from having been a newcomer in the East Side of New York, filled with brilliant immigrant talents in theater and the arts, to separation from its ways through education. M. E. Ravage, in his *An American in the Making* (1917) told of having been denounced as a traitor to his people because he had pursued higher education at Columbia College and elsewhere, and so separated himself from the new immigrants' attitudes and concerns. But such human pangs were inseparable from the mobility which gave individuals opportunities for union or alienation.

17. Various Issues

Prohibition was an important — almost a fatal — issue of the time. It is likely that its career did as much as anything to impugn the reputation of Progressivism. James H. Timberlake, in *Prohibition and the Progressive Movement 1900-1920* (1963) plots the movement's inevitable course. See also Peter H. Odegard, *Pressure Politics: The Story of the Anti-Saloon League* (1928). There have been a number of state histories of prohibition, of which Paul E. Isaac's *Prohibition and Politics: Turbulent Decades in Tennessee 1885-1920* (1965) is an example. All such works throw light on local and sectional differences, and deserve to be kept in mind for indications of changes in social climate. For none of the situations described were simple cases of right or wrong, strength or weakness. Ohio, for example, which produced the most powerful anti-spirits organization was also outstanding in the production of distilled liquors. John A. Krout's *The Origins of Prohibition* (1925), a scholarly work, tells much about American groups and organizations which brought about the phenomenal careers of the prohibitionists, and their equally sensational collapse, as detailed in Odegard's *Pressure Politics*, mentioned above.

See also Ernest H. Cherrington, general secretary of the World League against Alcoholism, who wrote *The Evolution of Prohibition in the United States of America* (1920) with formidable attention to details which probed the strength of his associates and the weakness of his enemies. It is important to distinguish such fighters from Progressives, who tended to be realistic, and in many cases to be drinkers themselves, as Finley Peter Dunne and his imaginary barkeep, Mr. Dooley, knew very well.

John Marshall Barker, *The Saloon Problem and Social Reform* (1905) exemplifies the realistic, responsible Progressive: concerned for the victims of drink, and working without spite or illusion for control of its dangers to life, character, and helpless dependents.

Insurance brought numerous publicists to the fore to criticize its often frustrating or cruel workings. It is best seen through the man who was raised to eminence by the issue, portrayed in Merle J. Pusey's *Charles Evans Hughes* (1951). Also interested in such questions was the greatest of the lawyer-Progressives, Louis D. Brandeis, who served rational societal goals up to and including his nomination for the Supreme Court. Alpheus T. Mason's *Brandeis* (1946) is definitive. *The Letters of Louis D. Brandeis*, edited by Melvin I. Urofsky and David W. Levy (1971–1973) are thus far in three volumes, and view him as urban reformer, People's attorney, and Progressive and Zionist.

Urofsky's *A Mind of One Piece: Brandeis and American Reform* (1971) sets down some of the editor's findings about his subject. Brandeis himself became a test case of Progressivism when reactionary forces of several sorts sought to keep him from ascending to the Supreme Court; see Alden L. Todd, *Justice on Trial: the Case of Louis D. Brandeis* (1964).

The children's cause ranked high with Progressives, and also linked at points with the desire of women for greater opportunity for themselves. Charles Larsen's *The Good Fight* (1972) surveys Ben B. Lindsey's career in this field and as a national symbol. When, in 1908, he was reelected to the Juvenile Court in Denver, the news attracted national attention. See also Elizabeth H. Davidson, *Child Labor Legislation in the Southern Textile States* (1939), and Jeremy F. Felt, *Hostages of Fortune: Child Labor Reform in New York State* (1965). Stephen B. Wood's *Constitutional Politics in the Progressive Era* (1967) deals with child labor. Walter I. Trattner covers the topic in *Crusade for the Children: A History of the National Child Labor Committee and Child Labor Reform in America* (1970).

A cause which touched on several causes, touching Lindsey and Brand Whitlock among others, produced the major figure of Thomas Mott Osborne, who publicized the deficiencies of prisons and developed such creative programs as the honor system and enlightened parole-board procedures; see Rudolph W. Chamberlain's *There Is No Truce* (1935), a life of Osborne. His own publications included *Within Prison Walls* (1914), an account of his own voluntary incarceration, and *Society and Prisons* (1916).

A sense of morality infused much of muckraking and Progressivism, and expressed itself in such a book as Philip L. Allen's *America's Awakening* (1906).

It expressed itself also in softening attitudes toward once stoutly held family relations; the changing record is reviewed in William L. O'Neill's *Divorces in the Progressive Era* (1967). The intrinsic cause — for more free personal choice of partners and sexual equality — was too radical a cause for most Progressives who, like Ida M. Tarbell (in her *The Business of Being a Woman* [1912]) assumed that women were housekeepers and little more than that, though she herself was a spinster.

See also Eleanor Flexner, *Century of Struggle: The Woman's Rights Movement in the United States* (1959). Once again, the state campaigns are individually of interest, as in A. Elizabeth Taylor's *The Woman Suffrage Movement in Tennessee* (1957). Peace was particularly a woman's cause, in which Jane Addams ranked high; see Marie Louise Degen, *The History of the Woman's Peace Party* (1939). David J. Pivar's *Purity Crusade: Sexual Morality and Social Control 1868-1900* (1973) needs to be used with care. Also related to this topic are David M. Kennedy's *Birth Control in America* (1970), which surveys Margaret Sanger's career, and Nathan G. Hale, Jr.'s *Freud and the Americans* (1972).

There was a radical wing to Progressivism which ran from Upton Sinclair, who was a socialist Progressive to Scott Nearing, whose autobiography is properly entitled *The Making of a Radical* (1972). Others closer to Sinclair than to Nearing, as earlier noted, included Robert Hunter, whose *Poverty* (1905) was a pioneer study, and John Spargo, whose *The Bitter Cry of the Children* (1906) broke similar ground. See also Sally M. Miller, *Victor Berger and the Promise of Constructive Socialism 1910-1920* (1973). William J. Ghent should be studied as a pioneer student of American society; his *Our Benevolent Feudalism* (1902) and *Mass and Class* (1904) warned against classes becoming frozen.

Morris Hillquit's *History of Socialism in the United States* (1903) helps define his party's role in the Progressive era, as does David Herreshoff's *American Disciples of Marx: From the Age of Jackson to the Progressive Era* (1967).

Strange though it may seem, free speech was a radical cause, even though the muckrakers had opened the way for treating sensitive themes before mass audiences. The reason was that "free speech" to its most uncompromising friends meant the right to challenge conventional public opinion not only on counts of patriotism and religion, but on sexual topics. Theodore Schroeder was the forward figure in this cause. His attitudes and life are not yet adequately available. See his *Free Speech Anthology* (1909), and also his *"Obscene" Literature and Constitutional Law: A Forensic Defense of Freedom of the Press* (1911). See also John P. Roche, "American Liberty: an Examination of the 'Tradition of Freedom'," in Milton R. Konvitz and Clinton Rossiter, eds., *Aspects of Liberty* (1958).

18. Progressives

Lincoln Steffens, having examined "the shame of the cities" to the satisfaction of his readers, turned (as did many other muckrakers and

Progressives) to the problem of constructive thinking. A product of Steffens's effort was his *Upbuilders* (1909), which, as earlier indicated, contained many insights which ought better to be revisited. For example he urged reformers to avoid the liquor issue, which, he insisted, confused perspectives and broke up movements. Steffens's heroes tended to be a combination of general civic concern plus some direct or indirect regard for law making or administration. Thus, E. A. Filene of Boston was heavily interested in turning merchandising into a civil pursuit. At the same time, he helped organize the American cooperative movement, the American credit union, and other instruments of industrial democracy. Although he did make efforts to refurbish Boston politics and life, they were not his main concern. Filene merits extended study, which will be provided by Mr. Kim McQuaid, presently of Northwestern University. Meanwhile there is Johnson's *Liberal's Progress*, previously noted as a study of Filene, and Filene's own writings, which include *Speaking of Change* (1939), a selection of his speeches and articles.

City, state, and national politics were assessed creatively by others of talent and personality, many, alas, lost to us in recent decades, and not able to feed us with their perceptions and experiences. Thus J. Allen Smith, a professor at the University of Washington, impressed many progressives with his *The Spirit of American Government: A Study of the Constitution: Its Origin, Influence and Relation to Democracy* (1907). Smith concluded that the Constitution was a reactionary document, and intended so to be. It was a view which did much to shake the fatalism of reformers who saw the Supreme Court as an impediment to change, and to give them new energy for social reform.

Charles Edward Merriam, a political scientist and progressive activist, offered contemporary help in explaining our "tendency toward centralization," in his detailed and instructive *American Political Ideas: Studies in the Development of American Political Thought 1865-1917* (1920).

The city was a major basin for progressive action, though, it must be insisted, it far from preempted that role. Frank M. Stewart, in *A Half-Century of Municipal Reform: The History of the National Municipal League* (1950), covers a valuable, though more formal aspect of the "revolt against formalism." Even the Single-Taxers contributed importantly to the modernization of the cities: a fact which can be forgotten, if one concentrates on the "failure" of their main idea; see A. N. Young, *The Single Tax Movement in the United States* (1916). Several larger studies hide as much as they reveal, in focusing attention on larger political combinations. For instance, Hoyt L. Warner's *Progressivism in Ohio 1897-1917* (1964) needs to be supplemented by looking into Clarence H. Cramer's *Newton D. Baker* (1961), since Baker not only succeeded Tom Johnson in Cleveland, but went on to become the Secretary of War under Woodrow Wilson. Brand Whitlock's *Letters and Journal*, edited by Allen Nevins (1936) touches crucially on Ohio affairs, and the larger world into which Whitlock went afterwards.

Other personalities and progressive configurations worth noticing include Ransom E. Noble, Jr., *New Jersey Progressivism before Wilson* (1946); Winifred G. Helmes, *John A. Johnson, the People's Governor* (1949), especially worth attention because Minnesota was so little "urbanized"; Fred Greenbaum, *Fighting Progressive: A Biography of Edward P. Costigan* (1971), an "old fashioned" biography which tells of a fine and courageous Colorado supporter of Ben Lindsey, of municipal ownership of public utilities, of commission government. It bears notice that the Republicans finally defeated Costigan by exploiting the "dry" vote. Hugh C. Bailey's *Edgar Gardner Murphy, Gentle Progressive* (1968) is noteworthy here as helping to break the syndrome of treating "southern" Progressives separately and in segregated pages, though, practically speaking, this must be done to some extent for orderly procedure (*see* Chapter II-20).

Richard Lowitt's *George W. Norris: The Making of a Progressive 1861–1912* (1963) adds scholarship to Norris's own autobiographical *Fighting Liberal* (1945). George E. Mowry's *The California Progressives* (1951) goes tandem with Spencer C. Olin's *California's Prodigal Sons: Hiram Johnson and Progressivism 1911–1917* (1968).

Norris is often seen along with Senator William E. Borah as a westerner and individualist. See Claudius O. Johnson, *Borah of Idaho* (1936) and Marian C. McKenna, *Borah* (1961).[8]

The quality of food was one of the most sensational of early progressive issues, as seen in the Upton Sinclair storm raised by *The Jungle* and the Congressional debates. Senator Albert J. Beveridge exercised himself greatly on the issue and worked to establish by law the Pure Food and Drug Administration. Oscar E. Anderson, Jr.'s *The Health of a Nation: Harvey W. Wiley and the Fight for Pure Food* (1958) reviews the events. Only a sidelight, yet as revealing as sidelights often are is Ella Reeve Bloor's autobiography, *We Are Many* (1940), written when she was a totally committed radical on the left. In earlier days she had been a socialist, and she tells of the research to which she contributed respecting the state of the Chicago stockyards.[9]

Experimental education was varied and vigorous in the Progressive era; see Lawrence A. Cremin, *The Transformation of the School: Progressivism in American Education, 1876–1957* (1961). Edward A. Ross's *Seventy Years of It* (1936) told of his thoroughly progressive career in education; his *Sin and Society* (1907) impressed his generation in arguing that corporations were making sin difficult to recognize; individual responsibility was lost in conglomerates. See also Sol Cohen, *Progressives and Urban School Reform* (1964), and H. K. Beale, *The History of Freedom of Teaching in American Schools* (1941).

19. La Follette

Frederic C. Howe's *Confessions of a Reformer* (1925) properly introduces some appropriate works dealing with this central figure in Progressivism, and his state, since Howe was a national reformer and also author of *Wisconsin: an Experiment in Democracy* (1912). A student of municipal government, author of *The City, the Hope of Democracy* (1905), and later commissioner of immigration for the Port of New York, Howe was one of the distinguished Progressives who ought to be better known.

La Follette's own *Autobiography* (1913) is a due starting point for assessing his career; for though it contains "inaccuracies" discoverable by academics of no consequence, it provides a point of view filled with nuances and achievements. It is implemented by Belle C. and Fola La Follette, *Robert M. La Follette* (1953), a "family" account nevertheless filled with valuable data and insights. Such books as A. T. Lovejoy, *La Follette and the Establishment of the Direct Primary in Wisconsin* (1941) and Edward N. Doan, *The La Follettes and the Wisconsin Idea* (1948), Chester C. Platt, *What La Follette's State is Doing* (1923) and W. F. Raney, *Wisconsin, a Story of Its Progress* (1940), and Ellen Torelle, comp., *The Political Philosophy of Robert M. La Follette* (1920), the last work by La Follette's own company, give some sense of the manner in which a state development was given a nationalized effect. See also Ernest W. Stirn, *An Annotated Bibliography of Robert M. La Follette* (1937).

Charles McCarthy's *The Wisconsin Idea* (1912) displays this vision of a combination of scientifically-acquired data and public responsibility which ultimately, in the Franklin D. Roosevelt Administration, became the "brains" or "brain trust"; see Filler, *Dictionary of American Social Reform*, p. 97. See also E. A. Fitzpatrick, *McCarthy of Wisconsin* (1944).

A strange recent tendency has been to derogate and depreciate La Follette in his own state. The present writer seems indirectly to have contributed to this unworthy impulse by suggesting in certain circles that La Follette ought not to be accepted with shining eyed nondiscrimination. Someone (he thought) must have voted for La Follette because of expectations of personal gain. Never in his wildest moments, however, did the present writer think that this was reason for a sense of unctuous superiority to La Follette. That the progressive movement in Wisconsin declined is quite evident; it declined everywhere. But it did not decline because of the defects in La Follette or his children so much as because of factors in a changing world which required new approaches but required as much the courage and competence of a La Follette. For continuity with his father's memoirs, see Philip F. La Follette's *Adventure in Politics* (1970), excellently edited by Donald Young. See also, for whatever light they throw on our present social circumstances Roger T. Johnson, *Robert M. La Follette, Jr., and the Decline of the Progressive Party in Wisconsin* (1970); Herbert T. Margulies, *Decline of the Progressive Movement in Wisconsin 1890–1920* (1968); Stanley P. Caine, *The Myth of a Progressive Reform: Railroad Regulation in Wisconsin 1903–1910* (1970), the last a peculiarly myopic production which evidently expected regulation to work automatically, in thermostat fashion. In reality, it behooves persons dissatisfied with any particular legislation or condition to bestir themselves, if they so desire.

Robert S. Maxwell's *La Follette and the Rise of the Progressives in Wisconsin* (1956) provides a modern account of the La Follette story. Maxwell, ed., *La Follette* (1969) prints a selection of La Follette's thoughts as well as views of him by contemporaries and historians. David P. Thelen's *The Early Life of Robert M. La Follette 1855–1884* (1966) is a "revisionist" view of the statesman which examines all his actions with suspicion and skepticism. See also Thelen, *The New Citizenship: Origins of Progressivism in Wisconsin 1885–1900* (1972), a monograph which finds Progressivism's roots in everything but idealism and integrity.

20. Southern White and Negro Progressivism

It has been noted elsewhere (*see* Chapter I-7) that Negro leaders had a need to encourage tolerance and respect among their white neighbors, but that they also felt sympathy for those among them who were impatient with social constraints and limitations and who sought drastic means for self-expression. White Progressives tended to judge actions in the Negro community largely on the basis of social usefulness and to be impatient of social weakness. Thus Samuel P. Orth, in his *Our Foreigners*, acknowledged the material advances of the freedmen since slavery, and named with approval the "beacon lights" of the Negroes. Nevertheless, he observed that "there is another side, nowhere better illustrated, perhaps, than in the neglected negro [sic] gardens of the South. Near every negro hut is a garden patch large enough to supply the family with vegetables for the entire year but it is usually neglected" (p. 64). He quoted a Tuskegee critic of his own people in support of his thesis and warned that the energy and talent of the new Italian immigrants might result in "economic doom" for the incapable Negro farmers.

Others, however, could point to the emergence of a tradition of outstanding Negroes in fields from the ministerial to invention; see William J. Simmons's important collection of *Men of Mark* (1887) which dealt with numerous such, especially of the hectic post-Civil War era, and featuring politicians who wielded considerable power in the shadow of Federal authority. Carter G. Woodson, "father of Negro history," dilated on the general subject of Negro achievements; one of his most distinguished works was *The Negro in Our History* (10th ed., 1962, revised and enlarged by Charles H. Wesley; original printing 1922). The volume was notable as repudiating separation, but seeing the Negro odyssey as a movement towards greater competence, greater opportunity, greater respect.

Less distinguished, but most useful and a valiant effort, was Merl R. Eppse's *The Negro, Too, in American History* (1938), prefaced by a photograph of

Abraham Lincoln. It collected numerous biographies integrating Negro thinkers and doers in the American pattern of life, told of the rise of Negro schools — a most progressive field — of denominational activities, and business ventures. It proudly detailed the Negro battle for votes, efforts at colonization, and the role of Negro soldiers during the Spanish-American War. Eppse realistically noted how the Civil Service Act meant jobs for Negroes as well as whites, and in other ways demonstrated that a history without Negroes was limited indeed.

Kelly Miller and J. R. Gay, *Progress and Achievements of the Colored People* (1917) was another such work which in the manner of Progressives emphasized opportunity and accomplishments.

Although he was dead by the time of Progressivism proper, Bishop Daniel Alexander Payne's *Recollections of Seventy Years* (1888) is a reminder of the labors numerous leaders put into the dream and substance of Negro education in the Progressive era and beyond. Although militants later argued that Negroes, educated or uneducated, were unwanted by white bigots, education trained whole generations of Negroes to social effectiveness, and few Negro extremists were brash enough to repudiate so saintly a person as Payne as an "Uncle Tom."

A patent cause of national, as well as southern concern, and a feature of the Progressive era, was the persistence of slavery under various shields of labor contracts, ignorance, malice, and related attitudes and laws. George Washington Cable, a Louisianan and novelist, had fought the convict-lease system which essentially enslaved both black and white unfortunates. His *The Silent South* (1885) had been rejected at home, and he had spent his last years in the North. (See also Cable's *The Negro Question* [1890].) But civic-minded southerners and humanitarians during the progressive years fought terror and law to reduce the disgrace of involuntary servitude, which persisted beyond Progressivism, and still persists; see Pete Daniel, *The Shadow of Slavery: Peonage in the South 1901–1969* (1972).

Whether Henry W. Grady's *The New South* (1890) can rate as a southern progressive statement — or, perhaps, a "right wing" progressive statement — with its emphasis on industry and separation of races is a moot question. See also Raymond B. Nixon, *Henry W. Grady: Spokesman of the New South* (1943). David W. Southern's *Malignant Heritage: Yankee Progressives and the Negro Question* (1968) sees nothing but darkness in the national heritage, to say nothing of the South. L. D. Reddick is more even-handed in his views of "The Negro as Southerner and American," in C. G. Sellers, Jr.'s *The Southerner as American* (1960) — this also includes essays by J. H. Franklin, David Donald, and others — pointing out how indistinguishable are most southern characteristics in both blacks and whites. Hugh C. Bailey's *Liberalism in the New South: Southern Social Reformers and the Progressive Movement* (1969) takes in such figures as the white Walter Hines Page and the black Booker T. Washington. A recognized progressive classic in this field is Ray Stannard Baker's *Following the Color Line* (1908) which treats great figures and small in complex array. William E. Larsen's *Montague of Virginia: The Making of a Southern Progressive* (1965) contrasts well with Emma Lou Thornborough's *T. Thomas Fortune: Militant Journalist* (1972). The latter reveals a hectic Negro career which deserves to be seen as human, rather than erratic.

There are further contrasts in Sheldon Hackney's *Populism to Progressivism in Alabama* (1969), which saw "neither revolution nor reform," but modernization, and Bruce Clayton's *The Savage Ideal: Intolerance and Intellectual Leadership in the South 1890–1914* (1972), a more judicious work than the title indicated. It saw, for example, the career of A. J. McKelway whole, noting his outstanding services against child labor, as well as his dedicated racism. Another point of view appears in Willis D. Weatherford's and Charles S. Johnson's (who taught sociology at Fisk University), *Race Relations: Adjustment of Whites and Negroes in the United States* (1934), and the famous Howard University professor Kelly Miller's *Race Adjustment* and *The Everlasting Stain*, (2 vols., reprinted 1968), which included such items as a defense of Booker T. Washington against Negro criticism, and an open letter to Woodrow Wilson.

W. E. B. Du Bois's life bestrode the Progressive and later eras. His life showed a growing militancy, but of a type different from that of another activist, Harvard-graduated William Monroe Trotter; see Stephen R. Fox, *The Guardian of Boston* (1970). Trotter was responsible for the so-called "Boston riot" of 1903, during which he and sympathizers publicly denounced Booker T. Washington as repressing Negro anger over their treatment as a people.

Du Bois's life was complicated by his high emotionalism, which was in conflict with his statesmanlike qualities. His *Autobiography* (1968) reflects both of his major characteristics. Julius Lester, ed., *The Seventh Son: The Thought and Writings of W. E. B. Du Bois* (2 vols., 1971) shows Du Bois's changing views and emphases. Sometimes, for example, he expresses high regard for Washington's leadership, at other times he becomes Washington's critic, impatient of his tactics, eager for change.

For a variety of works by Negroes which fought the progressive fight see: Booker T. Washington, *The Future of the American Negro* (1899) and *The Negro in Business* (1907); T. Thomas Fortune, *Black and White: Land, Labor, and Politics in the South* (1884) — a keen study which hoped to see the struggle for equal rights substitute for the racial struggle — and W. E. B. Du Bois, *The Souls of Black Folk* (1903).

Charles E. Wynes, ed., *Forgotten Voices: Dissenting Southerners in an Age of Conformity* (1967) included Cable, Lewis H. Blair, and, tragically, Thomas E. Watson of Georgia, whose emotional liberalism revealed its dangers when he turned into a venomous bigot; see C. Vann Woodward, *Tom Watson* (1938).

Unfortunately, Woodward chose to designate Watson as a Progressive, which he hardly was at any stage of his career. In fact, he moved from radical rhetoric to the rhetoric of crass reaction. It is an offense to fine, southern Progressives to identify such a person as Watson with them.

See also Francis B. Simkins, *Pitchfork Ben Tillman* (1944) for a South Carolinian equivalent to the Georgian Watson; and Luthin, *American Demagogues*, previously noted, for portraits of Theodore G. Bilbo of Mississippi, and Eugene Talmadge, who succeeded Watson in Georgia as a stirrer-up of the worst feelings of frustrated farmers.

Such politicians, to repeat, do not deserve mention in the same context as true Progressives, for all the limitations the latter may have had. Burton J. Hendrick, in *The Training of an American: The Earlier Life and Letters of Walter H. Page 1855-1913* (1928) shows a publisher and statesman who moved slowly toward racial equality, if at all, but posited civilized behavior on both sides of the racial line. The same perspective appears in Edgar Gardner Murphy's *Problems of the Present South* (1904) and *The Basis of Ascendency* (1909). See also V. O. Key, Jr., *Southern Politics* (1949).

Perspective on race is not easily obtained. C. Vann Woodward notes, in his *Origins of the New South* (1951), that "Progressivism had its day in the South as elsewhere, but it no more fulfilled the political aspirations and deeper needs of the mass of people than did the first New Deal administration. Otherwise, there is no explaining the rise of the [Cole L.] Bleases [blatant demagogues] in the earlier instance — nor of Huey Long in the latter" (p. 395). It is easy to forget the Weatherfords, Montagues, and Pages, and emphasize less gracious personages, as in Albert D. Kirwan, *The Revolt of the Rednecks: Mississippi Politics 1876-1925* (1951), and William D. Miller, *Memphis during the Progressive Era, 1900-1917* (1957). After all, were they not southern equivalents of recently touted northern bosses? But such emphases ignore the powerful meliorating forces emanating from both Negro and white society.

Progressivism was a large, strongly-pulsed movement. It would have been strange had it not included doubtful and undesirable elements. But it included also elements which organized the National Association for the Advancement of Colored People — an organization inconceivable without the firm cooperation of Negroes and whites. Especially helpful is such a work as B. Joyce Ross's *J. E. Spingarn and the Rise of the NAACP, 1911-1939* (1972), since it helps put in perspective such narrow-gauged works as *Malignant Heritage*, mentioned above. The NAACP was a progressive triumph: of Negro Progressivism and, of course, the much-larger Progressive movement. Without such workers as Spingarn, Charles Edward Russell, and William English Walling, no NAACP was possible; see Robert J. Jack, *History of the National Association for the Advancement of Colored People* (1943), and Charles Flint Kellogg, *NAACP* (1967).[10]

21. Labor and Capital

Labor was not so much progressive as it was a factor in Progressivism. Labor's tendency, thanks to the difficult conditions with which it lived, was to be *radical*; that is, to force upon capitalism a sense of its wrongs. William Cahn, ed., *A Pictorial History of American Labor* (1972) details some of the conditions which created this attitude. Burton J. Hendrick's *The Age of Big Business* (1919) is of interest as by a former quasi-muckraker and Progressive who, standing between labor and capital, sought to balance the count between them.

There are numerous books about business which deserve study in order to observe labor-capital relations in realistic terms. T. C. Cochran and William Miller, *The Age of Enterprise* (1942) is most readable; Elisha P. Douglass, *The Coming of the Age of American Business: Three Centuries of Enterprise, 1600–1900* (1971) is one of the latest. These two works do not sufficiently take into account the attitudes of Progressives as they affected business. Robert Wiebe's *Businessmen and Reform* (1962) is one study which does so. Its thesis is that Progressives saw a compatability of all classes and harbored a faith in individuality. Edward C. Kirkland, in *Dream and Thought in the Business Community, 1860–1900* (1956), describes the conservative situation in business against which Progressives had to contend. Samuel P. Hays, in *Response to Industrialism, 1885–1914* (1957), saw a process of modernization evolve out of the business community, but needed to perceive the human factor as operating in a native context.

Businessmen were varied and strongly individual, some welcoming aspects of Progressivism, others resisting it, sometimes to the bitter end. See, for example, Joseph G. Pyle's *The Life of James J. Hill* (2 vols., 1916–1917) which shows the "Empire Builder" developing his Great Northern Railway Company without land grants and without government subsidies. His own *Highways of Progress* (1910) suggests that more inspired his efforts than hunger for more and more wealth. See also William T. Hutchinson's *Cyrus Hall McCormick* (2 vols., 1930–1935) which again gives evidence that this inventor of the reaper, though forced into bitter legal battles, may have had motivations beyond those of greed. Progressives took such questions into account when they developed their critiques of capital.

The trust haunted the dreams of all Americans, and they sought guidance in connection with its power for good or evil. Charles R. Flint and others analyzed it in *The Trust: Its Book* (1902), a volume which was edited by James H. Bridge, himself author of an early, realistic study of the rise of Andrew Carnegie. See also *The Masters of Capital* (1919) by John Moody, a mild critic of business who, himself, became a symbol of business's power and prestige. See also Moody's sometimes moving and always enlightening autobiography, *The Long Road Home* (1933).

Two novels demand thoughtful reading. Frank Norris's *The Pit* (1903), which was intended to be part two of a trilogy; the first part was the famous *The Octopus* (1901) which told of the clash between farmers and the all-powerful Southern Pacific Railroad. *The Pit* took the action to the stock exchange, where it saw jungle forces unleashed. Norris's intention was, in a third volume, to show nature and humanity combining to hold in check the animal passions of men and force their cooperation and well-being. It was, perhaps, just as well that he did not finish his trilogy.

Theodore Dreiser was of more pessimistic temperament, and this was shown in his *The Financier* (1912), a novel based on the career of Charles T. Yerkes, who used force and chicanery which first brought him to imprisonment, then to affluence in the hectic politics of Chicago. Dreiser was no muckraker; he admired men of forcefulness, and saw nothing in nature conducive to morality. But he saw a side of human nature which others had to agree was there, and which Progressives took into account as they made their observations and programs.

Labor tended toward radicalism simply because it found itself harassed by the principles which employers followed. Graham Adams, Jr., in his *Age of Industrial Violence 1910-15* (1966), examines the findings of the United States Commission on Industrial Relations and finds them ruthless beyond tolerance. Ivy Lee, an innovator in public relations in behalf of business, in his *Human Nature and Railroads* (1914) made a plea for "leadership" as opposed to "mob rule" which, in effect, meant that the heads of industry ought to make all the rules for industrial relations and enforce them.

Such a point of view allowed labor spokesmen and advocates to defend violence on their side and yet maintain reputations for liberalism. This would be true of Eugene V. Debs, socialist leader, who was seen as saintly by his admirers. See David Karsner, *Talks with Debs in Terre Haute* (1922) and, with greater sophistication, Ray Ginger, *The Bending Cross* (1949), a biography of Debs.

More complex in some ways was Clarence Darrow, who began by defending labor leaders accused of violence, and in the 1920s fought to save the lives of the young murderers Richard Loeb and Nathan Leopold. Darrow's basic premise was the sanctity of human life and the valuelessness of capital punishment — humanistic tenets which many Progressives could accept. Darrow has attracted sentimental portrayals, almost of a folklore quality. His actual words make him more believable; see samples of his writings as reproduced in Arthur and Lila Weinberg, eds., *Clarence Darrow's Verdicts Out of Court* (1963).

Two figures of indubitable progressive tenets were Oscar Ameringer and Helen Keller. Ameringer was a socialist with Populist qualities who saw no reason for human want and poured wit and sarcasm over the frailties of American capitalism; see his autobiography, *If You Don't Weaken* (1940). Helen

Keller for a time lent her distinction to the socialist cause. See Philip S. Foner, ed., *Helen Keller: Her Socialist Years, Writings and Speeches* (1967), and Van Wyck Brooks, *Helen Keller: Sketch for a Portrait* (1956).

Nathan Fine's *Labor and Farmer Parties in the United States, 1828–1928* (1928) comes to grips with the fact that farmer-labor alliances were fluid, transcended "urban progressivism," and accomplished something positive for American society. See also Stuart A. Rice, *Farmers and Workers in American Politics* (1924). Central to the problem of labor was the dreaded labor injunction which could order embattled workers to cease and desist from striking, and thus take the heart out of their organizing efforts. Felix Frankfurter and N. V. Greene, in *The Labor Injunction* (1931), explain this significant point.

Results of such difficulties may be examined in numerous studies indicating radical and even anarchistic responses to acute troubles. See, for example, A. M. Simons's socialist *Class Struggles in America* (1903) and Sidney Lens's *The Labor Wars: From the Molly Maguires to the Sitdowns* (1973). Hutchins Hapgood's *The Spirit of Labor* (1907) is evocative, as is, with less art, Eli Ginzberg's and Hyman Berman's *The American Worker in the Twentieth Century: A History through Autobiographies* (1963).

The Progressives sought understanding, as in William English Walling's *American Labor and American Democracy* (1926); see also Irwin Yellowitz, *Labor and the Progressive Movement in New York State 1897–1916* (1965). However, they deprecated violence as an instrument for advancing labor's lot. George G. Suggs, Jr., in *Colorado's War on Militant Unionism* (1972), seems to suggest that they could not honor law and order and survive, but Progressives responded with such antagonistic books as John Spargo's *Syndicalism, Industrial Unionism and Socialism* (1913), and Robert Hunter's *Violence and the Labor Movement* (1914).

The classic criticism of business continues to be Henry Demarest Lloyd's *Wealth against Commonwealth*, earlier noted. It was answered at length in Allen Nevins's *Study in Power, John D. Rockefeller, Industrialist and Philanthropist* (1953), but not before Lloyd's book had influenced an entire generation of American social thinkers. The question of what the "facts" in the matter are is relevant. It must be noted, however, that much American social discourse has necessarily tended toward exaggeration, in order to underscore its points. Whether this helps such a book as James Weinstein, *The Corporate Ideal in the Liberal State 1900–1918* (1968), which sees business as needing "war as fulfillment," remains to be seen.

There were distinct Progressives among laborers. John Mitchell, coal miner and a founder of the United Mine Workers, was one such; see his *Organized Labor* (1903) and *The Wage Earner and His Problems* (1915). Far and above all of them was Samuel Gompers, who moved from labor radicalism to a program of opportunistic survival and growth. Although this offended his foes, including his biographer Bernard Mandel — see his *Samuel Gompers* (1963) — it helped keep labor out of the hands of short-sighted dreamers and enthusiasts. Gompers's own *Seventy Years of Life and Labor* (2 vols., 1925) explains and defends his viewpoint.

Capitalism also produced its statesmen, unwilling to give up its free enterprise prerogatives, but anxious to avoid devastating labor wars. Herbert Croly, in *Marcus Alonzo Hanna* (1912), treated this Republican manager as a great man: an interesting conviction, since it came from the founder of the liberal *New Republic*. Hanna was active in a mediating agency — some held its purpose was to dampen workers' organizing activism — and worked with Gompers to curb the more distressing labor-capital confrontations; see Marguarite Green, *The National Civic Federation and the American Labor Movement, 1900–1925* (1956). [11]

22. Progressivism at Peak

The basic fact about Progressivism as it moved to fulfill itself in legislation and political choices was enunciated by Charles Edward Russell in his muckraking *Business* (1911). He termed business "the heart of the nation," and so held that it needed to be firmly controlled in the interests of the body politic it was required to serve. The problem — and the problem for the entire progressive generation — was to determine just what would serve the nation best.

A vital fact about Progressivism was that it inspired some reformers who were essentially conservative, but who were closer to those who were consistent in their reform aspirations than to their hard and fast conservative associates. This gave power and breadth to Progressivism, but also created soft spots which would confine it and give its later critics grounds for derogating the entire movement, as in Gabriel Kolko's *The Triumph of Conservatism: A Reinterpretation of American History 1900–1916* (1963).

Yet distinctions must be made, if we are not to trap ourselves in our own presumptions. No great popular movement can advance if it is to be held in the hands of a few tight-fisted leaders. Progressives helped make William Howard Taft President, yet his collection of speeches, *Present-Day Problems* (1908), holds to legalism at the expense of human need. Albert J. Beveridge's *The Meaning of the Times and Other Speeches* (1908) is by another Republican, but demands that the human factor be honored. To be sure, Beveridge broke with Taft in 1912. John Wanamaker, a pioneer of department store development did not, but he was concerned for democratic ends and put his financial solvency on the line in defiance of would-be trusts; see Herbert Adams Gibbons, *John Wanamaker* (1926).

Arthur J. Eddy, in *The New Competition* (1912), reflected business's effort to work together, but in an effort (idealistically put, to be sure) to affect government in ways limiting to progressive intentions.

A progressive figure meriting recapture by a new generation was Frank Parsons, an intensely learned and intensely idealistic student of the American system. He is presently known only as the creator of vocational guidance. He was much more; see his *The Telegraph Monopoly* (1899), *The City for the People* (1899), and his *Railroads, the Trusts and the People* (1906). All of this was, however, subservient to his desire to lift public understanding through education and reform measures. See Howard V. Davis, *Frank Parsons, Prophet, Innovator, Counselor* (1969).

Muckraking differed from Progressivism in being more pertinaciously concerned for matters close to the individual consciousness. Although muckrakers and Progressives met at many points on key issues, muckraking tended more toward personalized and event-weighted approaches, Progressivism, toward larger views of national policy. Muckraking preceded Progressivism, setting up interest in the state of society by way of its reports on crime, fraud, the troubles of the poor, the women, the children, the immigrants. All such matters, vividly detailed, heightened the sensibilities of the reading public and prepared it for the rhetoric and passion which attended Progressivism at its peak.

Accordingly, new and concerted attention was given Progressives, individually and as a presumed movement. The apparent seriousness of their program may be seen in the opinion of some observers — Ray Stannard Baker, for example — that the Republican party was fated to disappear as the old Whigs had, to be succeeded by the Progressive party.

The overview of the situation from the legislative side may be considered in Kenneth Hechler's *Insurgency: Personalities and Politics of the Taft Era* (1940) and James Holt's *Congressional Insurgents and the Party System, 1909–1916* (1967). The participants saw themselves in S. Duncan-Clark's *The Progressive Movement: Its Principles and Program* (1913), with an introduction by Theodore Roosevelt; William English Walling's *Progressivism and After* (1914), Walling then viewing events from a socialist standpoint; and Benjamin Parke De Witt's *The Progressive Movement* (1915).

Thomas Dreier's *Heroes of Insurgency* (1910) gives a sense of the urgency which seemed to attend his subjects' efforts. In addition to other Progressives who have received mention elsewhere, there was William E. Borah of Idaho who, however, refused to follow Roosevelt out of the Republican party; some modern attitudes of disillusion with Progressivism may be perceived in such a book as LeRoy Ashby's *The Spearless Leader* (1972), a sour study of Borah, which would have, perhaps, required their subjects to leap out of their time into the 1970s for satisfying fulfillment.

Carl H. Chrislock, in *The Progressive Era in Minnesota, 1899–1918* (1970), shows farm issues as national issues, and helps explain how such solutions as they found were products of urban and rural thinking combined. The excitement conjured up in the Old Northwest is recounted in Robert L. Morlan, *Political Prairie Fire, the Non-Partisan League 1915–1922* (1955). Also worth notice, there being too few such compilations, is Colin B. Goodykoontz, ed., *The Papers of Edward P. Costigan . . . 1902–1917* (1941), Costigan having been previously identified as an outstanding Colorado Progressive.

The leader of the Progressives was universally recognized to be La Follette; why he should have failed to receive their nomination in 1912 wants closer attention than it has been given. Their major cause appeared to be monopoly, with its challenge to American traditions of freedom. That there were conservative aspects to the progressive campaign there can be no doubt; Americans had much to conserve; and, indeed, the issue of conservation became an outstanding one, giving momentum to Progressivism. The controversy which the country found most stirring was the so-called Ballinger Affair, involving the then Secretary of the Interior and the alleged give-away of Alaskan land claims thought to be valuable. The matter is discussed in Alpheus T. Mason, *Bureaucracy Convicts Itself* (1941); in Gifford Pinchot, *Breaking New Ground* (1947); in James Penick, Jr., *Progressive Politics and Conservation* (1968); and in Elmo R. Richardson, *The Politics of Conservation . . . 1897–1913* (1962). Pinchot himself is discussed in M. Nelson McGeary, *Gifford Pinchot, Forester Politician* (1960). See also Judson King, *The Conservation Fight: From Theodore Roosevelt to the Tennessee Valley Authority* (1959). A related issue in conservation, stretching over into another era, is J. Leonard Bates, *The Origins of Teapot Dome: Progressives, Parties and Petroleum, 1909–1921* (1963).

A key to Progressivism's great era was the rage for efficiency — in that time the equivalent impulse for what later became mass production, computer heroics, and electronics — efforts to produce more faster, presumably in the interests of a more substantial and fulfilled people. Progressivism was in many ways an efficiency movement, surrounded with an aura of eloquence and high hopes.

Samuel P. Hays, *Conservation and the Gospel of Efficiency . . . 1890–1920* (1959) provides a transition between two significant movements. The efficiency evangel was widely heard. Municipal workers stressed *forms* of city government; Vann Woodward observes, in his *Origins of the New South*, that it is too little recognized that the Commission Plan and the City-Manager Plan both originated in such southern cities as Galveston, Texas, and in Memphis, New Orleans, Greenville, and elsewhere. See also Harold A. Stone and others, *City Manager Government in the United States* (1940). Industrial analysts sought to streamline factory operations; the key work is Frederick Taylor, *Principles of Scientific Management* (1911). Gompers and others worried that workers might be forced to invest more labor and energy at no more pay, but efficiency was an instrument which could be used or misused. For a general study, see Samuel Haber, *Efficiency and Uplift: Scientific Management in the Progressive Era,*

1890–1920 (1964). See also Milton J. Nadworny, *Scientific Management and the Unions, 1900–1932* (1955). Other relevant works include Morris L. Cooke and Philip Murray, *Organized Labor and Production: Next Steps in Industrial Democracy* (1940); Sudhir Kakar, *Frederick Taylor: A Study in Personality and Innovation* (1970); and Richard M. Huber, *The American Idea of Success* (1971), the latter containing an excellent section on efficiency.

Railroads had accumulated an enormous amount of moral and technical lore. Although the Hepburn Act of 1906 was intended to strike a compromise between individual ownership, with its dangers of exploitation, and government ownership, with its dangers of bureaucracy, the question of authority and control hung over the Progressive movement. William Z. Ripley, an authority, in *Railroads: Rates and Regulation* (1912), said as much as any one man could to elucidate the matter. Gabriel Kolko's *Railroads and Regulation* (1965) attracted academic attention by seeing developments as a "triumph of conservatism," which they may well have been. Another point of view, however, is expressed in Albro Martin's *Enterprise Denied: Origins of the Decline of American Railroads, 1897–1917* (1971) which sees government meddling as having drained the railroads of vigor and resourcefulness.

Many of the developments of the time can be accounted for on the score of efficiency, but in such a work as Louis D. Brandeis accomplished, for example, a moral as well as modernizing element can be clearly discerned. Brandeis conducted legal suits in behalf of workers and middle class merchants and others who needed to overcome abstract law in defense of their savings, their safety on jobs, and other basics. The "Brandeis Brief" was established as a factual approach in court which demonstrated, through statistics and human interest cases, that definitions of freedom and civil rights had to be judged in terms of real conditions.

A wide variety of reforms of the time can be assessed in part in terms of the efficiency — or modernization — they augmented. Propaganda on their behalf can be found or discerned in years preceding the Woodrow Wilson Administrations, and built ground for them. Nevertheless scarcely one of these reforms lacked its eloquent spokesmen, or failed to ask regard in terms of human need. This was true of antitrust actions of the Taft Administration which, it was hoped, would serve American freedom and opportunity. In the long run, Americans opted for regulation of trusts, rather than their destruction; see Hans B. Thorelli, *The Federal Antitrust Policy* (1954). The popular election of senators had been advocated long before, and was a semirespectable topic of controversy, as shown in the preparation of an academic thesis, John Haynes's *Popular Elections of United States Senators* (Johns Hopkins University Studies in Historical and Political Science, Eleventh Series XI–XII, 1893). David Graham Phillips's "Treason of the Senate" articles in *Cosmopolitan* gave glamour and urgency to the cause. The Lorimer case, noted before (*see* Chapter II-15) helped, whether rightly or wrongly, to call further attention to the reform, which was brought to fulfillment (in 1913) by the adoption of the Seventeenth Amendment to the Constitution. See Robert and Leona Train Rienow, *Of Snuff, Sin and the Senate* (1965), especially "The Senate and Reform," (pp. 278 ff.).

The stockmarket could not achieve regulation in the Progressive era; Americans could not bring themselves to shed a sufficient quantity of their largely illusory hopes of making a "killing" in the market; see Cedric B. Cowing, *Populists, Plungers, and Progressives: A Social History of Stock and Commodity Speculation 1890–1936* (1965). They did, however, take steps to curb some of the more drastic by-products of speculation and monopoly power through income tax and trade regulation, as examined in Thomas C. Blaisdell, Jr.'s *The Federal Trade Commission: An Experiment in the Control of Business* (1932) and Sidney Ratner's *American Taxation: Its History as a Social Force in Democracy* (1942). Establishment of the Federal Reserve Bank, however, was a large step forward in modernization and innovative government intervention in business. It derived partly from the revelations in hearings of the famous Pujo Committee in Congress (1912), made strikingly clear in Louis D. Brandeis's *Other People's Money* (1914). Carter Glass's *An Adventure in Constructive Finance* (1927) may be read along with Rixey Smith's and Norman Beasley's *Carter Glass* (1939), and especially Samuel Untermyer's *Who Is Entitled to the Credit for the Federal Reserve Act? An Answer to Senator Carter Glass* (1927). See also Seymour E. Harris, *Twenty Years of Federal Reserve Policy* (1933).

Such were some of the achievements of Progressivism which, as stated, overlapped into Woodrow Wilson's era. Such measures as the above were strongly intended to be helpful to industry, and with no sense of selling out the Republic for that reason; Americans were presumed to have a stake in capital, and apparently agreed that such was the case. These measures were also intended to serve what was largely — overwhelmingly a majority — a white population and, again, without necessarily harming others. The Pujo Committee was a progressive triumph which held capital up to the mark of public responsibility. So was the United States Commission on Industrial Relations, which sorted out information, much of it painful, regarding inhumanity and the wounding of civil rights in respect to workers and their organizations; see Graham Adams, Jr., *The Age of Industrial Violence 1910–15* (1966). Hyman Weintraub's *Andrew Furuseth, Emancipator of Seamen* (1959) honors a leader of an oppressed minority of workers, but it was La Follette's Seaman's Act which began the long march for justice in the field. The NAACP has already been noted as a progressive triumph, but Negroes as early as 1912 could claim political clout. W. E. B. Du Bois, in his autobiography, declared that his people had elected Woodrow Wilson over Theodore Roosevelt: a debatable belief, but one complimentary to the democratic process.

Free Trade was a great issue in the Progressive era and contributed to William Howard Taft's decline in public esteem, and it was Woodrow Wilson's major cause in 1912 — one he had inherited from southern traditions extending back to the 1820s. Free Trade concerns us less now than it did the Progressives because it has become locked into international diplomacy. It merits understanding because it helps describe the world of the Progressives and their different ways of handling social differences. See Frank W. Taussig, *Tariff History of the United States* (1931). Also Festus P. Summers, *William L. Wilson and Tariff Reform* (1953). The tariff as a progressive issue can be assessed in studies and biographies of La Follette, Beveridge, Taft, Woodrow Wilson, and other figures of the time. See also Henry T. Wills, *Scientific Tariff Making* (1913).

Progressivism in 1912, then, was crystallizing around a new society intended to be, not so much "elite" — a word repulsive to the democratic tradition — as executive. That is, the industrial, urban-directed society appeared to need more and better administrators of its complex people and sectors. We have already seen ward-heelers sentimentally idealized as the true friends of the working man, and though this was a doubtful picture of reality, it contained grains of truth. There were pompous nativists who deemed themselves superior to new immigrants. There were malicious racists. Such books as Huthmacher's biography of Robert F. Wagner and John D. Buenker's *Urban Liberalism and Progressive Reform* (1973) were useful in tracing change in a new urbanism. The Progressives helped with vital research, as well as reform. Such a series as that edited by Clinton Rogers Woodruff for the National Municipal League was most enlightening. Typical was Graham R. Taylor's *Satellite Cities: A Study of Industrial Suburbs* (1915): a book which touched on a vital feature of American developments. Also in the series were books on city government, municipal utilities, women's work, the cost of living, and other topics by such worthies as Mary R. Beard, and the academician William Bennett Munro. If Andrew Jackson and the common thief Samuel Swartwout can be seen as associated in the currents of Progressivism in their time, it is not clear why Woodrow Wilson and Charles F. Murphy of Tammany Hall could not also be so regarded. "Moral" reformers kept the world of Jackson honest; and though religious zeal was low by the 1910s at the better political levels, there were good elements in society. There was Frances Perkins, later of the New Deal cabals, who was properly revolted by the dreadful fire in 1911, which charred almost one hundred and fifty girls working in a shirtwaist factory, to do something about the conditions which had permitted the tragedy to occur; see Leon Stein, *The Triangle Fire* (1962). Arthur Mann's *La Guardia: A Fighter against the Times, 1882–1933* (1959) deals with one worthy product of immigrant unrest and the will to better the conditions of the poor.[12]

23. Woodrow Wilson

Progressivism shared honors with other tendencies in American life for modernizing and assimilating new and old factors of its configuration, and did more than its share in seeking a balance between the old and the new. George W. Perkins was of the executive class, in John A. Garraty's book *Right-Hand Man* (1960) — that is, right-hand man to J. P. Morgan. As such he worked judiciously to build company relations to government and to the Progressive party and has been made, somewhat unfairly, a symbol of capitalistic influence in it. It was not surprising that there should have been some such influence, and not necessarily for the worst. Nevertheless there were understandings in politics which needed perennial attention. Thus, during the Hughes insurance investigation, it came out that an insurance company in which he was interested had given $48,000 to Roosevelt's 1904 campaign fund. Perkins was asked whether such gifts ought not to be made illegal, and he agreed that they should. However, it was others who led in the drawing up and legislative enactment of laws which changed the rules of special gifts, and special favors; people like Perkins helped little.

Both Democrats and Republicans needed to bring their party organizations up to date, and especially to refurbish the executive branch. The great book in the field was Herbert Croly's *The Promise of American Life* (1909). It derogated the reform movement as sentimental and, in the famous phrase, sought "Jeffersonian ends by Hamiltonian means." That is, it proposed a strong executive who served the interests of all the people. Croly later supplemented his views with *Progressive Democracy* (1914). For his *New Republic*, he found such persons to help explicate his views as Walter Lippmann and others who thought the nation needed masterful leaders rather than careless consensus.

The problem of an elite in a democracy is most complicated, since, in one sense, all societies inevitably precipitate elites, however they may designate themselves. Croly's biography, *Willard Straight* (1924), dealing with a wealthy American interested in Chinese financial affairs who subsidized the *New Republic*, is essentially a tale of elitists who hoped to run American affairs with a minimum of popular involvement. Graham Wallas's *The Great Society, a Psychological Analysis* (1914), a successor to this author's also important *Human Nature in Politics* (1908), in effect sought ways to manipulate public opinion, presumably in the public's best interests.

Walter Lippmann was persuaded to this point of view, though his long service as analyst of American domestic and foreign affairs gives insight into what happened to it over the years. See David Weingast, *Walter Lippmann, a Study in Personal Journalism* (1949); Marquis Childs and James Reston, eds., *Walter Lippmann and His Times* (1959); Clinton Rossiter and James Lare, eds., *The Essential Lippmann* (1965); E. L. and F. H. Schapmeier, *Walter Lippmann,*

Philosopher-Journalist (1969); John Luskin, *Lippmann, Liberty, and the Press* (1972).

That Woodrow Wilson should have emerged as a leader of elitists was a phenomenon of the time. He was the president of Princeton University, who esteemed himself a conservative Democrat, and of a southern heritage. In 1910, there was still a powerful national opinion sympathetic to the northern argument which had dominated the Civil War. George B. Tindall, in *The Emergence of the New South* (1967), makes much of Wilson as representative of his alert and resourceful section: one which was able to fight back and persuade the nation of its point of view. Wilson's vital tariff views are examined in William Diamond's *The Economic Thought of Woodrow Wilson* (1943). *Woodrow Wilson: Reform Governor* (1965), edited by David W. Hirst, examines the record which made him a national figure and the Democratic candidate for the election of 1912. An outstanding figure of Wilson's circle was Edward M. House, remarkable for having real influence in Wilson's presidential chambers, without having ever suffered the challenge of elections or of close public scrutiny. House was the anonymous author of *Philip Dru, Administrator: A Story of Tomorrow, 1920–1935* (1912), which Wilson admired as sketching the executive the nation needed, but who had at least several doubtful social attitudes. Charles Seymour, ed., *The Intimate Papers of Colonel House* (4 vols., 1926–1928) deserves closer study than it has recently received, for light on Wilson's and the nation's preconceptions.

Vann Woodward notes, in his *Origins of the New South* that "Progressivism — [was] for Whites Only" (pp. 369 ff.). It has been recently emphasized that the Wilson Administration did indeed seek to overthrow Republican patronage respecting Negroes, and especially to emphasize segregation in government such as Republicans had avoided. Although this was generally true, it was inaccurate to attaint all Progressivism with the policies of southerners or Democrats. Progressive achievements aiming toward equality have already been indicated, and were augmented by famous Progressives. The theory, which at the time gave the Wilson Administration distinction as one in which the greatest number of reform measures had passed, assumed that his reforms — in free trade, farmers' loans, antitrust action, and others — served all Americans, directly or indirectly.

Ray Stannard Baker, one of the most famous of the muckrakers, became an admirer and associate of Wilson, and later edited his papers; see Baker's *Woodrow Wilson: Life and Letters* (8 vols., 1927–1939). This series is now being superseded by Arthur S. Link and others, eds., *The Papers of Woodrow Wilson* in a continuous series of publications, beginning in 1966. Link himself has been long engaged in a definitive life of Wilson; for a brief summary of his views about this subject which has engaged him so long, see his *Woodrow Wilson* (1963).

The Wilson bibliography is immense, and it must suffice here to indicate some of the areas it takes in. Wilson's writings must themselves be taken into account; see, for example, his *Mere Literature and Other Essays* (1896) which helped make his reputation with the influential academic community. As president, first of Princeton University, then of the country, his writings multiplied. See Ray Stannard Baker and William E. Dodd, eds., *College and State: Educational, Literary and Political Papers (1875-1913)* (2 vols., 1925); Saul K. Padover, ed., *Wilson's Ideals* (1942), offering his epigrams on business, government, and politics; and August Heckscher, ed., *The Politics of Woodrow Wilson* (1956).

An evocative work is D. H. Elletson, *Roosevelt and Wilson: A Comparative Study* (1965). John Wells Davidson, ed., *A Crossroads of Freedom: The 1912 Campaign Speeches of Woodrow Wilson* (1956) is an intensely interesting account of Wilson's appeal to the country as it indeed stood at crossroads in 1912. Wilson became President because the Republican party divided into Regulars and Progressives. It thus becomes important to understand what that split involved; see Victor Rosewater's *Backstage in 1912: The Inside Story of the Split Republican Convention* (1932).

Colonel House's momentous influence on the White House helps define the Progressivism of Wilson; see A. D. H. Smith, *The Real Colonel House* (1918) and Alexander L. George and Juliette L. George, *Woodrow Wilson and Colonel House* (1956). William Allen White's *Woodrow Wilson* (1924) reflects a softer aspect of the Progressive drive. Wilson's southern character makes important that of his southern associates; see, for example, writings by Josephus Daniels, who was his Secretary of the Navy, *Tar Heel Editor* (1939), *Editor in Politics* (1941), and *The Wilson Era: Years of Peace, 1910-1917* (1944); and Robert Dallek, *Democrat and Diplomat: The Life of William E. Dodd* (1968).

Wilson was a personality as well as a political figure, and much can be discerned about him in such memoirs as Edith Bolling Wilson's *My Memoir* (1939), and Cary T. Grayson's (his physician) *Woodrow Wilson: An Intimate Memoir* (1960).

See also John M. Blum, *Joe Tumulty and the Wilson Era* (1951) and *Woodrow Wilson and the Politics of Morality* (1956).[13]

24. The Youth Movement

A movement which to a considerable extent was the wave of the future and, as such, helped qualify the force of Progressivism, was the emergence of youth as an all but separate entity in American life. Youth had heretofore been an adjunct of adult pursuits. Youth had sought to prove themselves worthy of attention by superior energy, superior ardor, and superior courage. It had been a count against William Jennings Bryan's 1896 candidacy that he *had* been young and presumably untried.

The rise of the city, with its impersonal circumstances, the drift of unattended youth to the big cities created new enclaves in New York, Chicago, and San Francisco, among other centers dedicated to new emphases upon self-expression, experimentation in the arts and education, and radical politics. Upton Sinclair had been young in the 1900s, but his social goals were the goals of his elders. Jack London had, to a degree, followed "bohemian" impulses in his career, but they were largely impulses of adventure, rather than a new life-style.

The new young were critical of national politics. They assessed reform in housing, pure food, and other fields as palliatives. They dreamed of an entirely new freedom which made of experiment a way of life, rather than a preliminary to settling down. In the 1910s they arrested attention for their eccentric (as it seemed) art, their tolerant attitudes toward sexual experimentation, their regard for the euphoria of strong drink not as a diversion from serious interests, but as a serious interest in itself. In the 1920s they were to reappear — following the trauma of wartime — not as eccentrics, but as having been the advance guard of an adult generation which went in for modern design, a new emphasis on fun, sports cars, and other evidences of a desire to be young for youth's own sake.

In the 1910s such pursuits seemed remote from the serious concerns of a President Wilson. Yet youth leaders thought themselves more serious than their elders. Thus Randolph Bourne, a hunchback with a great need for important goals in life, dreamed of transforming America into a land of beauty and equality; see Filler, *Randolph Bourne* (1966 ed.). Bourne wrote on experimental schools, youthful ideals, the linking of beauty in fiction and poetry with human need. A pacifist, he denounced American intervention in World War I, and became an inspiration to others who thought like him.

John Reed, son of a West Coast reformer, attended Harvard and drifted far from his father's ideas of responsible government conservation policies. Reed began as a bohemian and became a radical and founder of the Communist Party. His story has been told from the communist point of view by Granville Hicks, in *John Reed* (1936). Histories of radicalism tend to bring in such figures as Bourne and Reed as intellectuals concerned for workers' causes; see, for example, Lillian Symes's and Travers Clement's *Rebel America* (1934).

Hutchins Hapgood's *A Victorian in the Modern World* (1939) is of interest as by one who had been part of the Progressive era, though concerned artistically more for people than for national issues. Such books of his as *The Autobiography of a Thief* (1903) and *The Spirit of Labor* (1907) added color and depth to muckraking and progressive literature. In the 1910s he abandoned old associates to join the youthful experimenters and become deeply involved in subjective experiences.

Van Wyck Brooks was a total intellectual, but as such, set himself up in the 1910s as a critic of American aesthetics and attitudes. His search for a "usable past" amounted to a desire to repudiate much of the American past as crude and wasteful, and reflected a youthful desire actually to dig a gap between the older and younger generations. He then despised the Puritans as repressive of deep human feelings. His *America's Coming-of-Age* (1915) posited that much of the American past had been imitative, gauche, unmemorable, and that a new and emancipating spirit was being unfolded. All of this did not bode well for unifying factors between Progressives and youth. The oppression practiced by military and police on dissidents during World War I created bitterness in the harassed elements which deepened this first generation gap. In some way, John Dos Passos's trilogy, *U.S.A.* (1930–1938), composed of *The 42nd Parallel, 1919,* and *The Big Money,* was a monument to the tragedy of disaffection which took place between generations.

Audiovisual Aids

1. *Social Reform Movements,* EAV; *The Living Past, Parts 1–4,* FCE; *Issues in American Democracy,* ERS; *Muckraking,* EAV.

2. *The Progressive Era: Reform Works in America,* EBEC.

3. *Teddy the Rough Rider,* WB; *Theodore Roosevelt,* WOLPER; *America's Heritage—Theodore Roosevelt,* PATHE.

4. *Nationalism,* EBEC; *American Foreign Policy: Instrument of Intervention,* NBC.

5. *Who Shall Reap,* USDA; *America's Heritage — Our Farming Pioneers,* PATHE; *The Farmer in a Changing America,* EBEC.

6. *American Memoir — a Series: Sixty Years of Magazines,* WTTWTV.

7. *The Rise of the American City,* EBEC.

8. *The Progressives,* MGHF; *The Progressive Reformers, 1900 to 1920,* ERS.

9. *Stockyards: End of an Era,* WTTWTV.

10. *History of the American Negro,* ERS; *Anthology of Negro Poets in the U.S.A.,* EAV; *The Negro and the American Promise* and *The Negro and the South,* NET; *Booker T. Washington,* EBEC; *Black History: Lost, Stolen, or Strayed,* CBS.

11. *Trusts and Trust Busters,* MGHF; *The Rise of the Industrial Giants,* MGHF; *The Boyhood of Thomas Edison,* CORF; *American Business — Origin and Growth,* ERS; *The Rise of Big Business,* EBEC; *The Rise of Organized Labor,* MGHF; *With These Hands,* ILGWU; *The Rise of Labor,* EBEC.

12. *The City,* AMIP; *A City to Live In,* BFA; *Lewis Mumford on the City,* a series, NFBC.

13. *Woodrow Wilson,* SAUDEK.

III

Progressivism: Second Phase

Progressivism should, theoretically, have superseded Republicanism, in a nation which had preferred Woodrow Wilson and Theodore Roosevelt to Taft, and which had vigorously enacted a long series of reform measures; see speech of Thomas J. Walsh in *Three Years of the New Freedom* (1916). But the regular Republicans, along with their Warren G. Harding of Ohio, who had offered them Taft again at their 1912 convention, were far from spent. Whatever or whoever it was that "killed" the Progressive party, the deed was done by the next turn of Presidential elections. Something but not all of the tale appears in Amos R. E. Pinchot's *History of the Progressive Party, 1912-1916* (1958) edited by Helene M. Hooker.

Woodrow Wilson was able to continue in power, but the great reform drive was largely over, at least so far as domestic concerns was involved. It needs, however, to be recalled from time to time that many Americans, and certainly those in the White House, believed that their forays abroad involved a type of crusadership. N. Gordon Levin, in *Woodrow Wilson and World Politics* (1968), defines his subject's "liberal globalism" as hostile to both traditional imperialism and to revolutionary socialism.

The American position needs to be seen in both materialistic terms and ideals. David Healy, *United States Expansionism* (1970), believes that our adventures abroad destroyed the concept of separateness; but perhaps, tragically, not entirely. Americans were divided on the issue. Robert E. Osgood profitably discusses *Ideals and Self-Interest in American Foreign Relations* (1953); see also Julius W. Pratt, *America and World Leadership, 1900-1921* (1967). It might, perhaps, seem difficult to discern idealism in the "dollar diplomacy" which so much directed official American policy in the Caribbean and South America. But this would be, as before (*see* Chapter II-4), because American policy was seen as speaking for all American opinion, and because another species of idealism saw the southern nations involved, unrealistically, as composed of freedom-seekers. In any event, the confused good will of William Jennings Bryan wants being assessed as part of American policy; see Joseph V. Fuller, "William Jennings Bryan," in *The American Secretaries of State and Their Diplomacy*, edited by Samuel F. Bemis (1929), vol. X, and Dana G. Munro, *Intervention and Dollar Diplomacy in the Caribbean, 1900-1921* (1964). See also Isaac J. Cox, *Nicaragua and the United States* (1927), Sumner Welles, *Naboth's Vineyard, The Dominican Republic 1844-1924* (1928), and Arthur C. Millspaugh, *Haiti under American Control 1915-1930* (1931).

Particularly relevant to America's frame of mind, as a nation, was its relationship to Mexico. In general, it can be said that it furnished an inadequate dress rehearsal for America's coming involvement in the European War. Wilson's administration meant well; precisely what it could have done better it is difficult to say. The State Department operated in a combination of self-interest and republican preference. The general public ended by romanticizing the adventurer Pancho Villa as a symbol of liberty. Progressives were not effective in either regard; see Robert E. Quirk, *An Affair of Honor: Woodrow Wilson and the Occupation of Veracruz* (1962); Clarence C. Clendenen, *The United States and Pancho Villa* (1961).[1]

1. Progressives and World War I

The war, though not so perceived at the time, was the wound which would over the years bleed away much of the Progressives' reputation, and also that of their associated socialists who accepted it as a just war. Charles Edward Russell had been all but revered as the outstanding muckraker, socialist, and progressive figure. His eloquence, which had once held liberals and union workers breathless dried up with the war's end; and though he won some honors as a writer and liberal symbol, it was mostly as a symbol of the past. Upton Sinclair accepted the war, but continued his spirited attacks on capitalism, and on the suppression of civil rights during the war, as in his novel *100%* (1920), the sardonic saga of a false-hearted labor spy, all of which helped Sinclair's reputation with the new world. Jane Addams became a symbol of the Progressive who had not repudiated the *Newer Ideals of Peace* (1907) which she had once voiced, and who continued as a legend of justice. But overall Progressives suffered loss of esteem, and worse, killing draughts of indifference.

They suffered too by the fact that an extraordinary mood of exaltation was created to back the war effort, a mood which seemed to make their writings more effective than ever. The revulsion from that mood dragged down even their best efforts. Thus George Creel was a worthy head of the Committee on Public Information to publicize the war effort, and sought to curb false stories and antiliberal actions, as he reminded readers in *Rebel at Large* (1947); see also James R. Mock and Cedric Larson, *Words that Won the War* (1939). Yet later revelations that there had been lies promulgated by Allied writers, intended to turn American public opinion against Germany, carried Creel down along with the blatant atrocity peddlers.

Progressives served also legitimately in seeking to educate foreign language speaking Americans to their new tongue and mores. No doubt some of this program was intended to sell the war to them; but much of it laid the foundation for their adjustment to American conditions; see Edward G. Hartmann, *The Movement to Americanize the Immigrant* (1948). Samuel Gompers's case was as tragic, Gompers believing that a patriotic labor would be given new acceptance by other Americans. He therefore carried the organized labor movement into the war with him, for a consummation which did not materialize. See his *Labor and the Common Welfare* (1919) for his progressive program.

Progressives played honorable parts in the war; see, for example, Daniel R. Beaver, *Newton D. Baker and the American War Effort, 1917–1919* (1966) and Ruhl J. Bartlett, *The League to Enforce Peace* (1944) for accounts of Baker's efforts to carry out his mission without partisanship or regard for special interests and efforts to define goals for peace. Progressives, however, were unable to see far beyond the need to crush the German military machine. In the long run, protestants against war in general or in favor of socialism, or at least in appeals for civil rights, fared best. For an overall account, see William Preston, Jr., *Aliens and Dissenters: Federal Suppression of Radicals, 1903–33* (1963). The pacifist tale is told in Charles Chatfield, *For Peace and Justice: Pacifism in America 1914–1941* (1971). See also Merle E. Curti, *Bryan and World Peace* (1931).

Free speech was so much under duress as to draw sympathy for types without notable distinction. Frank Harris, a British literary buccaneer, was total opportunist, whose *England or Germany?* (1915) was written with more malice than penetration, but which antipatriots respected. George Sylvester Viereck's *Spreading Germs of Hate* (1930) included harsh truths about the activities of government agents, but was written by an agent of Germany with some light literary talent.

The war affected many people differently and often made violent changes in their lives. A. M. Simons had been a radical as editor of the *International Socialist Review*. His *Class Struggles in America* (1903) saw not a united nation, but one internally at war. His *Social Forces in American History* (1911) continued to maintain this view of life. Nevertheless, Simons was one who became persuaded that the future of civilization required that the German cause be quelled. Following the war's end, he spoke for others of his mind in *The Vision for which We Fought: A Study of Reconstruction* (1919). It soon became evident to him, as to others, that his "vision" was not that of the majority of his countrymen. The radical turned conservative; his next book was entitled *Personnel Relations in Industry* (1921). See Kent and Gretchen Kreuter, *An American Dissenter: The Life of Algie Martin Simons 1870–1950* (1969).

Dissent attracted many types of individual. Norman Thomas had a religious vocation. The war turned him into a socialist and front line fighter for civil liberties. His *The Conscientious Objector in America* (1923), introduced by Robert M. La Follette, is one of the distinguished works of the time. See Harry Fleischman, *Norman Thomas, a Biography* (1964). A. J. Nock despised the masses, and though he had also had a religious turn and known the muckrakers, his grim cause was the individual. Nock's *The Myth of a Guilty Nation* (1922) aided dissent, and even aspects of Progressivism, but Nock was too much himself to work with others, though, in the early 1920s, as editor of *The Freeman*, he encouraged free expression and a variety of literary talents.

Zachariah Chafee Jr.'s, *Free Speech in the United States* (1941 and Donald Johnson's *The Challenge to American Freedoms: World War I and the Rise of the American Civil Liberties Union* (1963) recount some of the circumstances and travails of dissidents — travails which grew more intense with hysteria. Horace C. Peterson and Gilbert C. Fite, *Opponents of War 1917–1918* (1957) and Robert K. Murray, *Red Scare: A Study in National Hysteria 1919–1920* (1955) describe events which Progressives did not often initiate, but which they could not control. Wilson himself, totally dedicated to his own crusade, did indulge vengeful feelings which did his democratic principles little honor.

Radicals, by the act of separating themselves from the war effort, often ensured themselves of better repute than the Progressives; see Louis B. Boudin, *Socialism and War* (1916) and Alexander Trachtenberg, ed., *The American Socialists and the War* (1917), two books published separately, and reprinted in 1973. More intensive work respecting Progressives would demonstrate their varied qualities and contributions in respect to such byproducts of war and peace as the great steel strike of 1919; see *Report on the Steel Strike. . .* by the Commission of Inquiry, the Interchurch World Movement (1920), and David Brody, *Labor in Crisis: The Steel Strike of 1919* (1965).

In the light of such national difficulties, it is possible to understand the disgust and repudiation implicit in Harold Stearns's *Liberalism in America: Its Origin, Its Temporary Collapse, Its Future* (1919), Stearns being one of the new youth who registered their feelings by leaving the country to reside in France. Nevertheless, a broader view which recognized that the youth were of varied qualities, just as were the Americans who stayed, could read with patience such a group of essays as was prepared under the auspices of the City Club of Chicago, *The Ideals of America* (1919), if only in order to have something to work with, and could read with pride Norman Hapgood's *Professional Patriots* (1919) which witheringly exposed the perpetrators of the "Red Scare." The mixed contribution of the Progressives is also evident in Christopher Lasch, *The American Liberals and the Russian Revolution* (1962).[2]

2. Prohibition, Woman Suffrage, and Progressivism

Prohibition has already received comment as a quasi-Progressive issue (*see* Chapter II-15, and II-17). The relationship between the two movements — for prohibition was a strong, separate movement — was muddled, in that prohibitionists tended to be Republicans in the North, Democrats in the South, and as progressive or nonprogressive as their political alliances required. Many of the Progressives drank; some of the muckrakers were close to drunkards. Thus a study of Prohibition which *identifies* it as Progressive (as

Vann Woodward's *Origins of the New South* would prefer) is doubtful when not false. Progressivism was not Prohibition.

Progressives did deplore the combination of liquor, vice, and crime, and wrote and agitated in opposition to the latter. To that extent prohibition was not merely a "rural crusade," since liquor as a lubricant of vice made its headquarters in the cities. Carry A. Nation of Kansas was no Progressive; indeed, her intolerance of liberalism in any form made her an opponent of free speech and free expression in ways repellant to Progressives. And though a syndrome of religion, small towns, and other elements made her a factor in Kansas, it made her a joke in New York where Progressives were no inconsiderable force. Frances Willard had, of course, been a Progressive in education, in woman suffrage, and in women's rights generally. During the Progressive era she ranked in memory (having died early, in 1898) as one of the greatest of American women, whom all honored, prohibitionists for her services to their cause, Progressives for her services to theirs.

Thus prohibition had a mixed status in progressive annals, which such strictures and generalizations as Vann Woodward's unfortunately muddled further. Progressivism and prohibition did not "march together." The student who recognizes that by and large the heavy censorship and authoritarianism of the aggressive teetotaler had little place in Progressivism proper, can put this matter readily in perspective. Lincoln Steffens did so in his *Upbuilders* (1909), as mentioned before, when he observed that all valid progressive crusades tended to lose perspective when identified with the temperance cause, and were best kept separate.

Woman suffrage, on the other hand, was clearly a progressive issue, though it became one of the ironies of the drive for the vote that the "emancipated" women in 1920, their first national Presidential election year, were enabled to contribute to the Warren G. Harding landslide.

Ernest H. Cherrington, in *The Evolution of Prohibition in the United States of America: A Chronological History* (1920) mentioned before, reveals the tireless organization which went into the long antiliquor campaign, and reminds the broadminded reader that there were good reasons for temperance, if not for prohibition. *The Liquor Problem: A Summary of Investigations, 1893–1903, by the Committee of Fifty* (1905) contributed to a research aspect of Progressivism, providing information and choices, though no solution. Maine continued to fancy prohibition, Massachusetts preferred local option, South Carolina state dispensaries. John Marshall Barker, professor of sociology in the school of theology, Boston University, has already been noted as having studied *The Saloon Problem and Social Reform* (1905). He set down sensible suggestions — public drinking fountains and toilet facilities, temperance work in trades unions and recreation areas — but could not build up the sense of urgency which prohibitionists engendered, and which Progressives could generate for some of their causes. Gilman M. Ostrander's *The Prohibition Movement in*

California, 1848–1933 (1957) is another of the important state histories, this one for a strategic state. Lewis L. Gould, in *Progressives and Prohibitionists: Texas Democrats in the Wilson Era* (1973) finds a positive relationship between Progressivism in that state and prohibition, and sees "conservatives" there as opposed to the augmented national authority which a prohibition victory would have gained. The book views Texas Progressivism negatively, noting that in the Wilson era, its practitioners did little for the needy farmer, were anti-Negro, and otherwise furnish no reminders of more distinguished Progressive achievements. Gould's hypothesis: that the pro-prohibition forces and antiprohibition forces were so well balanced that they expended inordinate energy on their main issue, helps suggest the kind of circumstances which influenced one or another achievement.

3. Forces Affecting Progressivism

The youth movement was a product of forces, rather than an instigator of them. Although the facade of Progressivism depicted an old America of standards, tolerance, and generosity, there were powerful elements beneath the surface which would be contained by law and order elements of society or rise to the surface. The compassionate articles of muckrakers, the work of organizations in behalf of women and children, the eloquence of La Follette, Norris, Beveridge and other legislators, the public indignation over the Ballinger-Pinchot affair — all this suggested that an alert electorate would see to it that human and industrial relations were increasingly beneficial to all.

Samuel Gompers, by enlisting labor for war, had anticipated that labor would emerge with a new credit with everyone, thus ensuring an era of industrial peace and plenty.

Various events, however, in the 1910s and overlapping into the 1920s, suggested that prejudice and group warfare was as alive as ever, and would help dull and raise questions about the eloquence which Woodrow Wilson and his cohorts had unleashed in behalf of their wartime promises.

Disappointments accumulated. American unwillingness to enter into the League of Nations — for which, in large part, the war had presumably been fought — left a sour taste in many liberal mouths. Although many sought to make Henry Cabot Lodge the villain of this situation — Karl Schriftgiesser, *The Gentleman from Massachusetts* (1944) held him responsible for the mountain of skulls of World War II — others saw Wilson as having contributed his own measure of errors to the event. See Thomas A. Bailey, *Woodrow Wilson and the Great Betrayal* (1945) and John A. Garraty, *Henry Cabot Lodge* (1953).

Bigotry reared its head in Georgia to accuse an innocent businessman, Leo Frank, of the atrocious killing of a young female worker in his factory in Atlanta. And though mountains of evidence exculpated him and a heroic governor commuted his sentence, Lynch Law prevailed. Christopher P. Connolly, for the muckrakers, exposed the hollowness of the evidence in *The Truth about the Frank Case* (1915), and editors across the country protested the verdict and aftermath, but none could stop the order of events. See Harry Golden, *A Little Girl Is Dead* (1965).

An acute pang was caused by revelations that the World Series of 1919 had been fixed. The distress caused by such cynical manipulation of the nation's good fellowship and play probably disillusioned more people than did evidence that the Allies, who were supposed to be fighting for a better world, were also interested in economic benefits. Along with such revelations came awareness of the rise of gangsters, from petty local groups to larger, interstate organizations. Gene Fowler's *The Great Mouthpiece: A Life Story of William J. Fallon* (1931) celebrated a brilliant lawyer who dedicated his talents to serving gangsters in court with outstanding success. Leo Katcher, *The Big Bankroll* (1959) told of Arnold Rothstein, whose power as gambler, "fixer," and general serviceman to criminals did not speak well for the democracy emerging from the war. The same could have been said of John Kobler's *Capone: The Life and World of Al Capone* (1971).

Especially unpromising for the new time was the attitude of those who were to act as liaisons between public and executives. Milton Plesur, ed., *Intellectual Alienation in the 1920's* (1970) told of H. L. Mencken's scorn of democracy, of F. Scott Fitzgerald's skepticism of adult tenets, of Irving Babbitt's humanistic fear of popular culture. As doubtful was Walter Lippmann's attitude as he emerged from the Crusade for Democracy. His *A Preface to Morals* (1928) saw life as essentially meaningless, with nothing but stoicism to sustain the living. Although his attitude gave an effect of honesty, it did not suggest any of the enthusiasm and sense of purpose which had once inspired Progressives.

There were, indeed, strong people and good organizations. The civil rights movement employed such talents as Arthur Garfield Hays, whose *City Lawyer* (1942) recounted good causes. Harold Rugg, the Progressive educator wrote with inexhaustible energy in his effort to reach children, as in his *That Men May Understand* (1941). The farmers raised good leaders to fight their battles for them; see Gilbert C. Fite's *George N. Peek and the Fight for Farm Parity* (1954). There were warm and varied journalists, such as Heywood Broun, who became a legend of good humor and well-meaning causes. See his *It Seems to Me* (1935) and Dale Kramer's *Heywood Broun* (1949).

But in general there was evidence that the *New Republic* editor, Walter Weyl had correctly sensed the spirit of those who had supported the war for idealistic reasons; see his *Tired Radicals and Other Papers* (1921). There were some of the older generation, like Charles Edward Russell, who would never give up. But prospects for Progressivism were at best enigmatic, as its partisans emerged triumphant from their assault on German Junkerism.

4. The Twenties Arrive

Herbert Croly, early in the 1920s, also complained that there did not seem to be as much liberal spirit, as many liberals on the scene as he had become used to in prewar years. He forgot that he had himself been interested only in a particular brand of liberalism, that of the elite quality. He had taken the "sentimental" liberals for granted, holding that they accomplished something, but not much with their popular perspective and prose. He does not seem to have made the connection between their retirement and the rise of a new elite, one which puts his own movers and shakers into the shadows. His associate, Walter Lippmann had asked for mastery rather than drift, but he had not looked sufficiently into how mastery was obtained or held. Woodrow Wilson who just the other day had been a world name, to which peasants from Italy to Cambodia had offered up prayers, was set aside with amazing rapidity. Walter Lippmann continued to offer up well-respected columns in the press, but his once proud sense of control over life and politics was muted; see David E. Weingast, *Walter Lippmann* (1949) (*see also* Chapter 11-23).

Times had patently changed for the Progressives, but enough remained of their traditions to sustain the shadow, if not the substance, of their work. Even the bland Democratic race for the Presidency of James M. Cox, the Ohio newspaper proprietor and governor, in 1920, could be seen by Charles E. Morris as *The Progressive Democracy of James M. Cox* (1920). (His Vice Presidential running-mate, Franklin D. Roosevelt, had earlier thought Herbert Hoover would make the best candidate for their party.) Wesley M. Bagby accurately described "Progressivism's Debacle: The Election of 1920" (University Microfilms, 1954). James C. Malin's *The United States after the War* (1930) as accurately recorded the new spirit, which was at one with the "normalcy" touted by the new President. William H. S. Stevens had once recorded disapproval of *Unfair Competition* (1914) in terms which President Wilson had popularized. A new prosperity dissolved much of the interest in the subject. Ray Stannard Baker in 1920 sought to pick up his old reputation as a responsible analyst of public affairs in his *The New Industrial Unrest*, and discovered the public was indifferent to his views. Arthur A. Ekirch, Jr. was later to see the period as contributing to *The Decline of American Liberalism* (1955). (His book ignored muckraking as either aiding or resisting this decline.) But he, like others, faced a dilemma. Bigness was inevitable; public as well as profiteers approved the business consolidations which made for mass production. How could it be obtained while also condoning stronger government intervention? Donald R. Richberg, a true Progressive and friend of business urged railroad organization which would be a model of efficiency and public service, and was forced to declare that it had been stymied by unfriendly forces; see his *Tents of the Mighty* (1930).

What confused prospects for clarifying public service was the fact that there were dreamers in every camp, whether liberal, radical, or conservative. Lewis Mumford's *The Story of Utopias* (1922) could inspire many program-makers. Students of 1974 would rub their eyes after discovering that Herbert Hoover's principles of individualism, decentralization, and voluntarism seemed reasonable to New Leftists as well as conservatives; see J. Joseph Huthmacher and Warren I. Susman, eds., *Herbert Hoover and the Crisis of American Capitalism* (1974). During the Twenties, Hoover's world-wide reputation for humanitarianism and efficiency, when approved by Progressives, seemed another nail in the coffin of their own good repute.

Although business and its attendant capitalism was held contemptible by a world network of radicals and revolutionaries, its manifest "success" in the 1920s created a complex social attitude of respect and derogation; see Sigmund Diamond, *The Reputation of the American Businessman* (1955) and Harold U. Faulkner, *The Decline of Laissez Faire, 1897-1917* (1951). Ida M. Tarbell's *The Life of Elbert H. Gary* (1925) was one of a number of such works by former muckrakers, which to the mind casually brought up on a Progressivism which saw itself in alliance with socialism and respectful of the Russian Revolution, could seem like the merest "sell out." Yet E. A. Filene, for example, saw no contradiction between capitalism and a coming era of cooperative developments which would bring out the best of capitalism. Filene was an admirer of Henry Ford, and seriously imagined that Ford might make a fine President of the United States, even though he had been persuaded during the past war to endorse impractical peace programs and, in the 1920s, was gulled by anti-Semites. Ford's positive qualities, which entitle him to some relationship to Progressivism, may be discerned in Allan Nevins's *Ford, the Times, the Man, the Company* (1954); a more critical view of Ford (and of Progressivism) may be discerned in Keith T. Sward, *The Legend of Henry Ford* (1948).

My Years with General Motors (1963) by Alfred P. Sloan, Jr., and edited by John McDonald, is another work which raises questions of a proper view of capitalism. Sloan took pride in his contribution to the evolution of the automobile, in his contributions to national defense, in his view of due labor relations, as in his program of incentive compensation. See also Harry Barnard, *Independent Man: The Life of Senator James Couzens* (1958) which deals with an associate of Ford who fought vigorously for good labor relations, and who, as police commissioner, mayor, and United States senator made civic efforts identifiable with Progressivism.

The need for a more concerted Progressivism was recognized in Oswald Garrison Villard's *Prophets True and False* (1928) which scorned William Randolph Hearst as a failure and derogated Colonel House, but displayed a variety of others for admiration: Anna Howard Shaw as an "Apostle of Justice"; Thomas J. Walsh, whose services ranged from condemnation of the antiradical raids, approved by A. Mitchell Palmer of the Department of

Justice, to fighting for American entrance into the World Court; and Borah, Norris, La Follette, and Alfred E. Smith of New York. See also Michael Wreszin, *Oswald Garrison Villard* (1965).

To the extent that progressive efforts to maintain justice might be deemed inadequate to the needs of labor, minority groups, notably Negroes, and others, new traditions compounded of radical components could be anticipated. This was implied in such books as Louis B. Boudin's *Government by Judiciary* (1932), which held the courts up for condemnation, Louis Adamic's *Dynamite: The Story of Class Violence in America* (1931), and Philip S. Foner's *History of the Labour Movement in the United States* (4 vols., 1947), books which indirectly suggested that the progressive policy of half-measures did not suffice.

Yet those half-measures contained substantial quantities of insight and the will to better things, as in the Chicago Commission on Race Relations' *The Negro in Chicago: A Study of Race Relations and A Race Riot* (1922) and Kate H. Claghorn's *The Immigrant's Day in Court* (1923). Walter White's *Rope and Faggot* (1929) expressed bitterness toward the cruel ways of Negrophobes, especially in the South of that time, but appealed to justice rather than counter-arson. John A. Ryan spoke outstandingly for Catholic liberalism, as in *The Catholic Church and the Citizen* (1928) and *Questions of the Day* (1931). And Clarke A. Chambers, in *Seedtime of Reform: American Social Service and Social Action 1918–1933* (1963), reviewed processes of civic improvement which could only be called progressive.

Gustavus Myers's *A History of Bigotry in the United States* (1943) was a novelty as by a former socialist-companion of muckrakers who had compromised his career with an unmitigated attack on Germans during the war, employing the dogmatism he had directed at business and politics in America. He now compiled evidence of bigotry which, however well interpreted, was not an attack on America, but on its interior foes.

Upton Sinclair, as we have seen (*see* Chapter 11-12) through the Twenties and beyond continued his tirade against special interests as he saw them in education, literature, and other fields: the most direct link with older muckraking and Progressivism which the era possessed.

Progressivism continued in the Old Northwest, emphasizing the farmers' cause. Charles Edward Russell, not yet retreating from muckraking and, indeed, taking up his earliest crusades as a midwesterner, wrote *The Story of the Nonpartisan League* (1920); see also Herbert E. Gaston, *The Nonpartisan League* (1920) and A. A. Bruce, *The Non-Partisan League* (1921). The interests served by this movement reached fulfillment in Robert La Follette's bid for the Presidency in 1924; see Kenneth C. McKay, *The Progressive Movement of 1924* (1947). Elizabeth Ring, in *Progressive Movement of 1912 and Third Party Movement of 1924 in Maine* (1933), adds dimensions to what is, however, a tale of limited effectiveness.

Most spectacular of distinctly progressive causes of a patently national character was that immortalized as Teapot Dome. It featured Thomas J. Walsh of Montana, who is yet to be fully assimilated into the American reform tradition, and Burton K. Wheeler, also of Montana, a stormy figure who made his reputation as a defender of labor, a fighter against the "Ohio Gang" which darkened Harding's administration, and against the great combines which became symbolized in Teapot Dome. Wheeler continued his work in the 1930s, as in his sponsorship of the Public Utilities Holding Company Act (1935), and in 1940 was seriously considered by Franklin D. Roosevelt as a running mate. But Wheeler was out of time as a noninterventionist in 1941, and as a sponsor of the America First organization which militants held to be "fascistic" in intent. Yet it was only 1939 when the script *The Man from Montana*, based on Wheeler's exposure of Attorney General Harry M. Daugherty's "Ohio Gang," furnished the inspiration for one of the most successful of motion pictures, *Mr. Smith Goes to Washington*, starring James Stewart. Long forgotten by then was the fact that Wheeler had been La Follette's running mate in 1924, on the National Independent Progressive Ticket. See also Burl Noggle, *Teapot Dome* (1962).

The Republican party rode high, but "urban liberalism" was able to display itself in 1928 with the candidacy of Alfred E. Smith. Such long time Progressives as Norman Hapgood stood behind this "Lincoln of the City Streets," but in that year they were doomed to awareness that their time had passed. Moreover, Smith himself emerged as a clear conservative when changing times gave his erstwhile follower, Franklin D. Roosevelt, the presidency he had sought. The same was true of others who saw more promise in what they recalled of Herbert Hoover's crusades than in the series of experiments and commitments which the new Roosevelt initiated; see Otis L. Graham, Jr., *An Encore for Reform: The Old Progressives and the New Deal* (1967).

For a seasoned view of the politics of the time, see Frank R. Kent, *The Democratic Party* (1928); see also R. V. Peel, *The 1928 Campaign* (1931) and Henry F. Pringle, *Alfred E. Smith: A Critical Study* (1927) which viewed with admiration Smith's regard for housing, education, welfare, and related subjects, as well as his opposition to loyalty tests. See also Smith's own *Progressive Democracy: Addresses and State Papers* (1928), with an introduction by the liberal Henry Moskowitz.[3]

5. Progressivism in Depression

The Thirties were not a good time for Progressives. The era asked for action, for change which Progressives were more than willing to grant, but with due respect accorded middle-class and individualist ideals. But though Charles Edward Russell and Clarence Darrow were asked to serve on advisory committees for the New Deal administration, they could not be strategic in program-making or slogan formulation, and they were not, even as grand old men. For an overview of circumstances and central characters, see Dixon Wecter, *The Age of the Great Depression* (1948) and Herbert Feis, *1933: Characters in the Crisis* (1966).

A species of Progressivism there certainly was in the national effort to ward off the worst possibilities of the Depression, though precisely how much of the effort could be credited to old principles, how much to new is a topic for debate. See, for example, Sidney Fine, *Laissez-Faire and the General Welfare State: A Study of Conflict in American Thought* (1966) and Harry K. Girvetz, *From Wealth to Welfare: The Evolution of Liberalism* (1963) which also ponders the meaning of welfare. A work which would have astonished partisans of the 1930s is Joan Hoff Wilson's *Herbert Hoover: Forgotten Progressive* (1975).

More familiar names may be found in "The Unofficial Observer" [J. F. Carter], *The New Dealers* (1934), who included Donald R. Richberg, Senator Robert F. Wagner, Gerard Swope, Rexford G. Tugwell, Henry A. Wallace, Frances Perkins, and Louis D. Brandeis. "Fallen angels" included E. M. House, Newton D. Baker, and Al Smith.

The Depression complicated many lives and principles, but their tendencies may be traced in such books as Allan Nevins's *Herbert Lehman and His Era* (1963), Bernard Sternsher's *Rexford Tugwell and the New Deal* (1964), and Bernard K. Johnpoll's *Pacifist's Progress: Norman Thomas and the Decline of American Socialism* (1970). Indeed, the passions of the 1930s seemed to make Thomas less than strategic to international and even national events. But Thomas's unrelenting adherence to humanistic principles continued to make him refreshing in a dogmatic time.

Needless to say, Franklin D. Roosevelt bestrode the time and, hated or adored, worked for a middle way. How well he succeeded may not here be judged. Frank Freidel's *Franklin D. Roosevelt: The Apprenticeship* (1952) is particularly useful since it enables one to judge his development out of the Progressive era proper. Frances Perkins's *The Roosevelt I Knew* (1946) is by an old-time "urban" Progressive. William E. Leuchtenberg's *Franklin D. Roosevelt and the New Deal* (1963) is a balanced report.

Since Drew Pearson became the outstanding latter-day muckraker of his time, his roots are of interest. See his *Washington Merry-Go-Round* (1935), done with Robert S. Allen. George Seldes's *Lords of the Press* (1938) indicates the complexities in assessing journalistic values by referring (pp. 356 ff.) to the publication *Better Times*, then published by the communist and communist-sympathizer faction of the staff of the *New York Times*, in which they expressed their dissatisfaction with the official policies of their paper.

The Roosevelt drive was to some degree an extension of what Al Smith had projected in 1928, but crisis conditions added urgencies to which the ward politicians could not respond in national political terms; see R. V. Peel and T. C. Donnelly, *The 1932 Campaign* (1932). Bruce M. Stave's *The New Deal and the Last Hurrah: Pittsburgh Machine Politics* (1970) saw the New Deal as assisting

Democratic politics with its patronage and machine building. But Edwin O'Connor's *The Last Hurrah* (1956), (*see* Chapter II-15) had seen a difference: a turning away of the ordinary citizen from his local boss to the powerful people in Washington.

The middle class, as social pivot and nurturer of ideals, was under duress, and there were those who hoped it was in process of dissolution; see Lewis Corey, *The Crisis of the Middle Class* (1935). It produced partisans of a Progressive cast, notably Alfred M. Bingham, editor of *Common Sense* which emphasized social techniques and efficiency for ending the crisis; see Bingham's "Program for America," in *Insurgent America: Revolt of the Middle-classes* (1935), and Bingham and Selden Rodman, eds., *Challenge to the New Deal* (1934), with an introduction by John Dewey, which brought together views by Thomas R. Amlie, Louis F. Budenz, John Chamberlain, and others.

Such programs and others — including Technocracy, an efficiency scheme — lacked the passion and human goals which had defined Progressivism at its most attractive best. But the times were limiting possibilities for Progressives. Most disturbing were those for the distraught farmers. William Lemke had been a Nonpartisan League leader. In 1936 he ran for President and drew some 900,000 votes. The fact that he was accorded the support of Father Charles E. Coughlin and Huey P. Long troubled some liberals with the prospect that agrarians might be joining fascist-type groupings and leaders for an assault on American freedoms.

The emergence of Harold L. Ickes as a New Deal leader created a distinct bond between the old Progressivism and the new times. The irascible Ickes was literally out of the old days: frank, picturesque, suspicious of big business, and still brooding over the killing, as he saw it, of his Progressive party, as he recounted in his *The Autobiography of a Curmudgeon* (1943). His was a vastly different personality from that of Frances Perkins, Secretary of Labor under President Franklin D. Roosevelt, who had come up into the New Deal from a career as a social worker and labor investigator, and who had been inspired to efforts in behalf of women and others by such tragedies as the Triangle Fire. See her 1912 report to a state factory investigating committee on fire hazards in factories and her other works, *A Plan for Maternity Care* (1918) and *People at Work* (1934).

Both Ickes and Perkins differed in the quality of their thought from Rexford G. Tugwell, an economics professor whose dream of an organized life of beauty and structure was reminiscent of H. G. Wells's views of human possibilities. In his *The Economic Basis of Public Interest* (1922), Tugwell had early posited government initiatives which went beyond progressive blueprints, but derived from them. Tugwell was made Undersecretary of Agriculture in 1934 and directed a Resettlement Administration which was literally intended to make America green. That it did not do so resulted from limited funds rather than limited vision.

There were others who were excited by the thought that the Depression was an opportunity for the creation of a new and renewed nation. Charles A. Beard and G. H. E. Smith hailed the New Deal in *The Future Comes* (1933), as had Paul H. Douglas, an economics professor and student of labor and wages, soon to be an outstanding liberal legislator, in his *The Coming of a New Party* (1932). E. T. Devine's *Progressive Social Action* (1933) also involved program-building. There was a species of muckraking in various analyses and exposés of politics and financial skulduggery, as in William B. and John B. Northrop's *The Insolence of Office: The Story of the Seabury Investigation* (1932) mentioned before, and Denis T. Lynch's expert journalism, *Criminals and Politicians* (1932). John McConaughy's *Who Rules America?* (1934) reflected the old fear of "invisible government," and M. R. Werner's *Privileged Characters* (1935) provided a bridge from Congressional investigation testimony on Republican scandals. Kenneth G. Crawford contributed to another muckraking tradition in *The Pressure Boys: The Inside Story of Lobbying in America* (1939).

Other links with Progressivism could be observed in Robert La Follette, Jr.'s Senate Committee on Education and Labor, which amassed evidence on *Violations of Free Speech and Assembly and Interference with the Rights of Labor* (1936); see also Roger N. Baldwin *Civil Liberties and Industrial Conflict* (1938); and Milton Derber and Edwin Young, *Labor and the New Deal* (1957). William L. Leiserson, a famous labor mediator, offered counsel to a fearful generation in his *Right and Wrong in Labor Relations* (1938).

Yet for all of the benign planning and operations of liberals in the 1930s, they were haunted by accusations of inadequacy. John Dewey was driven to write "Why I Am Not a Communist," as though the burden of proof was on him; see Filler, *The Anxious Years: America in the 1930's* (1963). As late as 1967, Murray B. Seidler deemed it correct to entitle his study *Norman Thomas, Respectable Rebel*, as though his socialism, his antiboss protests, his support of embattled labor were somehow not enough: Thomas himself wrote of *Socialism on the Defensive* (1938), and not from the "Right" but from the "Left." A later collective portrait of American socialists, consisting of tape-recordings of 1965–1966, was Betty Yorburg's *Utopia and Reality* (1969) which clearly reflected a tired and puzzled socialist leadership.

Hence, although there was "muckraking" and even "Progressivism" which was distinct from older varieties, they did not act to build up relations between the old and the new. A tragic case was that of Harold Rugg, a brilliant and informed partisan of progressive education, whose *Foundations for American Education* (1947) were far from any vacuous formulations which could be identified with mere permissiveness. Rugg became the target of patriotic organizations of the more closed-minded variety which succeeded in driving his textbooks from the schools, with none to fight his battles for him.

John Roy Carlson (Arthur Derounian) was as genuine a muckraker as the times produced, disinterestedly and at the cost of personal danger exposing the plots and dangers of fascist and communist organizations. It was Carlson who revealed the sad relations between Burton K. Wheeler and fascist adventurers, and similar circumstances in *Undercover* (1943) and *The Plotters* (1946). Though the books circulated well for a time, they seemed to lack the institutional relations which could give them significant impact. Congress exposed labor racketeering and its findings were reflected in Harold Seidman's *Labor Czars* (1938) and Leo Huberman's *The Labor Spy Racket* (1937). But, again, such revelations failed to give new glamour to leaders representing older preferences for individuality and probity.

George Seldes was of interest in believing himself a direct descendent of the old muckrakers, with a special stake in free speech and truth. His publication, *In Fact*, emphasized these points during the 1940s and early 1950s. Earlier he wrote his *Iron, Blood and Profits: An Exposure of the World-Wide Munitions Racket* (1934). His *Freedom of the Press* (1935) and *Lords of the Press* (1938) built directly on the method Upton Sinclair had employed in his *The Brass Check* (1919). Seldes's *Witch Hunt: The Technique and Profits of Redbaiting* (1940) revealed inadvertently how much liberal ground had been lost between the conservative and radical sides.

Leo Gurko's view of the time as *The Angry Decade* (1947) highlighted one of its major qualities: that it could not appeal to pride in Americanism in its strictures against the nation's deficiencies. Robert Morss Lovett, a professor of English concerned for liberal causes, in his autobiography *All Our Years* (1948), expressed bitterness over harassment he and others like himself had suffered at conservative hands better than he did faith in the nation's principles such as an earlier liberal generation had managed. Frank A. Warren III's *Liberals and Communism: The "Red Decade" Revisited* (1966) was, in effect, a record of a demoralized liberalism either in despair or actively seeking new guidelines for a new time. Philip S. Foner, ed., *The Bolshevik Revolution, Its Impact on American Radicals, Liberals and Labor* (1967) focused on one momentous fact to which old Progressives had been unable to reconcile themselves. It seemed a matter of promise to others who were able to swallow without dismay such revelations of communist chicanery as appeared in Benjamin Gitlow's *I Confess* (1939), and in John Dos Passos's disillusioned *Adventures of a Young Man* (1939), the protagonist of which had gone with generous heart to aid the "Republican" cause during the Spanish civil war.

Sinclair Lewis's *It Can't Happen Here* (1935), a tale of fascism come to America, was a work of liberal intent which, however, inadvertently gave comfort to illiberal views of the "Left," some of which are described in Richard H. Pells, *Radical Visions and American Dreams: Culture and Social Thought in the Depression Years* (1973). John L. Spivak had a long career exposing fascist-type plottings, North and South, and detailing the horrors of the southern chain-gang. His autobiographical *A Man in His Time* (1967) told of worthy enterprises in exposing the troubled and aggressive "Right," but could not accurately be designated as progressive in viewpoint.

Interestingly, the Communists themselves were willing to identify themselves as Progressive when it suited them, as it did when they assessed midwestern possibilities; thus the Communist Party in Wisconsin issued the pamphlets, *Communism and the Farmer-Labor Progressive Federation* (1936) and *The La Follette Third Party; Will It Unite or Split the Progressive Forces* (1938), the latter, presumably, including themselves. Many of their cohorts, however, disdained such casuistries; Granville Hicks, their literary chief at the time, denounced the *New York Times* for not giving their works and viewpoints full coverage, in consideration of its alleged liberalism, but added that they would not reciprocate, since they did not believe in liberal principles!

There were certainly worthy enterprises of various types which, whether they honored Progressivism or not, merited honor themselves. Richard Wright began his career as an author on the Federal Writers Project of the New Deal's W. P. A.: a stormy but generally successful effort at government sponsorship of the arts in Depression times. Wright later told in the *Atlantic* (August-September, 1944) how "I Tried to Be a Communist." He broke away from the importunities of the hard-line radicals, but doing so did not give him progressive principles or increase his love for America; he left it to live the life of an expatriate. Erskine Caldwell and Margaret Bourke-White's volume of photographs and texts, *You Have Seen Their Faces* (1937), was moving and enlightening of life in the South, but once again left no progressive residue.

Even E. A. Filene, who had sponsored cooperatives, credit unions, peace projects, research projects intended to sort out feasible from unfeasible economic systems, and who had wholeheartedly endorsed the New Deal, concluded that his fellow-millionaires were incorrigible. They would not learn that there had to be change, and that social anguish would not cure itself. At the end of his life, Filene was turning toward socialism directly in seeking alternatives to bull-headed capitalism; see Gerald W. Johnson, *Liberal's Progress* (1948).

Edmund Wilson set down "Meditations of a Progressive," but all his thoughts were Marxist at this stage of his career; see Filler, *The Anxious Years* (1963) (pp. 120ff.). If anyone was outstandingly liberal, and sustaining what could be sustained of the progressive torch, it was President Roosevelt himself, working as best he could with restless and not wholly responsible social tendencies and giving support to such distinct Progressives in his administration as Ickes and Frances Perkins. There were quasi-Progressives like Max Lerner, editor of *The Mind and Faith of Justice Holmes* (1943), who held on to his subject's large, liberal principles, though in so loose a fashion as to show the editor's potential for endorsing many positions. In sum, Progressivism was revealed as under such pressures in a world of many "isms," few liberal, that though still alive, it was precariously situated between hammers and anvils which threatened its very existence.[4]

Writers of the time like John Steinbeck and Erskine Caldwell wrote tales which involved, if not a species of muckraking, at least an adjunct to it. See also F. Jack Hurley, *Portrait of a Decade: Roy Stryker and the Development of Documentary Photography in the Thirties* (1972).

6. Post-Depression Conditions

World War II radically changed prospects for Progressivism, for good or ill. A feature of Depression politics had been the activities of the Committee on Un-American Activities, dominated by Martin Dies of Texas. Dies hardly represented muckraking or Progressivism since his mission, which was to investigate fascist and communist subversive activities, rapidly turned into an intensive concern for the latter. Dies himself reported to the nation in his *The Trojan Horse in America* (1940) which elicited some approval and storms of indignation and retorts. With the coming of war and the forging of the Grand Alliance, Dies became useless and an embarrassment to a nation which was honoring the Soviet dictator and his cause, and Dies sank out of sight, not again to emerge into view.

World War II, unlike its predecessor, was considered a just war; in addition, the armed services had learned sophistication in their treatment of conscientious objectors. Hence there was little occasion for muckraking during the war crisis, except in the one distressing area of Japanese-American mistreatment. West coast hysteria and individual or group bigotry forced a reluctant government, headed by President Roosevelt, to withdraw the Japanese-Americans from their legal homes and pursuits, and maintain them in compounds far away from the sensitive coastal areas. All this was necessary in order to appease senators and congressmen who had to satisfy their anxious constituencies in order to get on with war measures. No one has ever responsibly defended these wartime measures. Liberals like Governor Earl Warren joined as best they could to make the tragic conditions as comfortable and morale-building as possible. Camp directors and Army officials were for the most part in accord with these goals.

What was in many ways unforeseen and unexpected was the reaction to this catastrophe of the Japanese-Americans themselves. They comported themselves with extraordinary grace and courage. It had been feared that their family structure might be compromised by this peremptory uprooting. Youth were expected to turn surly, or show other signs of demoralization. A relatively few Japanese-Americans accepted the government offer to leave the country and "repatriate" — though they were not Japanese, but Americans — to Japan. The rest, for the most part, carved out one of the finest of wartime records as citizens and as soldiers. At the end of wartime hostilities they went back to work and could look upon children who, as a group, led the field in educational achievement.

Although following the war a number of books were published written in bitterness by non-Japanese respecting Japanese Relocation, they could hardly be described as muckraking, since the facts were generally known and appreciated, and in some cases constituted reports rather than revelations. The Japanese-Americans themselves, through their organizations and otherwise, wrote in appreciation of the positive efforts which had been made in their behalf, during a time of trouble and uncertainty.

A phenomenon of the time that could only be called progressive was Wendell L. Willkie, an Indiana lawyer who, as president of the Commonwealth and Southern Corporation, had fought against the creation of the Tennessee Valley Authority: the chain of dams and power-producing installations sponsored by the New Deal. In 1940 he was the Republican party's nominee for President on a free enterprise platform. Although he was defeated, he maintained an attractive image, was chosen by President Roosevelt as a symbol of unity across party lines on the war issue — Willkie refused to join other Republicans in an isolationist stand — and toured the world as Roosevelt's personal representative. Willkie returned home with a vision he embodied in *One World* (1943) which showed astonishing growth in social perspectives and informed the viewpoint of his *An American Program* (1944).

Willkie was turned down by his party in 1944 and given no second chance with the electorate. Suddenly, that same year, he was dead and became a legend of ideals and potential; see Joseph Barnes, *Willkie: The Events He Was Part Of, The Ideas He Fought For* (1952); Mary E. Dillon, *Wendell Willkie 1892–1944* (1952); Donald B. Johnson, *The Republican Party and Wendell Willkie* (1960); Ellsworth Barnard, *Wendell Willkie, Fighter for Freedom* (1966).

7. Progressives: 1948

Postwar reaction to the Grand Alliance might have seemed most unpromising for Progressivism, yet it produced a Progressive party: one which might have puzzled the elder La Follette in some of its aspects — its regard for international solidarities, for example — but which claimed a heritage from the Wisconsin hero, and much besides. It needs to be recalled that the war itself had been touted as being fought by freedom-loving peoples, at least as compared to those living under the Nazi terror. Whatever the truth behind the Grand Alliance, there had at least been a sense of commitment to international principles which restrained nationalists and anticommunists to a degree. The death of President Roosevelt made Hitler dance and liberals weep, but the emergence of Truman as his successor gave arms to liberals as well as patent reactionaries.

Labor had been made big labor by the war. Amd the farmers who had seemed beyond redemption politically, and needing crutches for survival, now found that they had gained strength by being able to tip the balance between the adherents of business and those of the unions. The farmers who made Truman President in his own right in 1948 were not the idealists of yore, but they produced one idealist who gave, perhaps, the last hurrah for Progressivism as such.

Henry A. Wallace was a big Iowa farmer, and some of his Thirties critics from the "Left" accused him of having initiated, as Secretary of Agriculture, policies to help farmers like himself, rather than the small and harassed farmer. In fact, his general policy had intended to help all farmers whether affluent or otherwise; Wallace was a sincere New Dealer. Whether he was equipped intellectually to understand and cope with the twists and turns of domestic and foreign policy was another matter; see his diary for 1942–1946 in John M. Blum, *The Price of Vision* (1943). Karl M. Schmidt, in *Henry Wallace* (1960), saw his as a "quixotic crusade" — a crusade rendered more difficult by revelations that he had solicited spiritualist guidance of a bizarre type, and accepted cooperation from patently communist sources; see pamphlets by Earl Browder, *How to Halt Crisis and War: An Economic Program for Progressives* (1949) and Eugene Dennis, *The Third Party and the 1948 Elections* (1948), both communist leaders. See also F. Ross Peterson, *Prophet without Honor: Glen Taylor* (1973), the latter being his running mate. William B. Hesseltine, *The Rise and Fall of Third Parties* (1948) provides valuable perspective on the relationship of third parties to Progressivism.

No one can read C. D. MacDougal's three volumes of *Gideon's Army* (1965) without crediting some of Wallace's followers with earnestness and intelligence. They fought bigotry and they pointed directly at disparities in American life which merited notice. In addition, they polled over a million votes. Nevertheless, they used up Progressive moral and political credit, rather than creating new credit, and they were an end, rather than a beginning. Allen Yarnell, in *Democrats and Progressives: The 1948 Presidential Election as a Test of Postwar Liberalism* (1974), argues that Wallace accomplished nothing, no more than freeing Truman to take hardline positions on foreign policy issues, and thus aiding him in his victory.

8. The McCarthy Era and Adlai

Nationalism — but not a Progressive nationalism — was heightened by the uprising of the Red Chinese on their mainland, which drove the Chinese Nationalists into the sea. American nationalism was further enhanced by the discovery that information about the making of the Atom Bomb, once apparently secure in American hands, had been transmitted to the Russians by traitors, and that American lives might well be jeopardized by this gift.

A major beneficiary of this transaction was Senator Joseph R. McCarthy of Wisconsin, who rose to national and international headlines, as he made accusations of treason which moved sweepingly from the lower ranks of public servant and individual to the highest. It is not easy to determine what qualities singled him out for distinction, so that the McCarthy Era would be meaningful for everybody, whether his friend or foe, and why an anti-Communist era found no further use for Martin Dies, though he sought recognition. Dies was, if anything, more expert in the field than McCarthy, yet his fame or notoriety was securely buried in congressional documents and a number of studies.

McCarthy, on the other hand, stirred readers on every level, advanced in senate influence, caused investigations and endless television coverage, and was finally censured by a senate which had had enough of him. So began the decline of one who had in 1946 ended the progressive senatorship of Robert M. La Follette, Jr. by a vigorous anti-Communist campaign which he had carried triumphantly into Washington. A literature developed on the McCarthy theme which makes clear how little Progressivism was able to interpose its reputation or principles against an adventurer who claimed to speak in the name of American principles, to no valid purpose. Allen J. Matusow, ed., *Joseph R. McCarthy* (1970) is a sound collection of pro and con materials. Many books treat of communist subversion, but David Shannon's *The Decline of American Communism* (1959) more judiciously assesses its actual influence, and indirectly shows how polarized opinions preempted attention, at the expense of the larger center which would ultimately decide the issues involved.

This larger center became the target of disapproval by intellectuals who held that McCarthy's demagoguery could be directly traced to Populist roots; see, for example, Daniel Bell, ed., *The New American Right* (1955). This doctrine, which spread widely among academics, was denied on the basis of fact by others, as in Michael P. Rogin, *The Intellectuals and McCarthy* (1967).

The problem with appraising McCarthyism, or anti-McCarthyism, lay in determining a proper attitude toward communists at home or abroad. During World War II, Winston Churchill, not famous for his love of communists, had said that he was interested in anyone who would kill German soldiers: an antihumanistic opinion which was intended to emphasize the need to win the war. Thus it was not enough for McCarthy or anyone else to prove that communists had duel loyalties, or anticapitalistic perspectives, or whatever. It was necessary to give evidence that American freedoms were in jeopardy, and that anti-communist measures did not contribute to such assaults on constitutional rights.

It was myopia on such topics which made futile or worse McCarthy's attacks on Adlai E. Stevenson of Illinois, who became the Democratic Presidential nominee in 1952, the same year that McCarthy won reelection to the Senate. McCarthy worked strenuously to identify Stevenson with "soft" attitudes toward communists, at home and abroad, and with persons for example associated with the ADA (Americans for Democratic Action), which he held was sympathetic to communists. To make his case against Stevenson, he had to overlook the latter's regard for civil rights, for a pluralistic society, and for international peace. Stevenson had limitations as a leader, limitations which enabled General Dwight D. Eisenhower to overwhelm him at the polls in 1952 and again in 1956. He would not study the feelings and vocabularies of grassroots voters. He was uncalculatedly flippant ("Eggheads of the world, unite; you have nothing to lose but your yokes"). But he added a touch of intellect to politics, and his causes, which ranged from opposing the loyalty oath in Illinois to fighting for a Fair Employment Act (FEPC) did him and his candidacy honor. Something of the progressive tradition clung to him. For all his remoteness from the generality of people, there was a kindliness about him and his purposes which related him to them.

See Kenneth S. Davis, *A Prophet in His Own Country* (1957) and *The Politics of Honor* (1967). See also *Adlai's Almanac: The Wit and Wisdom of Stevenson of Illinois*, Bessie R. James and May Waterstreet, comp. (1952), and Stevenson, *Speeches* (1952), with a foreword by John Steinbeck; also Stevenson's *The New America*, Seymour E. Harris, John B. Martin, Arthur Schlesinger, Jr., eds. (1957). Stevenson died in 1965; retrospective views include Herbert J. Muller, *Adlai Stevenson: A Study in Values* (1967) and Richard J. Walton, *The Remnants of Power: The Tragic Last Years of Adlai Stevenson* (1968).[5]

9. Vestiges of Muckraking and Progressivism

Although there seemed large tendencies toward polarization and accommodation, elements continued to assert themselves as regardful of older values, or as heirs to them. Richard S. Childs was a long-tried partisan of civic reform, and his *Civic Victories: The Story of an Unfinished Revolution* (1952) doubtless spoke for older perspectives. But Paul H. Douglas, writing on *Ethics in Government* (1952) and George A. Graham, voicing concern for *Morality in American Life* (1952), expressed sentiments which haunted even the most flatulent of those who had sold out their memories of Depression and war service for aimless prosperity and Organization Man routines.

Drew Pearson was not deterred by the exasperated criticism he provoked from Franklin D. Roosevelt and Harry S. Truman from continuing to look for bad faith and corruption in government, and lesser men seized opportunities, sometimes partisan, to expose chicanery of one sort or another. There were difficulties in pinning down public concern. Discovery that the "$64,000 Question" television show was rigged brought blank surprise from some editors whose first impulse was to play down the whole situation. It ought not to be taken too seriously, they thought. What difference did it make? Everyone knew that wrestling bouts were fixed. Why not? They were no more than entertainments.

Nevertheless, the "$64,000" show was quietly retired, along with some of its promoters, and "Payola" scandals — involving disc jockeys who pushed particular records over others for bribes — pained and embarrassed many participants. The country slept uneasily. Meanwhile, it was able to look over a genuine scion of Progressivism, a Tennessean who had joined the House of Representatives in 1939, and in 1947 called for *A Twentieth-Century Congress*, in a book which was in a foreword given the blessing of the unseated Robert La Follette, Jr. Estes Kefauver looked confidently to the grassroots to be concerned, as he was, for crime, for graft, and for uncontrolled power. He expressed these fears in congressional hearings which were widely seen, and in his books *Crime in America* (1951) and *In a Few Hands: Monopoly Power in America* (1965), released after his death in 1963.

Kefauver sought his Democratic party's Presidential nomination in 1952, but was turned back; some thought the party feared him more than it did Stevenson. In 1956 Kefauver beat out John F. Kennedy for the Vice-Presidential place, but it was a loser's victory. Kefauver's unfulfilled ambitions seemed to prove that if Progressivism was ever to return, it would have to be under some guise other than he had assumed; see Joseph B. Gorman, *Kefauver: A Political Biography* (1971).

In addition to an old Progressivism, there was also an old radicalism which seemed no more able to penetrate American apathy. George Seldes continued to carry on with criticisms of big business in ways he described in his autobiographical *Tell the Truth and Run* (1953). I. F. Stone, an old socialist and admirer of Upton Sinclair wrote *The Hidden History of the Korea War* (1952) and *The Truman Era* (1953), critical works which made little impression at the time.

10. New Frontiers

Progressivism, or any other "ism," seemed of secondary interest to a nation rolling in affluence. Yet there were anxieties associated with the threat of major war coming out of the East or West, for which policies needed to be sought. It was understandable that Albert C. Ganley should have entitled his study *The Progressive Movement: Traditional Reform* (1964). The debates between Richard M. Nixon and his Presidential challenger John F. Kennedy in 1960 took no account of traditional approaches outside of party. Viewers on television concentrated on their different personalities. The one emphasized classical Republican regard for business; the other classical Democratic empathy with labor and minority demands; see Sidney Kraus, ed., *The Great Debates* (1962). See also John F. Kennedy's posthumous *A Nation of Immigrants* (1964), with an introduction by Robert F. Kennedy. The nation responded by dividing its votes almost in half for the candidates.

As President, Kennedy received the good wishes of the country which enjoyed his youth and family, approved his efforts at creating good will with

Russia, with South America, and elsewhere, and it absorbed the tragedy of the Bay of Pigs with relatively little anger or chagrin. Although the nation needed large health, conservation, transportation, ecological, and other remedial measures, it did not urgently demand action in these fields. Nor did it ask for rapid action to implement the Supreme Court's great decision of 1954 calling for desegregation. It was significant that the original Progressives had been suspicious of a generally conservative Court. Their remedy had been a stronger Executive. The continuing good times of the early 1960s seemed to make stepped-up government action unnecessary. Kennedy's death brought no crisis assessments, but regrets over the promise and charisma he had displayed; see Allan Nevins, ed., *The Burden and the Glory: Hopes and Purposes of . . . Second and Third Years as Revealed in His Public Statements* (1964).

His successor, Lyndon B. Johnson, made it his ambition to out-New Deal the New Deal, and government funds circled freely to every sector of society. Yet the fact that they flowed in good times distinguished them from the earlier moneys more judiciously directed at the needy, and more carefully accounted for. Johnson's "give aways," although well-intended, lacked the element of responsibility which would have given them better title to Progressivism. In any event, they did not help Johnson's credit with the electorate when his Vietnam program turned into a nightmare.

The decisive force was the television which, though accused of dulling the public's mind with hollow situation comedies and sports, had the potential for seizing the public mind as the old popular magazines once had. The novel condition which now emerged was the public's ability to watch the mounting war in Vietnam on television, and realize that it was revealing an administration which was unable either to win the war or to give up its stake in the adventure. As Johnson's credibility with his constituency diminished, he felt able only to continue policies which left the public adrift and unable to answer firmly the questions and criticisms posed by a reinvigorated radical movement, much of it composed of youth.

This movement took many forms, but the two major ones involved an egalitarian drive for Negro rights, on one hand, and a swelling antiwar protest movement, on the other. Informed partisans despised Theodore Roosevelt as an imperialist. They belittled Woodrow Wilson as a racist. They thought of progressive reforms as mean and insignificant. Having money, they despised money. Youth rates on planes enabled them to move swiftly from place to place seeking "action," and ways to express their contempt for an effete America, yet dangerous, as they thought, to the peace of the world.

C. Wright Mills was a figure of consequence to them: one who had moved from The Establishment in his classic — and corrosive — *White Collar: The American Middle Classes* (1951) to *The Power Elite* (1956) which Mills saw as oppressive in its unity. His *Listen Yankee* (1960) not only hailed the Cuban Revolution but expressed disaffection from the United States as did many of his American admirers. Others joined him in creating a jaundiced view which, in effect, aimed at dividing the country, rather than finding ways to achieve an American consensus.

Out of the ranks of the young rose a political group determined to affect American politics. It created a drive which momentarily made Senator Eugene J. McCarthy of Minnesota a spokesman for their discontent, thanks to his lack of faith in the war Johnson was waging. "Vietnam," wrote McCarthy, "is a military problem, Vietnam is a political problem; and as the war goes on it has become more clearly a moral problem." (Eugene J. McCarthy, *The Limits of Power; America's Role in the World* [1967], p. 187.) This search for morality gave him structure at a time which had made do with mere expedience. Both he and Johnson soon left the field, and left the problem of morality to others.

Audiovisual Aids

1. *American Foreign Policy — Instrument of Intervention*, NBC.
2. *U. S. Neutrality, 1914–1917*, CBS; *World War I*, PSP *What Price Glory*, a famous motion picture allegedly pacifist, but with implications the directors may not have themselves realized, FOX; *All Quiet on the Western Front*, made after Erich Maria Remarque's famous novel, and compassionately giving the German version of front-line services, UNIVERSAL; *America Gets Involved*, BBC
3. *The Golden Twenties*, MOT; *Mr. Smith Goes to Washington*, COL; *America, on the Edge of Abundance*, NET.
4. *The Great Depression, The Grapes of Wrath, Between the Wars*, EAV; *The Great McGinty*, a full-length satire on politics, posited on Progressive tenets of good government, PAR.
5. *All the King's Men*, based on Robert Penn Warren's novel dealing with the problems of political idealism and reform, COL; *The Last Hurrah*, from Edwin O'Connor's novel based on the life of Boss James M. Curley of Boston, whom Filene had once dreamed could be a popular leader opposing corrupt politics of the common stamp, COL; *Born Yesterday*, an outstanding comedy depicting political corruption in Washington, COL.

iv

Search for Values

1. The Anguish of Change

Although in the 1960s and early 1970s thousands of books poured from presses in behalf of embattled youth and Negroes, almost none of them could be identified with progressive ideals or experience. The very concept of "Blacks," which momentarily preempted the Negro field, implied a militancy defiant of the facts of history and ethnology and a determination to politicalize the subject; see Filler, "Negro Materials of the 1960's," *Choice*, April 1968, 1-6. Jack T. Kirby, in *Darkness at the Dawning* (1972), identified bigotry with Progressivism in the South. Opportunistic arguments veered from derogating the abolitionists, Abraham Lincoln, and the Civil War as racist to, in one historical study, discovering that "[by] 1900 blacks were less in the mainstream of American life than they had been in the previous four decades," David M. Katzman, *Before the Ghetto: Black Detroit in the Nineteenth Century* (1973). A host of civil rights laws and institutional efforts failed to shake the convictions behind this premise.

"New Left" writing moved on and off the campuses, as in Edward J. Bacciocco, Jr., *The New Left in America: Reform to Revolution, 1956-1970* (1974) and Barton J. Bernstein, ed., *Towards a New Past: Dissenting Essays in American History* (1968), which featured well-regarded protestants like Staughton Lynd, who sought to see "Beyond [Charles A.] Beard," and Eugene D. Genovese who offered Marxist interpretations of the Slave South. Leon Friedman, in *The Wise Minority* (1971), made a premise of "conscientious law-breaking" as a necessary part of the American political process. It had indeed been a part of protest and even liberal crusades to test the law, but usually after having first sought to prove to the electorate and its minions the intrinsic loyalty to American ideals and experience which the crusades embodied.

Nevertheless, a variety of writings sought to find middle ground which would better identify with the citizenry in its ordinary pursuits and attitudes. Books on housing reform, the operations of Social Security, the workings of the American Medical Association, "senior citizens" — who were becoming conspicuous as equally momentous with the problems of child care — appeared, though rarely linked with the work of reformers and legislators who could give a public impetus to the arguments. Environment became a conspicuous subject, though the need for factory products and natural resources often caused businessmen and politicians to call a halt on conservation and pollution measures, on grounds that necessity compelled their decisions. Fred Carvell and Max Tadlock, eds., *It's Not Too Late* (1971) offered a volume of textbook essays on environment saving. The campuses were interested, but how far they could affect public thinking in the field was unclear.

A variety of books treated serious subjects with authority, but were unable to link them with related subjects, thus giving strength to all of them. Edward M. Swartz's *Toys that Don't Care* (1971) was such a subject, and was aggravating to people who were outraged that careless manufacture could result in the maiming of children. Nevertheless, there was little the upset parent could do, even if he was persistent in letter-writing to congressmen and others.

Some statesmen were interested. Senator Charles H. Percy wrote *Growing Old in the Country of the Young* (1974), and in it indicated the need for action in behalf of the old. Senator Warren G. Magnuson with Elliot A. Segal examined costs in *How Much for Health?* (1974). John W. Gardner, highly respected as leader of *Common Cause*, an effort to create an army of concerned citizens, wrote an introduction for Milton Silverman and Philip R. Lee's *Pills, Profits & Politics* (1974). But the catalytic action which had once created landmark laws and organizations in the Progressive era did not seem to materialize, at least to the level which society's needs seemed to demand. One of the problems was defining individual responsibility. Those, for example, who made a free speech cause of pornography, and persuaded serious people that individual rights were at stake in the issue, were not required to prove themselves equally interested in civic concerns. Indeed, with "squares" having been made a word of contempt, and "The Square Deal" seeming as remote as the reign of Tutankhamen, the equation of personal principles with civic principles was at best hazy. Fred J. Cook, a "crusading journalist," expressed nostalgia in *The Muckrakers* (1972), a simplistic work which could little serve the new, complex times. Elliott M. Sanger, in *Rebel in Radio: The Story of WQXR* (1973), spoke of a station (which later became the station of the *New York Times*), which had emerged out of its conservative past to become a leader in explorations intended to renew its own deteriorated city and others, and to provide policy partial to all dissatisfied factions, whether women or "Gays."

A phenomenon of the time was "the new journalism," which promised to add a new dimension of excitement and reality to social events. Norman Mailer, the novelist, claimed to read contemporary events with intimate understanding of their psychological and even mystic reality. Tom Wolfe, discoverer of "the new journalism" borrowed language, gestures, and feelings from the people he examined in order to bring the reader as close to their condition as possible. The new method seemed to have some relevance to larger social concerns in such a *tour de force* as Joe McGinnis's *The Selling of the President* (1969), in which he entered behind the scenes of Republican campaign headquarters to reveal their principals in their casual and unpremeditated roles. Yet seen in review, as in the anthology edited by Tom Wolfe and E. W. Johnson, *The New Journalism* (1973), the new journalists seemed more zippy than illuminating.

Louis Harris indirectly characterized all such phenomena of social intercourse, with their inevitable confusions of purpose and their attempts at new style and modernity, in *The Anguish of Change* (1973): a time of discouragement with leaders, the long Vietnam agony, the poverty which had somehow emerged from prosperity, the low quality of living as well as of material production, the status of women, labor, and youth. Alfred Steinberg, in *The Bosses* (1972), revisited an old theme which Warren Moscow hopefully personalized in the case of one he called *The Last of the Big-Time Bosses: The Life and Times of Carmine De Sapio and the Rise and Fall of Tammany Hall* (1971). Others were less sanguine than Moscow, predicting that a tired and disillusioned nation would gladly hand back power to party leaders who would deliver a minimum of protection and services for their payoffs.

Other writings, which attracted more or less public interest included Ronald B. Taylor, *Sweatshops in the Sun: Child Labor on the Farm* (1973); Leopold Lippmann and I. Ignacy Goldberg, *Right to Education: Anatomy of the Pennsylvania Case and Its Implications for Exceptional Children* (1973); and Louis H. Masotti and Jeffrey K. Hadden, eds., *The Urbanization of the Suburbs* (1973), a massive volume of essays which recognized that suburbia was here to stay and had to be objectively assessed. A topic of concern was the decline of the magazine, usually laid to the rise of television, but which threatened to leave the nation without matter which it could reread and rethink. *Collier's* had gone down despite money and prestige. The fall of the *Saturday Evening Post* created a sensation, especially since part of its failure, at least, was the result of its effort at muckraking, which cost it several defeats in the courts at the expense of millions of dollars, and may have hurt reader and advertiser's interest; see Matthew J. Culligan, *The Curtis-Culligan Story* (1970) for one account of its collapse. A partially revived *Saturday Evening Post* returned to its old principles of optimism, good humor, and a generally "positive" view of life.

At the same time, a portion of the nation's press and readers continued to approve and patronize aspects of social criticism and reform. Drew Pearson, and Jack Anderson stated *The Case Against Congress;. . .Corruption on Capitol Hill* (1968), and I. F. Stone received a moment of glory as the grand old man of dissident journalism; see Neil Middleton, ed., *The I. F. Stone Weekly Reader* (1973). Marlise James's *The People's Lawyers* (1973) focused on a wide spectrum of civil rights advocates, and made it clear that they were here to stay. Thus Sylvia A. Law's *Blue Cross: What Went Wrong?* (1974), was prepared by a law professor under university auspices, and published by a university press, and seemed the harbinger of other studies which would bring public interest law to bear on social problems of many kinds. James Colaianni's *The Catholic Left in the Crisis of Radicalism within the Church* (1968) had helped indicate the dimensions of the social crisis.

2. Nader

The sensation of sensations, however, in public interest law, in civil rights concern, in the responsibility of the private sector of American affairs, and in the ramifications of government actions as they related to city and nation was Ralph Nader who, on emerging as a public figure, became immediately identified with muckraking, if not with classical Progressivism. Nader was striking in the utter cleanliness of his personal deportment, a fact reminiscent of Charles A. Lindbergh's earlier charisma but contrasting with later attitudes which made "mod" clothing, free-wheeling sexuality, and drunkenness matters of civil rights, rather than signs of superficiality or lack of control. Even the use of marijuana was treated by some partisans as an issue of freedom, and the use of cigarettes defended by persons critical of the Pure Food and Drugs Administration for accomplishing less than it should.

Nader's "square" attitude toward social responsibility combined with his clean-cut personal appearance were to make him a favorite of organizations which sponsored his talks at high lecture fees, which he was said to turn back to his organizations in furtherance of their work. His studies of industrial malfeasance kept him modestly but effectively employed in the first stages of his career. His book, *Unsafe at Any Speed: The Designed-in Dangers of the American Automobile* (1965) was at first modestly successful. But Nader had, in addition, worked with members of Congress to look into such matters. Their hearings provided a link with journalism and publicity which harked directly back to muckraking and progressive days.

What has been insufficiently noticed, however, was that it was not the alleged inadequacy of automobile manufacture which lifted Nader to fame, or even the revelations, such as they were, of official investigations. After all, the public in part determined which cars they preferred to buy and which hearings they cared to patronize with their attention. It was learning that Nader had been shadowed by General Motors agencies, who had sought maliciously to build up invidious information respecting his character and motives which roused public attention. It humanized Nader and dehumanized General Motors, and gave the public a stake in the former's career.

The true hero of these proceedings was television itself. Watching the public humiliation of General Motors officials as they admitted their degrading surveillance of Nader made spectators realize the difference between the exposed power of corporations to hurt, and the "public defender" confections which TV regularly served up with happy endings. Television was revealed as having a potential such as had not been available since the time of the muckraking magazines. It had only to produce its Lincoln Steffenses and

David Graham Phillipses to affect positively the course of social communication. See Thomas Whiteside, *The Investigation of Ralph Nader, General Motors vs. One Determined Man* (1972) and Robert F. Buckhorn, *Nader: The People's Lawyer* (1972).

Nader went on to attract a formidable army of young law students and lawyers inspired by his example — "Nader's Raiders" — and to become a favorite of journalists and lawmakers. His various teams of investigators compiled information of many sorts respecting industrial products, congressional operations, environmental needs, professional ethics, and other fields, and began a flow of publications intended to enlighten the public on particular problems and the legislative action which was required. Moreover, their work got results. Bills were passed in Congress which affected gas pipeline safety, radiation control, meat and poultry inspection standards, coal mine health and safety measures, and even affected entire operations, like the workings of the Federal Trade Commission.

The list of publications was actually formidable, and the individual volumes were written with verve and authority. Typical was the book edited by a former editor-in-chief of the Harvard Civil Rights-Civil Liberties Law Review, Mark J. Green, *The Monopoly Makers: Ralph Nader's Study Group Report on Regulation and Competition* (1973). There was even a volume by Charles Peters and Taylor Branch, eds., *Blowing the Whistle: Dissent in the Public Interest* (1972) which attempted to speak to the question of "Old Muck, New Rakers." It examined individuals and groups which it saw as resisting the good work of Nader, Daniel Ellsberg, and other "whistle blowers." In effect, it sought to encourage others to join them in a new muckraking effort.

Still the haunting question remained whether Nader was a useful person whose career activated other useful persons, or whether he was the flying wedge of a movement, calculated to create an understanding between the average citizen and the official world which he elected or endorsed. Progressivism had premised a thinking and active citizen supportive of the best. It had premised an imaginative citizenry, capable of being stirred to worthy goals by such achievements as Upton Sinclair's *The Jungle* and John Steinbeck's *The Grapes of Wrath*. Many of the literary successes of the 1950s and 1960s were skillful and of literary merit, as in the cases of Jack Kerouac's *On the Road* and Philip Roth's *Portnoy's Complaint*, but they were not calculated to contribute to such campaigns as Nader fancied. There was always the danger that the Nader type of enterprise serviced the facades of civilization rather than its essence.

3. Watergate

As memorable as Nader was, his causes had to give way to those implied by Watergate. It took time for it to catch on; first responses were similar to those which had accompanied "Payola" revelations: What could you do? What do you expect? Investigative reporting had made the difference, combined with television coverage which took readers from books to television screens and back again. Seymour Hersh had, in *Cover Up* (1972), stirred the country with his account of the Army's secret investigation of the massacre of My Lai, and had been awarded the Pulitzer Prize for his efforts. Jack Anderson had uncovered the "Eagleton Affair" which had given bizarre overtones to the McGovern campaign in 1972; see *The Anderson Papers*, previously mentioned. An Anderson-Eagleton confrontation on television had added excitement and raised questions which were both educational and evocative.

Now two young *Washington Post* newspapermen activated themselves in ways they were to describe in Carl Bernstein's and Bob Woodward's *All the President's Men* (1974). Numerous other journalists contributed bits and pieces to the problem. Ultimately, there were hearings which riveted the attention of the public, and massive confrontations between public officials of various kinds and the President himself which made it clear that a public crisis was in progress. It was constitutional, but it also involved the nature of American society. Vice President Spiro T. Agnew, a heartbeat away from the Presidency, and forced to retire from office, complained that he had been victimized by what he termed "post-Watergate morality," and, indeed, every manner of skulduggery was now exposed in the news involving corruption, bribes, private manipulation of public funds, undermining of civil rights, much of which would have passed unnoticed before. *The Watergate Hearings, Break-In and Cover-Up: Proceedings of the Senate Select Committee*, as edited by Gerald Gold and the staff of the *New York Times* (1973) was filled with evidence of the most serious infringement of personal rights, sometimes justified on the grounds of national security, but often involving only partisan or private interests. William V. Shannon's *They Could Not Trust the King: Nixon, Watergate, and the American People* (1973) spelled out the problem of authority in a democracy.

One of the keys to the meaning of Watergate was the question of "cover-up." To how much privacy were government officials entitled? How much investigatory journalism did the public want? Watergate accomplices believed themselves hounded by unfair and partisan reporters. In the last analysis, it would be their readers who would decide the "truth" of the matter, simply by their decisions on what to read and why. As events closed in on the President, who stood responsible for what his Administration had done and intended, it was clear that congressmen would have to determine how they themselves stood with their consciences, and with their constituencies. In effect, the President had already concluded to trust the people in his own way by releasing his version of the controversial tapes, unforeseen at the beginning of the Watergate investigation, but now become an issue in public as distinguished from private communication. See *The Presidential Transcripts*, with commentary by the staff of the *Washington Post* (1974). There were those who denounced the transcripts as crude, cynical, and filled with revelations of fraud. The President evidently believed that the common reader for whom he targetted them would see them in more sympathetic light.

For the ends he envisioned, this was not to be. The nation had been stunned by the fall of the Vice President, Spiro T. Agnew, from a proud summit on which he had criticized the opposition in words of utter virtue. It was not only that his liberal foes who had pursued him were triumphant; his conservative admirers were left chastened and disarmed. The long and persistent probings which acccompanied the Watergate investigation, by journalists as well as lawyers, kept Nixon giving out line until he was firmly enmeshed, and forced by his own party to resign.

All of this helped muckraking, but whether it helped Progressivism could not be known. Bernard James, in *The Death of Progress* (1972), argued that old anticipations of progress were not only illusory, but deceiving. We needed, he thought, to find means for survival, if only by peremptory approaches to people and conditions. In short, he said, we might have to resign some of our old definitions of humanity. One hoped that he was wrong, but there did appear to be notes of pessimism and soured disposition in some modern considerations of public events. Progressives had appealed to good will, hope, a desire for better things. V. O. Key's *Techniques of Political Graft in the United States* (1936) and Louise Overacker's *Money in Elections* (1932) had been in the progressive tradition. Even Harvey O'Connor's *Mellon's Millions* (1933), though written with socialist anticipations, had overlapped with progressive attitudes, as Upton Sinclair had once had a foot in both camps.

Modern estimates tended to range in tone from querulous to funereal. Footnote brigades continued to see failure everywhere, as in R. Alan Lawson's *The Failure of Independent Liberalism 1930–1941* (1971), though a less blurred vision might have seen achievement in the work of Stuart Chase, Lewis Mumford, and John Dewey, even as independent thinkers. Numerous books seemed to presume a noble electorate gulled by crafty men, but failed to explain how they had attained election: a question which to Lincoln Steffens had once seemed the basic question. Gordon Fellman and Barbara Brandt, *The Deceived Majority: Politics and Protest in Middle America* (1973) and Walter Karp, *Indispensable Enemies: The Politics of Misrule in America* (1973) both suffered from the same defect of seeing conspiracies where there were relationships tolerated which were insufficiently rooted in the best American experience, and which could not be explained in terms of them. As we have seen, old Progressives had been given lip-service rather than study or regard. A "new morality" such as publicists lightly discussed in magazine articles and books could not easily be fitted into "post-Watergate morality." The nation would have to make up its mind what it expected of its legislators, and also of itself.

Books about corruption could be read with profit, if they were not read with unction, for example Walter Goodman's *A Percentage of the Take* (1971), Robert N. Winter-Berger's *The Washington Pay-off: An Insider's View of Corruption in Government* (1972), and Carl J. Friedrich's *The Pathology of Politics: Violence, Betrayal, Corruption, Secrecy, and Propaganda* (1972). James C. Scott's *Comparative Political Corruption* (1972) also suggested science as well as indignation.

American apathy and individualism had produced strange fruit which critics at home and abroad could satirize: poverty in the midst of plenty, discomfort in the midst of every efficiency machine. Sheer self-preservation would have seemed to make it a priority for Americans to seize hold of their welfare system, their tax structure, their control of industry and labor, environment, and education, health, culture, and social justice systems, and shake them until they produced results. Such books as Marc Pilisuk and Phyllis Pilisuk, eds., *Poor Americans: How the White Poor Live* (1971) and Anthony Sampson, *The Sovereign of ITT* (1973), though useful, lacked some component of social awareness and involvement which could be noted in the first stages of Nader's campaign and in aspects of Watergate. Despite the storm which the youth drive of the 1960s had caused, Americans were not yet synchronized in purpose to create overlapping interest groups which could incite each other to purposeful reform.

A special word deserved to be said for writers. Investigatory journalism was all very well, as bread for social change. But society yearned for wine as well, and some of the earlier muckrakers or Progressives had been able to provide it. Lincoln Steffens's *Autobiography* was a classic which could be read as literature as well as life. Upton Sinclair (the late Perry Miller to the contrary) had sometimes written memorably, and made his point by his writing skill as well as his facts. Jack London, Finley Peter Dunne, and others, read with care and discrimination could serve the present as well as the past, as could autobiographies by Robert M. La Follette and Brand Whitlock, without in the slightest interfering with the research and careers of new scholars in the field.

It was one of the strong points of the Communist world that it could often furnish inspiration to its people where it could not furnish bread. Progressivism in the past had given some imaginative inspiration along with its data and clear prose. Its cultural torchbearers were not well remembered, and often scorned. Scorn had even, incredibly, touched Vachel Lindsay, an American genius and Progressive, if ever there was one. A choice had unnecessarily been posed between progressive ideals and those followed by later individualists. A newer Progressivism, if it should ever materialize, would have to find ways to speak to human emotions as well as to the mind and pocketbook.

Old clichés of the businessman as Babbitt would have to be abandoned. Businessmen were sometimes crude, they were sometimes sensitive; the poet Wallace Stevens had been in business, so had T. S. Eliot, and others; and technical "intellectuals" did not always read or even think. A serious program for America, determined to be effective, would shrug off empty attitudes and judge persons rather than professions, especially if it intended to influence a wide range of people.

It seemed desirable to lay aside the literature of wailing and woe, usually the product of limited reading and experience and, in any event, liable to the error of the "self-fulfilling prophecy." Henry Kariel, *The Decline of American Pluralism* (1961), Robert P. Wolff, *The Poverty of Liberalism* (1968), Theodore Lowi, *The End of Liberalism* (1969) — it was difficult to see what purpose such works served. Even a formidable pessimism needed a program for living and the enjoyment of living which made it worthwhile in the first place.

It was promising that there were more reasonable approaches to America's troubles than the above use of paper and printing offered, and that more creative thinking in connection with those troubles might be expected. Fred Harris was not a fanciful litterateur or bureaucrat, but a legislator with a sense of people, and his *The New Populism* (1973), however controversial in details, did represent a program for reform. Nor was reform the sole prerogative of professed liberals. It needed to be noted over and over again that reform had derived from liberals, yes, but it had also derived from conservatives, as any random sample of distinguished names in American reform could show. A reviewer for the *New York Post* (John Barkham, January 17, 1974) observed that "Conservatism is so widely equated with negativism that it is something of a shock to discover William F. Buckley, the voice of conservatism, preaching reform in his best Addisonian prose." Buckley's *Four Reforms: A Program for the Seventies* (1973) won mixed responses from his critic. He approved Buckley's proposal for tax reform, noted that Buckley's suggestion that the Fifth Amendment, which protects the citizen against self-incrimination, be repealed had practically no chance of being accepted, agreed that the welfare situation cried out for reform, but thought Buckley was going about it in the wrong way, and drily noted as impractical Buckley's call for a constitutional amendment which would permit aid to parochial schools.

However, there was thinking going on, perhaps temporarily swamped by the continuing urgencies of Watergate. It seemed likely that muckraking would continue. It was an American method of social communication to which Americans were habituated. But Progressivism? In the 1973 Manhattan telephone directory there were 29 listings beginning with "Progress," including the Progress Republican Club and the Progress Realty Corporation. There were 55 listings which began with Progressive. Several of these seemed to hark back to earlier connotations, as with *The Progressive Farmer*, a publication with its hint of Populism, and the Progressive Labor Party which doubtless considered itself forward looking. But though more persons in this brief sample identified themselves with Progressive than with Progress, most of the former were active in such categories as Progressive Cleaners and Progressive Wig Suppliers than in political theory.

There seemed no gain in attempting to prejudge how Americans might, in their more positive moods, prefer to see themselves, as Progressives, perhaps, as solid Democrats or Republicans, as Nonpartisans, or Social Democrats. What was important was that they have some sense of their heritage, and that of the people they intended to influence. People did not ponder all their options. If options did not make themselves apparent, people passed on the way. There had been a long and continuing tradition of Progressivism under many names, tending toward realism and materialism, but catching fire on great occasions to inspire idealists and memorable leaders. It seemed reasonable to review the record and determine what of it could be brought to bear on living events.[1]

Audiovisual Aids

1. *Television: A Political Machine*, NET; *America's Critics Abroad*, USDD; *America and the Americans*, NBC; *America: The Greatness that Is Ours*, DOUGLS; *An American Ballad*, details the life of Rabbi Henry Cohen of Texas, a fighter against discrimination, JTS.

   Numerous films treat of American problems: *Harvest of Shame*, which details oppressive practices relating to migrant workers, CBS; *America's Untapped Asset*, which explains the proper use of people with physical disabilities, NSCCA; *The Urban Crisis*, lectures by a Health, Education and Welfare official and *Water Pollution, Air Pollution*, EAV.

Bibliography
and Author Index

ADAMIC, LOUIS. *Dynamite: The Story of Class Violence in America.* New York: Viking Press, 1931. 31-5359. 92

ADAMS, GRAHAM, JR. *Age of Industrial Violence 1910–15.* New York: Columbia University Press, 1966. 66-17857. 68, 74

ADDAMS, JANE. *My Friend, Julia Lathrop.* New York: Macmillan, 1935. 35-33985. 54

_____. *Newer Ideals of Peace.* New York: Macmillan, 1907. 7-4377. 84

_____. *The Second Twenty Years at Hull-House.* New York: Macmillan, 1930. 30-31867. 54

_____. *Twenty Years at Hull-House.* New York: Macmillan, 1910. 10-27333. 54

ADLER, SELIG. *The Isolationist Impulse.* New York: The Free Press, 1957. 31

AGUINALDO, EMILIO, and PACIS, VICENTE ABANO. *A Second Look at America.* New York: R. Speller, 1957. 57-11884. 34

AINLEY, LESLIE. *Boston Mahatma: The Public Career of Martin Lomasney.* Boston: W. M. Pobrendible, 1949. 49-51315. 53

ALLEN, FREDERICK LEWIS. *The Big Change: America Transforms Itself 1900–1950.* New York: Harper, 1952. 52-8455. 25

ALLEN, PHILIP L. *America's Awakening.* New York: Revell, 1906. 63-8914. 58

ALLSWANG, JOHN M. *A House for All Peoples: Chicago's Ethnic Groups and Their Politics, 1890–1936.* Lexington: University Press of Kentucky, 1971. 76-119810. 57

AMERINGER, OSCAR. *If You Don't Weaken.* New York: H. Holt and Co., 1940. 40-27504. 68

ANDERSON, JACK. *The Anderson Papers.* New York: Random House, 1973. 72-11407. 5, 114

ANDERSON, OSCAR E., JR. *The Health of a Nation: Harvey W. Wiley and the Fight for Pure Food.* Chicago: University of Chicago Press, 1958. 58-11945. 61

ANDREWS, WAYNE. *Battle for Chicago.* New York: Harcourt, Brace, 1946. 46-11934. 54

ARNETT, ALEX M. *The Populist Movement in Georgia: A View of the "Agrarian Crusade" in the Light of Solid-South Politics.* New York: Columbia University, 1922. 23-263. 38

ARON, RAYMOND. *Progress and Disillusion: The Dialectics of Modern Society.* rev. New York: Praeger, 1968. 67-22287. 4

ASBURY, HERBERT. *Carry Nation.* New York: A. A. Knopf, 1929. 29-21266. 52

_____. *The Gangs of New York.* New York: A. A. Knopf, 1928. 28-10023. 52

_____. *The Great Illusion.* Garden City, N.Y.: Doubleday, 1950. 50-10358. 52

_____. *Sucker's Progress: An Informal History of Gambling in America.* New York: Dodd, Mead & Company, 1938. 38-34335. 53

_____. *Up from Methodism.* New York: A. A. Knopf, 1926. 26-17134. 52

ASHBY, LEROY. *The Spearless Leader.* Urbana: University of Illinois Press, 1972. 74-170963. 71

BACCIOCCO, EDWARD J., JR. *The New Left in America.* Stanford: Hoover Institution Press, 1974. 73-75887. 109

BAGBY, WESLEY M. "Progressivism's Debacle: The Election of 1920." Ann Arbor: University Microfilms, 1954. Mic A 54-2007. 90

BAILEY, HUGH C. *Edgar Gardner Murphy, Gentle Progressive.* Coral Cables, Fla.: University of Miami Press, 1968. 68-29705. 61

———. *Liberalism in the New South.* Coral Gables, Fla.: University of Miami Press, 1969. 78-81620. 64

BAILEY, THOMAS A. *The Man in the Street: The Impact of American Public Opinion on Foreign Policy.* New York: Macmillan, 1948. 48-6857. 28

———. *Theodore Roosevelt and the Japanese American Crises: An Account of the International Complications Arising from the Race Problem on the Pacific Coast.* Stanford: Stanford University Press, 1934. 34-38008. 28

———. *Woodrow Wilson and the Great Betrayal.* New York: Macmillan, 1945. 45-5994. 88

BAKER, RAY STANNARD. *American Chronicle.* New York: C. Scribner's Sons, 1945. 45-2441. 43, 65

———. *Following the Color Line.* Garden City, N. Y.: Doubleday, Page & Co., 1908. 8-31180. 65

BAKER, THOMAS HARRISON. *The Memphis Commercial Appeal: The History of a Southern Newspaper.* Baton Rouge: Louisiana State University Press, 1971. 74-165066. 39

———. *The New Industrial Unrest.* Garden City, N. Y.: Doubleday, Page & Co., 1920. 20-8811. 90

———. *Woodrow Wilson: Life and Letters.* 8 vols. Garden City, N. Y.: Doubleday, Page & Co., 1927–1939. 27-25411. 77

———, and DODD, WILLIAM E., eds. *Public Papers, College and State: Educational, Literary and Political Papers of Woodrow Wilson.* 2 vols. New York: Harper, 1925. 25-3224. 78

BALDWIN, ROGER N. *Civil Liberties and Industrial Conflict.* Cambridge: Harvard University Press, 1938. 38-27405. 96

BANNISTER, ROBERT C., JR. *Ray Stannard Baker: The Mind and Thought of a Progressive.* New Haven: Yale University Press, 1966. 66-12486. 44

BARKER, CHARLES ALBRO. *Henry George.* New York: Oxford University Press, 1955. 55-6251. 23

BARKER, JOHN MARSHALL. *The Saloon Problem and Social Reform.* Boston: The Everett Press, 1905. 5-33983. 58, 87

BARNARD, ELLSWORTH. *Wendell Willkie, Figher for Freedom.* Marquette: Northern Michigan University Press, 1966. 66-19668. 100

BARNARD, HARRY. *Eagle Forgotten: The Life of John Peter Altgeld.* New York: Duell, Sloan and Pearce, 1948. A50-9082. 38

———. *Independent Man: The Life of Senator James Couzens.* New York: Scribner, 1958. 58-7⁵ 3. 91

BARNES, JOSEPH. *Willkie.* New York: Simon and Schuster, 1952. 52-13324. 100

BARNETT, S. A., CANON and wife. *Towards Social Reform.* New York: Macmillan, 1909. 9-9823. 56

BARRETT, JAMES WYMAN, ed. *The End of the World: A Post Mortem, by its Intangible Assets.* New York: Harper, 1931. 31-10073. 40

———. *Joseph Pulitzer and His World.* New York: Vanguard Press, 1941. 41-21082. 40

———. *The World, the Flesh and the Messrs Pulitzer.* New York: Vanguard Press, 1931. 31-8398. 40

BARROWS, ESTHER G. *Neighbors All.* Boston: Houghton Mifflin, 1929. 29-18086. 56

BARTLETT, RUHL J. *The League to Enforce Peace.* Chapel Hill: University of North Carolina Press, 1944. 44-5804. 85

BATES, J. LEONARD. *The Origins of Teapot Dome,* rev. Urbana: University of Illinois Press, 1963. 63-17045. 72

BEALE, HOWARD K. *The History of Freedom of Teaching in American Schools.* New York: C. Scribner's Sons, 1941. 41-5920. 61

———. *Theodore Roosevelt and the Rise of America to World Power.* Baltimore: Johns Hopkins Press, 1956. 56-10255. 28

BEALS, CARLETON. *The Great Revolt and Its Leaders: The History of Popular American Uprisings in the 1890's.* London and New York: Abelard-Schuman, 1968. 68-16745. 37

BEAN, WALTON E. *Boss Ruef's San Francisco.* Berkeley: University of California Press, 1952. 52-7946. 51

BEARD, CHARLES AUSTIN, ed. *A Century of Progress.* New York and London: Harper, 1933. 33-23949. 4

———. *Contemporary American History, 1877–1913.* New York: Macmillan, 1914. 14-3118. 25

———, and MARY R. *The Rise of American Civilization.* rev. ed. New York: Macmillan, 1949. A51-2586. 3

———, and SMITH, G. H. E. *The Future Comes.* New York: Macmillan, 1933. 33-37474. 96

BEAVER, DANIEL R. *Newton D. Baker and the American War Effort, 1917–1919.* Lincoln: University of Nebraska, 1966. 66-10334. 85

BEECHER, HENRY WARD. *Evolution and Religion.* New York: Fords, Howard & Hulbert, 1885. 31-14248. 7

BELL, DANIEL, ed. *The New American Right.* New York: Criterion Books, 1955. 55-11024. 102

BELLAMY, EDWARD. *Looking Backward, 2000–1887.* Boston: Ticknor, 1888. 6-11710. 19

BEMIS, EDWARD, W., ed. *Municipal Monopolies.* New York: T. Y. Crowell & Company, 1899. 4-31389. 36

BEMIS, SAMUEL F., ed. *The American Secretaries of State and Their Diplomacy.* New York: A. A. Knopf, 1927–1929. 27-8473. 83

BENT, SILAS. *Ballyhoo.* New York: Boni and Liveright, 1927. 27-23331. 5

BERGER, MEYER. *The Story of the New York Times, 1851–1951.* New York: Simon and Schuster, 1951. 51-6775. 40

BERGSON, HENRI LOUIS. *Creative Evolution* trans. by Arthur Mitchell. New York: Henry Holt, 1911. 11-3948. 8

BERMAN, MILTON. *John Fiske, the Evolution of a Popularizer.* Cambridge, Mass.: Harvard University Press, 1961. 62-7334. 33

BERNHEIMER, CHARLES. *Half a Century in Community Service.* New York: Association Press, 1948. 48-9228. 56

BERNSTEIN, BARTON J., ed. *Towards a New Past.* New York: Pantheon Books, 1968. 67-19177. 109

BERNSTEIN, CARL, and WOODWARD, BOB. *All the President's Men.* New York: Simon and Schuster, 1974. 73-22334. 114

BEVERIDGE, ALBERT J. *The Meaning of the Times and Other Speeches.* Indianapolis: Bobbs-Merrill Co., 1908. 8-12769. 70

———. *The Russian Advance.* New York: Harper, 1903. 3-32459. 30

BIERCE, AMBROSE. *Letters.* San Francisco: Book Club of California, 1922. 23-7856. 42

BIERSTADT, EDWARD HALE. *Aspects of Americanization.* Cincinnati: Stewart Kidd Co., 1922. 22-11161. 57

BILLINGTON, RAY ALLEN. *The Protestant Crusade 1800–1860: A Study of the Origins of American Nativism.* New York: Macmillan, 1938. 38-38025. 13

BINGHAM, ALFRED M. *Insurgent America: Revolt of the Middle-classes.* New York: W. W. Norton & Co., 1938. 39-10744. 95

———, and RODMAN, SELDEN, eds. *Challenge to the New Deal.* New York: Falcon Press, 1934. 34-28579. 95

BIZZELL, WILLIAM BENNETT. *The Green Rising, an Historical Survey of Agrarianism.* New York: Macmillan, 1926. 26-24178. 37

BLACKWELL, ALICE STONE. *Lucy Stone, Pioneer of Woman's Rights.* Boston: Little, Brown, 1930. 30-25807. 12

BLAIR, LEWIS HARVIE. *The Prosperity of the South Dependent upon the Elevation of the Negro.* Richmond, Va.: E. Waddey, 1889. 52-55645. 15

BLAISDELL, THOMAS C., JR. *The Federal Trade Commission.* New York: Columbia University Press, 1932. 32-34346. 74

BLAU, JOSEPH LEON, ed. *Social Theories of Jacksonian Democracy: Representative Writings of the Period 1825–1850.* Indianapolis: Bobbs-Merrill, 1954. 55-169. 4

BLISS, WILLIAM DWIGHT PORTER, ed. *The Encyclopedia of Social Reform: Including Political Economy, Political Science, Sociology and Statistics.* New York: Funk & Wagnalls, 1897. 2-19652. 19

———. *A Handbook of Socialism: A Statement of Socialism in its Various Aspects and a History of Socialism in All Countries.* New York: Scribners, 1895. 2nd ed. 1907. 4-10433. 19

BLOOMER, DEXTER C. *Life and Writings of Amelia Bloomer.* Boston: Arena Publishing Co., 1895. 14-15880. 13

BLOOR, ELLA REEVE. *We Are Many.* New York: International Pub., 1940. 41-2883. 61

BLOTNER, JOSEPH. *The Political Novel.* Garden City, N. Y.: Doubleday, 1955. 55-6672. 45

BLUM, JOHN M. *Joe Tumulty and the Wilson Era.* Boston: Houghton Mifflin, 1951. 51-5295. 78

_____, ed. *The Price of Vision*. Boston: Houghton Mifflin, 1973. 72-6806. 101

_____. *The Republican Roosevelt*. Cambridge: Harvard University Press, 1954. 54-5182. 51

_____. *Woodrow Wilson and the Politics of Morality*. Boston: Little, Brown, 1956. 56-10643. 78

BLUMBERG, DOROTHY ROSE. *Florence Kelley: The Making of a Social Pioneer*. New York: A. M. Kelley, 1966. 65-16982. 55

BOK, EDWARD. *The Americanization of Edward Bok*. New York: C. Scribner's Sons, 1920. 20-17333. 43

BOODIN, JOHN Elof. *Cosmic Evolution: Outlines of Cosmic Idealism*. New York: Macmillan, 1925. 25-25852. 8

BOOTH, WILLIAM. *In Darkest England and the Way Out*. New York: Funk & Wagnalls, 1890. 4-3813. 41

BOUDIN, LOUIS B. *Government by Judiciary*. New York: W. Godwin, 1932. rev. 32-5954. 92

_____. *Socialism and War*. New York: New Review Pub. Ass'n, 1916. 16-14448. 86

BOURNE, RANDOLPH. SILLIMAN. *The Gary Schools*. Boston: Houghton Mifflin, 1916. 16-7521. 25

BOWDEN, ROBERT. *Boies Penrose*. New York: Greenberg, 1937. 37-1850. 54

BOWERS, CLAUDE GERNADE. *Beveridge and the Progressive Era*. Boston: Houghton Mifflin, 1932. 32-22530. 30

BRANDEIS, LOUIS D. *Other People's Money*. New York: Frederick A. Stokes, 1914. 14-6184. 74

BRANYAN, ROBERT L., and LARSEN, LAWRENCE H., eds. *Urban Crisis in Modern America*. Lexington, Mass.: Heath, 1971. 71-164935. 36

BREMNER, ROBERT H. *American Philanthropy*. Chicago: University of Chicago Press, 1960. 60-7246. 55

_____. *From the Depths: The Discovery of Poverty in the United States*. New York: New York University Press, 1956. 56-7622. 17, 54

BRIDGE, JAMES H., ed. *The Trust: Its Book*. New York: Doubleday, Page & Co., 1902. 9-16118. 67

BRIFFAULT, ROBERT. *Rational Evolution (The Making of Humanity)*. New York: Macmillan, 1930. 30-29276. 4

BRODY, DAVID. *Labor in Crisis: The Steel Strike of 1919*. Philadelphia: Lippincott, 1965. 65-23205. 86

BROOKS, VAN WYCK. *America's Coming-of-Age*. New York: B. W. Huebsch, 1915. 15-27963. 80

_____. *Helen Keller: Sketch for a Portrait*. New York: Dutton, 1956. 55-11080. 69

BROUN, HEYWOOD. *It Seems to Me*. New York: Harcourt, Brace, 1935. 35-27802. 89

BROWN, ERNEST FRANCIS. *Raymond of the Times*. New York: Norton, 1951. 51-5183. 39

BROWN, HALLIE QUINN, ed. *Homespun Heroines and Other Women of Distinction*. Xenia, Ohio: Aldine Publishing Company, 1926. 26-18256. 12

BROWNE, RAY B., *et al.*, eds. *New Voices in American Studies*. West Lafayette, Ind.: Purdue University Studies, 1965. 66-63485. 48

BROWNELL, BLAINE A., and STICKLE, WARREN A., eds. *Bosses and Reformers*. Boston: Houghton Mifflin, 1973. 72-4798. 53

BRUCE, A. A. *The Non-Partisan League*. New York: Macmillan, 1921. 21-12012. 92

BRYAN, WILLIAM JENNINGS. *The First Battle*. Chicago: W. B. Conkey Co., 1896. 12-14597. 35

BRYCE, JAMES. *The American Commonwealth*. London and New York: Macmillan, 2nd rev. ed. 1889. 9-13056. 23

BUCK, SOLON J. *The Agrarian Crusade*. New York: Yale University Press, 1921. A23-836. 37

_____. *The Granger Movement*. Cambridge: Harvard University Press, 1913. 13-19662. 37

BUCKHORN, ROBERT F. *Nader: The People's Lawyer*. Englewood Cliffs, N.J.: Prentice-Hall, 1972. 76-38579. 113

BUCKLEY, WILLIAM F. *Four Reforms: A Program for the Seventies*. New York: Putnam, 1973. 73-78608. 117

BUENKER, JOHN D. *Urban Liberalism and Progressive Reform*. New York: Scribner, 1973. 73-1314. 75

BURNS, EDWARD MCNALL. *The American Idea of Mission: Concepts of National Purpose and Destiny*. New Brunswick, N.J.: Rutgers University Press, 1957. 57-10961. 33

BURROUGHS, JOHN. *Time and Change*. Boston and New York: Houghton Mifflin, 1912. 12-25134. 8

BURTON, DAVID HENRY. *Theodore Roosevelt: Confident Imperialist*. Philadelphia: University of Pennsylvania Press, 1968. 68-9737. 28

BUTCHER, MARGARET JUST. *The Negro in American Culture: Based on Materials Left by Alain Locke*. 2nd ed. New York: Knopf, 1972. 74-38321. 14

CABLE, GEORGE W. *The Negro Question*. New York: C. Scribner's Sons, 1890. 11-1447. 64

_____. *The Silent South*. New York: C. Scribner's Sons, 1885. 12-31083. 64

CAHN, WILLIAM. *A Pictorial History of American Labor*. New York: Crown Publishers, 1972. 70-185099. 67

CAINE, STANLEY P. *The Myth of a Progressive Reform: Railroad Regulation in Wisconsin 1903–1910*. Madison: State Historical Society of Wisconsin, 1970. 75-630131. 62

CALDWELL, ERSKINE, and BOURKE-WHITE, MARGARET. *You Have Seen Their Faces*. New York: Viking Press, 1937. 38-457. 98

CALLOW, ALEXANDER B., JR. *The Tweed Ring*. New York: Oxford University Press, 1966. 66-24440. 18

CARGILL, OSCAR. *Intellectual America: Ideas on the March*. New York: Macmillan, 1941. 41-21084. 25

_____, ed. *The Social Revolt: American Literature from 1888 to 1914*. New York: Macmillan, 1933. 33-10099. 45

CARLSON, JOHN ROY. *Undercover*. New York: E. P. Dutton, 1943. 43-51232. 97

CARLSON, OLIVER. *Brisbane: A Candid Biography*. New York: Stackpole Sons, 1937. 37-31251. 5

_____. *The Man Who Made News: James Gordon Bennett*. New York: Duell, Sloan and Pearce, 1942. 42-24810. 39

——, and BATES, ERNEST SUTHERLAND. *Hearst, Lord of San Simeon.* New York: Viking, 1936. 36-9254. 5

CARMAN, ALBERT RICHARDSON. *The Ethics of Imperialism: An Enquiry Whether Christian Ethics and Imperialism are Antagonistic.* Boston: H. B. Turner & Co., 1905. 5-17965. 30

CARTER, J. F. *The New Dealers.* New York: Simon and Schuster, 1934. 34-7597. 94

CARTER, PAUL ALLEN. *The Spiritual Crisis of the Gilded Age.* DeKalb: Northern Illinois University Press, 1971. 72-156938. 20

CARVELL, FRED, and TADLOCK, MAX, eds. *It's Not Too Late.* Beverly Hills, Calif.: Glencoe Press, 1971. 73-146944. 110

CARVER, CHARLES. *Brann and the Iconoclast.* Austin: University of Texas Press, 1957. 57-8822. 6

CASE, VICTORIA, and CASE, ROBERT ORMOND. *We Called It Culture.* Garden City, N.Y.: Doubleday, 1948. 48-5380. 40

CHAFEE, ZACHARIAH, JR. *Free Speech in the United States.* Cambridge: Harvard University Press, 1941. A41-4297. 86

CHALMER, DAVID M. *Hooded Americanism: The. . .Ku Klux Klan, 1865-1965.* Garden City, N.Y.: Doubleday, 1965. 64-19266. 55

——, ed. *The Muckrake Years.* New York: Van Nostrand, 1974. 73-14370. 44

——, *The Social and Political Ideas of the Muckrakers.* New York: Citadel Press, 1964. 64-15960. 50

CHAMBERLAIN, JOHN. *Farewell to Reform, Being a History of the Rise, Life and Decay of the Progressive Mind in America,* 2nd ed. New York: The John Day Co., 1933. A40-1986. 24, 26

CHAMBERLAIN, RUDOLPH W. *There Is No Truce.* New York: Macmillan, 1935. 35-3612. 50

CHAMBERS, CLARKE A. *Seedtime of Reform.* Minneapolis: University of Minnesota Press, 1963. 63-23058. 92

CHATFIELD, CHARLES. *For Peace and Justice: Pacifism in America 1914-1941.* Knoxville: University of Tennessee Press, 1971. 70-142143. 85

CHERRINGTON, ERNEST H. *The Evolution of Prohibition in the United States of America.* Westerville, Ohio: American Issue Press, 1920. 20-21319. 58, 87

Chicago Commission on Race Relations. *The Negro in Chicago.* Chicago: University of Chicago Press, 1922. 22-21190. 92

CHILD, LYDIA MARIA. *Letters of Lydia Maria Child, with a Biographical Introduction by John Greenleaf Whittier,* 4th ed. Boston: Houghton, Mifflin, 1884. 21-21177. 13

CHILDS, MARQUIS, and RESTON, JAMES, eds. *Walter Lippmann and His Times.* New York: Harcourt, Brace, 1959. 59-10255. 76

CHILDS, RICHARD S. *Civic Victories.* New York: Harper, 1952. 52-12041. 103

CHRISLOCK, CARL H. *The Progressive Era in Minnesota, 1899-1918.* St. Paul: Minnesota Historical Society, 1971. 79-178677. 71

City Club of Chicago. *Ideals of America.* Chicago: A. C. McClurg & Co., 1919. 19-16553. 86

CLAGHORN, KATE H. *The Immigrant's Day in Court.* New York: Harper, 1923. 23-4538. 92

CLAYTON, BRUCE. *The Savage Ideal*. Baltimore: Johns Hopkins University Press, 1972. 70-184955. 65

CLENDENEN, CLARENCE C. *The United States and Pancho Villa*. Ithaca, N.Y.: Cornell University Press, 1961. 61-18097. 84

CLEVELAND, GROVER, Pres. U.S. *Letters of Grover Cleveland, 1850–1908*; selected and edited by Allan Nevins. Boston: Houghton Mifflin, 1933. 33-35003. 33

COBB, FRANK IRVING. *Frank I. Cobb of "The World," a Leader in Liberalism;* compiled from his editorial articles and public addresses by John L. Heaton. New York: E. P. Dutton & Co., 1924. 24-17976. 40

COCHRAN, NEGLEY DAKIN. *E. W. Scripps*. New York: Harcourt, Brace, 1933. 33-6361. 40

COCHRAN, T. C., and MILLER, WILLIAM. *The Age of Enterprise*. rev. New York: Macmillan, 1942. 42-22792. 67

COHEN, SOL. *Progressives and Urban School Reform*. New York: Teachers College, Columbia University, 1964. 64-18682. 61

COIT, STANTON. *Neighborhood Guilds*. London: S. Sonnenschein & Co., 1891. 6-14627. 56

COLAIANNI, JAMES. *The Catholic Left in the Crisis of Radicalism within the Church*. Philadelphia: Chilton, 1968. 68-29313. 111

COLETTA, PAOLO E. *William Jennings Bryan, Political Evangelist, 1860–1908*. Lincoln: University of Nebraska Press, 1964. 38

_____. *William Jennings Bryan, Progressive Politician and Moral Statesman, 1909–1915*. Lincoln: University of Nebraska Press, 1969. 38

COLLIN, RICHARD H., ed. *Theodore Roosevelt and Reform Politics*. Lexington, Mass.: Heath, 1972. 74-176364. 51

COLQUHOUN, ARCHIBALD ROSS. *Greater America*. New York: Harper & Brothers, 1904. 4-9147. 33

COMMAGER, HENRY STEELE. *The American Mind: An Interpretation of American Thought and Character Since the 1880's*. New Haven: Yale University Press, 1950. 50-6338. 25

Commission of Inquiry, Interchurch World Movement. *Report on the Steel Strike*. New York: Harcourt, Brace, 1920. 20-16529. 86

COMMONS, JOHN R. *Myself*. New York: Macmillan, 1934. 34-38714. 19

_____. *Races and Immigrants*. New York: Macmillan, 1907. 7-17894. 57

CONNOLLY, CHRISTOPHER P. *The Devil Learns to Vote*. New York: Covici, Friede, 1938. 38-8780. 50

_____. *The Truth about the Frank Case*. New York: Vail-Ballou Co., 1915. 40-19437. 89

COOK, ANN, et al., eds. *City Life 1865–1900*. New York: Praeger, 1973. 78-95675. 52

COOK, FRED J. *The Muckrakers*. Garden City, N.Y.: Doubleday, 1972. 71-168287. 110

COOKE, MORRIS L., and MURRAY, PHILIP. *Organized Labor and Production*. New York: Harper & Bros., 1946. 46-7283. 73

COREY, LEWIS. *The Crisis of the Middle Class*. New York: Covici, Friede, 1935. 35-33155. 95

COWING, CEDRIC B. *Populists, Plungers, and Progressives*. Princeton, N.J.: Princeton University Press, 1965. 65-12988. 74

Cox, Isaac J. *Nicaragua and the United States.* Boston: World Peace Foundation, 1927. 28-3858. 83

Cramer, Clarence H. *Newton D. Baker.* Cleveland: World Pub. Co., 1961. 61-5805. 60

Crane, Stephen. *The Red Badge of Courage.* rev. New York: D. Appleton, 1895. 49-36615 42

Crawford, Kenneth G. *The Pressure Boys.* New York: J. Messner, 1939. 39-27853. 96

Creel, George. *Rebel at Large.* New York: G. P. Putnam's Sons, 1947. 47-11611. 84

Creelman, James. *On the Great Highway.* Boston: Lothrop, 1901. 1-27696. 42

Cremin, Lawrence A. *The Transformation of the School: Progressivim in American Education, 1876-1957.* New York: Knopf, 1961. 61-11000. 61

Croly, Herbert. *Marcus Alonzo-Hanna.* New York: Macmillan, 1912. 12-9163. 70

_____. *Progressive Democracy.* New York: Macmillan, 1914. 14-18928. 76

_____. *The Promise of American Life.* New York: Macmillan, 1909. 9-28528. 76

_____. *Willard Straight.* New York: Macmillan, 1924. 24-12001. 76

Crooks, James B. *Politics & Progress: The Rise of Urban Progressivism in Baltimore.* Baton Rouge: Louisiana State University Press, 1968. 68-21805. 52

Crouthamel, James L. *James Watson Webb: A Biography.* Middletown, Conn.: Wesleyan University Press, 1969. 70-82536. 39

Cudlipp, Hugh. *Publish and Be Damned!* London: A. Dakers, 1953. A54-8802. 6

Culligan, Matthew J. *The Curtis-Culligan Story.* New York: Crown, 1970. 72-93406. 111

Curley, James M. *I'd Do It Again.* Englewood Cliffs, N.J.: Prentice-Hall, 1957. 57-8558. 54

Curti, Merle E. *Bryan and World Peace.* Northampton, Mass.: Dept. of History, Smith College, 1931. 32-21510. 85

_____. *The Social Ideas of American Educators.* New York: C. Scribner's Sons, 1935. 35-4578. 24

Dabney, Virginius. *Liberalism in the South.* Chapel Hill: University of North Carolina Press, 1932. 32-30107. 15

Dallek, Robert. *Democrat and Diplomat: The Life of William E. Dodd.* New York: Oxford University Press, 1968. 78

Daniel, Pete. *The Shadow of Slavery: Peonage in the South 1901-1969.* Urbana: University of Illinois Press, 1972. 70-174779. 64

Daniels, George H., ed. *Darwinism Comes to America.* Waltham, Mass.: Blaisdell, 1968. 68-21635. 20

Daniels, Josephus. *Editor in Politics.* Chapel Hill: University of North Carolina Press, 1941. 41-1166. 78

_____. *Tar Heel Editor.* Chapel Hill: University of North Carolina Press, 1939. 39-29441. 78

_____. *The Wilson Era.* Chapel Hill: University of North Carolina Press, 1946. 46-25158. 78

DANIELS, ROGER. *The Politics of Prejudice: The Anti-Japanese Movement in California and the Struggle for Japanese Exclusion.* Berkeley: University of California Press, 1962. 62-63248. 28

DARROW, CLARENCE. *Farmington.* Chicago: A. C. McClurg & Co., 1904. 4-25700. 46

———. *The Story of My Life.* New York: C. Scribner's Sons, 1932. 31-28682. 51

DAVID, HENRY. *History of the Haymarket Affair.* New York: Farrar & Rinehart, 1936. 36-36485. 35

DAVIDSON, ELIZABETH H. *Child Labor Legislation in the Southern Textile States.* Chapel Hill: University of North Carolina Press, 1939. 39-16618. 58

DAVIDSON, JOHN WELLS, ed. *A Crossroads of Freedom: The 1912 Campaign Speeches of Woodrow Wilson.* New Haven: Yale University Press, 1956. 56-11796. 78

DAVIS, ALLEN F. *American Heroine:. . . Jane Addams.* New York: Oxford University Press, 1973. 73-82664. 56

———. *Spearheads for Reform.* New York: Oxford University Press, 1967. 67-25457. 56

DAVIS, ELMER HOLMES. *History of the New York Times, 1851–1921.* New York: New York Times, 1921. 21-26721. 40

DAVIS, HOWARD V. *Frank Parsons: Prophet, Innovator, Counselor.* Carbondale: Southern Illinois University Press, 1969. 69-11514. 71

DAVIS, KENNETH S. *A Prophet in His Own Country.* Garden City, N.Y.: Doubleday, 1957. 57-5784. 103

DAVIS, REBECCA HARDING. "Life in the Iron Mills," *Atlantic Monthly* (1861). 430-451. 42

DAVIS, RICHARD HARDING. *Cuba in War Time.* New York: R. H. Russell, 1897. 3-8729. 42

DEFOREST, JOHN WILLIAM. *Honest John Vane: A Story.* New Haven, Conn.: Richmond & Patten, 1875. 6-3 392. 40

———. *Miss Ravenal's Conversion from Secession to Loyalty.* New York: Harper & Brothers, 1939. 42-43995. 40

———. *Playing the Mischief: A Novel.* New York: Harper & Brothers, 1875. 6-40002. 40

———. *A Volunteer's Adventures: A Union Captain's Record of the Civil War.* New Haven: Yale University Press, 1946. A46-3486. 40

DEGEN, MARIE LOUISE. *The History of the Woman's Peace Party.* Baltimore: Johns Hopkins Press, 1939. 40-5486. 59

DELL, FLOYD. *Upton Sinclair.* New York: George H. Doran Co., 1927. 27-15372. 47

DENNETT, TYLER. *Roosevelt and the Russo-Japanese War.* Garden City, N.Y., Doubleday, Page & Co., 1925. 25-8548. 28

DERBER, MILTON, and YOUNG, EDWIN, eds. *Labor and the New Deal.* Madison: University of Wisconsin, 1957. 57-9813. 96

DEROUNIAN, ARTHUR. See Carlson, John Roy.

DEVINE, E. T. *Misery and Its Causes.* New York: Macmillan, 1909. 9-13279. 56

———. *Progressive Social Action.* New York: Macmillan, 1933. 33-4012. 96

DEWEY, JOHN. *Characters and Events, Popular Essays in Social and Political Philosophy.* New York: H. Holt, 1929. 29-11299. 25

_____. *Democracy and Education: An Introduction to the Philosophy of Education*. New York: Macmillan, 1916. 16-7522. 25

_____. *The Influence of Darwin on Philosophy, and Other Essays in Contemporary Thought*. New York: H. Holt, 1910. 10-10721. 8

_____. *Moral Principles in Education*. Boston: Houghton Mifflin, 1909. 9-18944. 25

_____, and DEWEY, EVELYN. *Schools of Tomorrow*. New York: E. P. Dutton, 1915. 15-12861. 25

DEWITT, BENJAMIN PARK. *The Progressive Movement*. New York: Macmillan, 1915. 15-6479. 71

DIAMOND, SIGMUND. *The Reputation of the American Businessman*. New York: Harper, 1955. 67-82357. 91

DIAMOND, WILLIAM. *The Economic Thought of Woodrow Wilson*. Baltimore: Johns Hopkins Press, 1943. 44-5332. 77

DIES, MARTIN. *The Trojan Horse in America*. New York: Dodd, Mead, 1940. 40-33230. 99

DILLON, MARY E. *Wendell Willkie 1892–1944*. Philadelphia: Lippincott, 1952. 52-5091. 100

DINSMORE, HERMAN H. *All the News that Fits*. New Rochelle, N.Y.: Arlington House, 1969. 69-16945. 40

DOAN, EDWARD N. *The La Follettes and the Wisconsin Idea*. New York: Rinehart, 1947. 47-6998. 62

DOMBROWSKI, JAMES. *The Early Days of Christian Socialism in America*. New York: Columbia University Press, 1936. 37-14017. 19

DONALD, DAVID HERBERT. *Lincoln Reconsidered: Essays on the Civil War Era*. 2nd ed. New York: Knopf, 1961. 56-5785. 9

DONNELLY, IGNATIUS. *Caesar's Column: A Story of the Future by Ignatius Donnelly*. Chicago: Syndicate Publishing Co., 1906. 6-28454. 38

DORFMAN, JOSEPH. *Thorstein Veblen and His America*. New York: Viking, 1934. 34-39873. 19, 25

DORN, JACOB HENRY. *Washington Gladden; Prophet of the Social Gospel*. Columbus: Ohio State University Press, 1968. 67-17173. 20

DORR, RHETA LOUISE CHILDE. *What Eight Million Women Want*. Boston: Small, Maynard & Company, 1910. 10-28964. 12

_____. *A Woman of Fifty*. New York and London: Funk & Wagnalls, 1924. 25-26024. 12, 43

DOS PASSOS, JOHN. *Adventures of a Young Man*. New York: Harcourt, Brace, 1939. 39-27434. 97

_____. *The Big Money*. New York: Harcourt, Brace, 1936. 36-17476. 80

_____. *1919*. New York: Harcourt, Brace, 1932. 32-26235. 80

_____. *The 42nd Parallel*. New York: Harper and Bros., 1930. 30-5538. 80

_____. *U.S.A.* New York: Harcourt, Brace, 1937. 38-27019. 80

DOUGLAS, PAUL H. *The Coming of a New Party*. New York: Whittlesey House, McGraw-Hill Book Co., 1932. 32-20216. 96

——. *Ethics in Government.* Cambridge: Harvard University Press, 1952. 52-9386. 103

DOUGLAS, WILLIAM ORVILLE. *Mr. Lincoln and the Negroes: The Long Road to Equality.* New York: Atheneum, 1963. 63-17851. 14

DOUGLASS, ELISHA P. *The Coming of the Age of American Business.* Edited by Philip S. Foner. Chapel Hill: University of North Carolina Press, 1971. 78-132254. 67

DOUGLASS, FREDERICK. *The Life and Writings of Frederick Douglass.* Ed. by Philip S. Foner. New York: International Publishers, 1950-1955. 4 vols. 50-7654. 14

DREIER, THOMAS. *Heroes of Insurgency.* Boston: Human Life Pub. Co., 1910. 10-27625. 71

DREISER, THEODORE. *The Financier.* New York: Harper & Brothers, 1912. 12-24487. 68

DRESCHER, Seymour, comp. and translated by, *Tocqueville and Beaumont on Social Reform.* New York: Harper & Row, 1968. 68-13576. 23

DU BOIS, W. E. B. *Autobiography.* New York: International Pub., 1968. 68-14103. 65

——. *The Souls of Black Folk.* Chicago: A. C. McClurg, 1903. 3-11173. 65

DUFFUS, ROBERT L. *Lillian Wald, Neighbor and Crusader.* New York: Macmillan, 1938. 38-27777. 56

DUNCAN-CLARK, S. *The Progressive Movement.* Boston: Small, Maynard & Co., 1913. 13-25956. 71

DUNN, JACOB PIATT, JR. *Massacres of the Mountains: A History of the Indian Wars of the Far West 1815-1875.* New York: Harper & Brothers, 1886. 3-55. 16

DUNNE, FINLEY PETER. *The World of Mr. Dooley.* Edited with an introd. by Louis Filler. New York: Collier Books, 1962. 62-15806. 41

DURDEN, ROBERT F. *The Climax of Populism: The Election of 1896.* Lexington: University of Kentucky Press, 1965. 65-11824. 38

DYKEMAN, WILMA. *Prophet of Plenty: The First Ninety Years of W. D. Weatherford.* Knoxville: University of Tennessee Press, 1966. 66-26067. 15

——, and STOKELY, JAMES. *Seeds of Southern Change: The Life of Will Alexander.* Chicago: University of Chicago Press, 1962. 62-13923. 15

EAST, JOHN PORTER. *Council-Manager Government: The Political Thought of Its Founder, Richard Childs.* Chapel Hill: University of North Carolina Press, 1965. 65-19386. 54

EATON, CLEMENT. *Freedom of Thought in the Old South.* Durham, N.C.: Duke University Press, 1940. 40-5232. 15

EDDY, ARTHUR J. *The New Competition.* New York: D. Appleton, 1912. 12-24164. 70

EISENSTADT, SHMUEL NOAH. *Modernization: Protest and Change.* Englewood Cliffs, N.J.: Prentice-Hall, 1966. 66-22805. 4

EISENSTEIN, LORIN, and ROSENBERG, ELLIOTT. *A Stripe of Tammany's Tiger.* New York: R. Speller, 1966. 66-29504. 53

EKIRCH, ARTHUR A., JR. *The Decline of American Liberalism.* New York: Longmans, Green, 1955. 55-11447. 3, 90

——. *Progressivism in America: A Study of the Era from Theodore Roosevelt to Woodrow Wilson.* New York: New Viewpoints, 1974. 72-2455. 3

ELLETSON, D. H. *Roosevelt and Wilson: A Comparative Study.* London: J. Murray, 1965. 65-6281. 78

ELLIS, ELMER. *Mr. Dooley's America: A Life of Finley Peter Dunne.* New York: Knopf, 1941. 41-21089. 41

ELLIS, JOHN TRACY. *American Catholicism.* Chicago: University of Chicago Press, 1956. 56-11002. 93

EPPSE, MERL R. *The Negro, Too, in American History.* Chicago: National Education Pub. Co., rev. 1938. 38-29984. 63

ERSHKOWITZ, HERBERT. *The Attitudes of Business toward American Foreign Policy 1900–1916.* University Park: Pennsylvania State University, 1967. 67-65348. 31

ESTHUS, RAYMOND A. *Theodore Roosevelt and Japan.* Seattle: University of Washington Press, 1966. 66-19567. 28

———. *Theodore Roosevelt and the International Rivalries.* Waltham, Mass.: Ginn-Blaisdell, 1970. 71-102172. 28

EVANS, I. O., ed. *An Upton Sinclair Anthology.* New York: Farrar & Rinehart, 1934. 34-20052. 47

FARRELL, JOHN C. *Beloved Lady: A History of Jane Addams' Ideas on Reform and Peace.* Baltimore: Johns Hopkins Press, 1967. 67-16916. 54

FAULKNER, HAROLD U. *The Decline of Laissez-Faire, 1897–1917.* New York: Rinehart, 1951. 51-5244.25, 91

———. *Politics, Reform, and Expansion, 1890–1900.* New York: Harper, 1959. 56-6022. 26

———. *The Quest for Social Justice, 1898–1914.* New York: Macmillan, 1931. 31-5574. 26

FEIS, HERBERT. *1933: Characters in the Crisis.* Boston: Little, Brown, 1966. 66-10982. 94

FELLMAN, GORDON, and BRANDT, BARBARA. *The Deceived Majority.* New Brunswick, N.J.: Transaction Books, 1973. 72-82197. 115

Fellowship of Reconciliation (United States). *Moral and Technical Implications of Peace on Earth.* New York: Fellowship of Reconciliation, 1965. 10

FELT, JEREMY F. *Hostages of Fortune: Child Labor Reform in New York State.* Syracuse, N.Y.: Syracuse University Press, 1965. 65-11676. 58

FILENE, E. A. *Speaking of Change.* New York: Priv. Pub., 1939. 39-3576. 60

FILLER, LOUIS. *Appointment at Armageddon: Muckraking and Progressivism in the American Tradition.* Westport, Conn.: Greenwood Press, 1976. 23

———, ed. *The Anxious Years.* New York: Putnam, 1963. 62-18266. 96, 98

———. *Crusaders for American Liberalism,* rev. ed. University Park, Pa.: Penn State Press, 1975. 5, 23, 44

———. *A Dictionary of American Social Reform,* new ed. New York: Greenwood Press, 1969. 74-90505. 23, 62

———. "John Chamberlain and American Liberalism." *Colorado Quarterly* 6 (1957/58), 200–211. 24

———. "Negro Materials of the 1960's," *Choice* 5 (1968), 161-170. 109

———. *Randolph Bourne.* New York: Citadel Press, 1966. 67-89260. 79

_____. "The Reputation of David Graham Phillips," *Antioch Review*, 11 (1951), 475-488. 48

_____. *The Unknown Edwin Markham.* Yellow Springs, O.: Antioch Press, 1966. 66-25696. 44

FINE, NATHAN. *Labor and Farmer Parties in the United States 1828-1928.* New York: Rand School of Social Science, 1928. 28-24182. 34, 69

FINE, SIDNEY. *Laissez-Faire and the General Welfare State*, rev. ed. Ann Arbor: University of Michigan Press, 1956. 56-62500. 94

FINLEY, RUTH EBRIGHT. *The Lady of Godey's, Sarah Josepha Hale.* Philadelphia: J. B. Lippincott, 1931. 31-28307. 12

FISKE, JOHN A. *Century of Science, and Other Essays.* Boston: Houghton Mifflin, 1899. 0-48. 8

_____. *Excursions of an Evolutionist.* Boston: Houghton Mifflin, 1884. 8-6759. 8

FITE, GILBERT C. *George N. Peek and the Fight for Farm Parity.* Norman: University of Oklahoma Press, 1954. 54-5934. 89

FITZPATRICK, E. A. *McCarthy of Wisconsin.* New York: Columbia University Press, 1944. A44-1122. 62

FLEISCHMAN, HARRY. *Norman Thomas, a Biography.* New York: Norton, 1964. 62-12282. 85

FLEXNER, ELEANOR. *Century of Struggle: The Woman's Rights Movement in the United States.* Cambridge: Harvard University Press, 1959. 59-9273. 12, 59

FLOAN, HOWARD RUSSELL. *The South in Northern Eyes, 1831-1861.* Austin: University of Texas Press, 1958. 57-8824. 15

FLOWER, B. O. *Progressive Men, Women and Movements of the Past Twenty-five Years.* Boston: New Arena, 1914. 15-1489. 43

FLYNN, EDWARD. *You're the Boss.* New York: Viking, 1947. 47-30772. 53

FLYNT, JOSIAH. *My Life.* New York: Outing Pub. Co., 1908. 8-30135. 43

FOLSOM, JOSEPH KIRK. *Culture and Social Progress.* New York: Longmans, Green, 1928. 28-9538. 4

FONER, PHILIP S., ed. *The Bolshevik Revolution, Its Impact on American Radicals, Liberals and Labor.* New York: International Publishers, 1967. 67-26742. 97

_____, ed. *Helen Keller: Her Socialist Years.* New York: International Pubs., 1967. 67-13214. 69

_____. *History of the Labor Movement in the United States.* New York: International Pubs., 1947-55, 1962-64. 66-59541. 92

_____. *The Spanish-Cuban-American War and the Birth of American Imperialism, 1895-1902.* New York: Monthly Review Press, 1972. 79-187595. 31

FORTUNE, T. Thomas. *Black and White: Land Labor and Politics in the South.* New York: Fords, Howard, & Hulbert, 1884. 12-2876. 65

FOSSUM, PAUL ROBERT. *The Agrarian Movement in North Dakota.* Baltimore: Johns Hopkins Press, 1925. 25-8941. 38

FOULKE, WILLIAM DUDLEY. *Fighting the Spoilsmen: Reminiscences of the Civil Service Reform Movement.* New York: G. P. Putnam's, 1919. 19-4045. 17

FOWLER, GENE. *The Great Mouthpiece: A Life Story of William J. Fallon*. New York: Covici, Friede, 1932. 32-9397. 89

FOX, STEPHEN R. *The Guardian of Boston*. New York: Atheneum, 1970. 78-108822. 65

FRANKFURTER, FELIX, and GREENE, N. V. *The Labor Injunction*. New York: Macmillan, 1930. 30-2892. 69

FREIDEL, FRANK. *Franklin D. Roosevelt: The Apprenticeship*. Boston: Little, Brown, 1952. 52-5521. 94

——. *The Splendid Little War*. Boston: Little, Brown, 1958. 58-10069. 34

FRIEDMAN, JACOB A. *The Impeachment of Governor William Sulzer*. New York: Columbia University Press, 1939. 39-12451. 53

FRIEDMAN, LEON. *The Wise Minority*. New York: Dial Press, 1971. 77-92733. 109

FRIEDRICH, CARL J. *The Pathology of Politics*. New York: Harper & Row, 1972. 79-138723. 116

FULLER, MARGARET, *see* Ossoli, Margaret Fuller.

GANLEY, ALBERT C. *The Progressive Movement: Traditional Reform*. New York: Macmillan, 1964. 64-3425. 26

GARDNER, GILSON. *Lusty Scripps: The Life of E. W. Scripps*. New York: Vanguard Press, 1932. 32-5611. 40

GARLAND, HAMLIN. *Main-Traveled Roads*. Boston: Arena, 1891. 17-26999. 37

——. *A Son of the Middle Border*. New York: Macmillan, 1917. 17-22272. 37

GARRATY, JOHN A. *Henry Cabot Lodge*. New York: Knopf, 1953. 53-6852. 88

——. *Right-Hand Man*. New York: Harper, 1960. 60-10404. 76

GASTON, HERBERT E. *The Nonpartisan League*, rev. ed. New York: Harcourt, Brace and Howe, 1920. 20-6358. 92

GAVREAU, EMILE. *My Last Million Readers*. New York: E. P. Dutton, 1941. 41-17181. 6

GEIGER, LOUIS G. *Joseph W. Folk of Missouri*. Columbia: University of Missouri, 1953. 53-7464. 51

GEORGE, ALEXANDER L., and GEORGE, JULIETTE L. *Woodrow Wilson and Colonel House*. New York: John Day, 1956. 56-13372. 78

GEORGE, HENRY, JR. *The Life of Henry George*. New York: Doubleday & McClure, 1900. 0-6530. 19

GERT, BERNARD. *The Moral Rules: A New Rational Foundation for Morality*. New York: Harper & Row, 1970. 74-105227. 11

GETTLEMAN, MARVIN E. *The Dorr Rebellion: A Study in American Radicalism, 1833–1849*. New York: Random House, 1973. 72-14312. 3

GHENT, WILLIAM J. *Mass and Class*. New York: Macmillan, 1904. 4-29347. 59

——. *Our Benevolent Feudalism*. New York: Macmillan, 1902. 2-26876. 59

GIBBONS, HERBERT ADAMS. *John Wanamaker*. New York: Harper & Bros., 1926. 26-18311. 70

GIDDINGS, FRANKLIN HENRY. *Democracy and Empire: With Studies of Their Psychological, Economic, and Moral Foundations*. New York: Macmillan, 1900. 0-1270. 33

GILDER, RICHARD WATSON. *Letters of Richard Watson Gilder*. ed. by Rosamond Gilder. Boston: Houghton Mifflin, 1916. 16-22427. 17

GINGER, RAY. *Age of Excess: The United States from 1877 to 1914*. New York: Macmillan, 1965. 65-12151. 24

———. *Altgeld's America*. New York: Funk & Wagnalls, 1958. 58-11362. 34

———. *The Bending Cross*. New Brunswick, N.J.: Rutgers University Press, 1949. 49-9524. 68

GINZBERG, ELI, and BERMAN, HYMAN. *The American Worker in the Twentieth Century*. New York: Free Press of Glencoe, 1963. 63-10649. 69

GIRVETZ, HARRY K. *From Wealth to Welfare: The Evolution of Liberalism*. Stanford: Stanford University Press, 1950. 51-165. 94

GITLOW, BENJAMIN. *I Confess*. New York: E. P. Dutton, 1940. 40-27077. 97

GLAAB, CHARLES, ed. *The American City: A Documentary History*. Homewood, Ill.: Dorsey Press, 1963. 63-19883. 35

———, and BROWN, A. THEODORE. *A History of Urban America*. New York: Macmillan, 1967. 67-15198. 35

GLAD, PAUL W. *McKinley, Bryan, and the People*. Philadelphia: Lippincott, 1964. 64-11853. 35

GLADDEN, WASHINGTON. *Recollections*. Boston: Houghton Mifflin, 1909. 9-28138. 20

———. *Tools and the Man: Property and Industry under the Christian Law*. Boston: Houghton, Mifflin, 1896. 4-3805. 20

GLASS, CARTER. *An Adventure in Constructive Finance*. Garden City, N.Y.: Doubleday, Page & Co., 1927. 74

GLASS, HIRAM BENTLEY, et al., eds. *Forerunners of Darwin, 1745-1859*. Baltimore: Johns Hopkins Press, 1959. 59-9978. 7

GOLD, GERALD, et al., ed. *The Watergate Hearings*. New York: Viking, 1973. 73-14191. 114

GOLDEN, HARRY. *A Little Girl Is Dead*. Cleveland: World Pub. Co., 1965. 65-25775. 89

GOLDMAN, ERIC FREDERICK. *Rendezvous with Destiny: A History of Modern American Reform*. New York: Knopf, 1952. 52-6418. 24

GOLDMARK, JOSEPHINE C. *Impatient Crusader*. Urbana: University of Illinois Press, 1953. 52-12408. 55

GOMPERS, SAMUEL. *Labor and the Common Welfare*. New York: E. P. Dutton, 1919. 20-224. 85

———. *Seventy Years of Life and Labor*. 2 vols. New York: E. P. Dutton, 1925. 25-5990. 70

GOODMAN, WALTER. *A Percentage of the Take*. New York: Farrar, Straus and Giroux, 1971. 72-137751. 116

GOODYKOONTZ, COLIN B., ed. *The Papers of Edward P. Costigan. . .1902-1917*. Boulder: University of Colorado, rev. 1941. 42-36621. 72

GORMAN, JOSEPH B. *Kefauver*. New York: Oxford University Press, 1971. 77-159645. 104

GOSNELL, HAROLD F. *Boss Platt and His New York Machine*. Chicago: University of Chicago Press, 1924. 24-2633. 51

_____. *Machine Politics: Chicago Model.* Chicago: University of Chicago Press, 1937. 37-20974. 54

GOTTESMAN, RONALD. *Upton Sinclair: An Annotated Checklist.* Kent, Ohio: Kent State University Press, 1973. 72-634010. 46

GOULD, LEWIS L. *Progressives and Prohibitionists: Texas Democrats in the Wilson Era.* Austin: University of Texas Press, 1973. 72-10861. 88

GRADY, HENRY W. *The New South.* New York: R. Bonner Sons, rev. 1890. A14-1410. 64

GRAFF, HENRY FRANKLIN, ed. *American Imperialism and the Philippine Insurrection: Testimony Taken from Hearings on Affairs in the Philippine Islands before the Senate Committee on the Philippines, 1902.* Boston: Little, Brown, 1969. 69-11430. 31

GRAHAM, GEORGE A. *Morality in American Life.* New York: Random House, 1952. 52-7142. 103

GRAHAM, OTIS L., JR. *An Encore for Reform.* New York: Oxford University Press, 1967. 67-15126. 93

GRANTHAM, DEWEY W. *Hoke Smith and the Politics of the New South.* Baton Rouge: Louisiana State University Press, 1958. 58-9209. 51

GRAYSON, CARY T. *Woodrow Wilson: An Intimate Memoir.* New York: Holt, Rinehart and Winston, 1960. 60-10998. 78

GREELEY, ANDREW M. *That Most Distressful Nation: The Taming of the American Irish.* Chicago: Quadrangle Books, 1972. 74-182501. 14

GREEN, MARGUARITE. *The National Civic Federation and the American Labor Movement 1900–1925.* Washington: Catholic University of America Press, 1956. 56-4315. 70

GREEN, MARK J., ed. *The Monopoly Makers.* New York: Grossman, 1973. 72-77614. 113

GREENBAUM, FRED. *Fighting Progressive: A Biography of Edward P. Costigan.* Washington: Public Affairs Press, 1971. 70-168553. 61

GREENE, THEODORE P. *America's Heroes.* New York: Oxford University Press, 1970. 70-117214. 42

GREENWOOD, GRACE. *Eminent Women of the Age; Being Narratives of the Lives and Deeds of the Most Prominent Women of the Age.* Hartford, Conn.: S. M. Betts, 1868. 18-23471. 11

GREER, THOMAS H. *American Social Reform Movements: Their Pattern since 1865.* New York: Prentice-Hall, 1949. 49-1202. 23

GRIMES, ALAN PENDLETON. *The Political Liberalism of the New York Nation.* Chapel Hill: University of North Carolina Press, 1953. 53-62070. 43

GRISWOLD, A. WHITNEY. *Farming and Democracy.* New York: Harcourt, Brace, 1948. 48-6511. 34

GROSS, THEODORE L., ed. *A Nation of Nations: Ethnic Literature in America.* New York: Free Press, 1971. 79-142365. 16

GRUNDER, GAREL A., and LIVEZEY, WILLIAM E. *The Philippines and the United States.* Norman: University of Oklahoma Press, 1951. 51-6997. 31

GUILFOYLE, JAMES H. *On the Trail of the Forgotten Man.* Boston: Peabody Master Printers, 1933. 33-22170. 54

GURKO, LEO. *The Angry Decade.* New York: Dodd, Mead, 1947. 47-11236. 97

HABER, SAMUEL. *Efficiency and Uplift*. Chicago: University of Chicago Press, 1964. 64-15828. 72

HACKNEY, SHELDON. *Populism to Progressivism in Alabama*. Princeton, N.J.: Princeton University Press, 1969. 68-56311. 65

HAGEDORN, HERMANN. *The Roosevelt Family of Sagamore Hill*. New York: Macmillan, 1954. 54-11834. 27

HALE, NATHAN G., JR. *Freud and the Americans*. New York: Oxford University Press, 1971. 74-151184. 59

HALE, SARAH JOSEPHA. *Woman's Record; or, Sketches of All Distinguished Women, from the Creation to A. D. 1868*. 3rd ed., New York: Harper & Brothers, 1873. 19-16342. 12

HALLOWELL, ANNA DAVIS, ed. *James and Lucretia Mott, Life and Letters*. Boston: Houghton, Mifflin, 1884. 12-32973. 13

HALSTEAD, MURAT. *Aquinaldo and His Captor: The Life Mysteries of Emilio Aquinaldo and Adventures and Achievements of General Funston. Historical Stories of Two Memorable Men*. Cincinnati: Halstead, 1901. 1-10174. 33

_____. *Pictoral History of America's New Possessions, the Isthmian Canals, and the Problems of Expansion*. Chicago: The Dominion Co., 1898. 99-3933. 31

HAMILTON, ALICE. *Exploring the Dangerous Trades*. Boston: Little, Brown, 1943. 43-51090. 56

HAMMOND, BRAY. *Banks and Politics in America, from the Revolution to the Civil War*. Princeton, N.J.: Princeton University Press, 1957. 57-8667. 9

HANAFORD, PHEBE ANN. *Daughters of America; or Women of the Century*. Augusta, Me.: True and Co., 1883. 15-25674. 11

HANDLIN, OSCAR. *Al Smith and His America*. Boston: Little, Brown, 1958. 57-6446. 53

_____, ed. *Immigration as a Factor in American History*. Englewood Cliffs, N.J.: Prentice-Hall, 1959. 59-9516. 57

HANSEN, MARCUS LEE. *The Immigrant in American History*. Cambridge: Harvard University Press, 1940. 40-35768. 56

HAPGOOD, HUTCHINS. *The Autobiography of a Thief*. New York: Fox, Duffield & Co., 1903. 3-13389. 79

_____. *The Spirit of Labor*. New York: Duffield & Co., 1907. 7-8549. 69, 79

_____. *A Victorian in the Modern World*. New York: Harcourt, Brace, 1939. 39-25183. 43, 79

HAPGOOD, NORMAN. *The Changing Years: Reminiscences of Norman Hapgood*. New York: Farrar & Rinehart, 1930. 30-30906. 4, 43

_____. *Industry and Progress*. New Haven: Yale University Press, 1911. 11-6498. 4

_____, ed. *Professional Patriots*. New York: A. & C. Boni, 1927. 27-12081. 86

HAPGOOD, WILLIAM POWERS. *The Columbia Conserve Company*. new ed. Philadelphia: Porcupine Press, 1974. 4

HARBAUGH, WILLIAM HENRY. *Power and Responsibility: The Life and Times of Theodore Roosevelt*. New York: Farrar, Straus and Cudahy, 1961. 61-10128. 27

HARRIS, FRANK. *England or Germany?* New York: Wilmarth Press, 1915. 15-13322. 85

HARRIS, FRED. *The New Populism*. New York: Saturday Review Press, 1973. 72-88653. 117

HARRIS, LOUIS. *The Anguish of Change*. New York: Norton, 1973. 73-11473. 111

HARRIS, SEYMOUR E. *Twenty Years of Federal Reserve Policy*. Cambridge: Harvard University Press, 1933. 33-13062. 74

HARRISON, CARTER, JR. *Stormy Years*. Indianapolis: Bobbs-Merrill, 1935. 35-21225. 51

HARRISON, JOHN M., and STEIN, HARRY, eds. *Muckraking, Past, Present, and Future*. University Park: Pennsylvania State University Press, 1973. 73-11204. 44

HART, ROBERT A. *The Great White Fleet: Its Voyage Around the World, 1907-1909*. Boston: Little Brown, 1965. 65-20742. 28

HARTMANN, EDWARD G. *The Movement to Americanize the Immigrant*. New York: Columbia University Press, 1948. 48-9245. 56, 84

HAWORTH, PAUL LELAND. *America in Ferment*. Indianapolis: Bobbs-Merrill, 1915. 15-3779. 25

HAYNES, FRED E. *James Baird Weaver*. Iowa City, Ia.: State Historical Society of Iowa, 1919. 19-27188. 37

———. *Third Party Movements since the Civil War*. Iowa City, Ia.: State Historical Society of Iowa, 1916. 16-6948. 37

HAYNES, JOHN. *Popular Elections of United States Senators*. Baltimore: Johns Hopkins University Studies, 1893. 6-34039. 73

HAYS, ARTHUR GARFIELD. *City Lawyer*. New York: Simon and Schuster, 1942. 42-17237. 89

HAYS, SAMUEL P. *Conservation and the Gospel of Efficiency*. Cambridge: Harvard University Press, 1959. 59-9274. 72

———. *Response to Industrialism, 1885-1914*. Chicago: University of Chicago, 1957. 57-6981. 67

HEALY, DAVID F. *United States Expansionism: The Imperialist Urge in the 1890's*. Madison: University of Wisconsin Press, 1970. 71-121769. 31, 83

———. *The United States in Cuba, 1898-1902: Generals, Politicians, and the Search for Policy*. Madison: University of Wisconsin Press, 1963. 63-13742. 34

HEARD, GERALD. *Pain, Sex and Time: A New Outlook on Evolution and the Future of Man*. New York: Harper & Brothers, 1939. 39-23842. 8

HEARST, WILLIAM RANDOLPH. *Selections from the Writings and Speeches of William Randolph Hearst*. San Francisco: Pub. priv., 1948. 49-1505. 5

HECHLER, KENNETH. *Insurgency, Personalities and Politics of the Taft Era*. New York: Columbia University Press, rev. 1940. 40-33640. 71

HECHT, BEN, and MACARTHUR, CHARLES. *The Front Page*. New York: Covici-Friede, 1928. 28-22077. 6

HECKSCHER, AUGUST, ed. *The Politics of Woodrow Wilson*. New York: Harper & Bros., 1956. 56-1842. 78

HELMES, WINIFRED G. *John A. Johnson, the People's Governor*. Minneapolis: University of Minnesota Press, 1949. 49-47259. 61

HENDRICK, BURTON J. *The Age of Big Business.* New York: Yale University Press, 1921. A23-830. 67

———. *The Training of an American: The Earlier Life and Letters of Walter H. Page 1855-1913.* Boston: Houghton Mifflin, 1928. 28-11821. 66

HERRESHOFF, DAVID. *American Disciples of Marx.* Detroit: Wayne State University Press, 1967. 67-11584. 59

HERSH, SEYMOUR. *Cover Up.* New York: Random House, 1972. 77-119900. 114

HESSELTINE, WILLIAM B. *The Rise and Fall of Third Parties.* Washington: Public Affairs Press, 1948. 48-6147. 101

HICKS, GRANVILLE. "David Graham Phillips: Journalist," *Bookman* 73 (1931), 257-266. 48

———. *John Reed.* New York: Macmillan, 1936. 36-9661. 79

HICKS, JOHN D. *The Populist Revolt.* Minneapolis: University of Minnesota Press, 1931. 31-30954. 37

HIGHAM, JOHN. *Strangers in the Land.* New Brunswick, N.J.: Rutgers University Press, 1955. 55-8601. 55

HILL, JAMES J. *Highways of Progress.* New York: Doubleday, Page & Co., 1910. 10-14659. 67

HILLQUIT, MORRIS. *History of Socialism in the United States.* New York: Funk & Wagnalls, 1903. 3-25752. 59

HIRST, DAVID W., ed. *Woodrow Wilson: Reform Governor.* Princeton, N.J.: Van Nostrand, 1965. 65-4440. 77

HIXSON, WILLIAM B. *Moorfield Storey and the Abolitionist Tradition.* New York: Oxford University Press, 1972. 78-179359. 30

HOAR, GEORGE FRISBIE. *Autobiography of Seventy Years.* New York: C. Scribner's Sons, 1903. 3-29308. 33

HOBSON, JOHN ATKINSON. *Imperialism: A Study.* New York: J. Pott, 1902. 2-27510. 32

HOFFMAN, CHARLES. *The Depression of the Nineties: An Economic History.* Westport, Conn.: Greenwood, 1970. 78-90790. 38

HOFSTADTER, RICHARD. *The Age of Reform: From Bryan to F. D. R.* New York: Knopf, 1955. 54-7206. 24, 38

———. *The Progressive Historians; Turner, Beard, Parrington.* New York: Knopf, 1968. 68-23944. 25

———. *Social Darwinism in American Thought 1860-1915.* rev. ed., New York: G. Braziller, 1959. 59-9543. 7

HOLDEN, ARTHUR C. *The Settlement Idea.* New York: Macmillan, 1922. 22-939. 55

HOLLI, MELVIN. *Reform in Detroit.* New York: Oxford University Press, 1969. 69-17762. 52

HOLT, HAMILTON, ed. *The Life Stories of Undistinguished Americans as Told by Themselves.* New York: J. Potts, rev. 1906. W6-170. 57

HOLT, JAMES. *Congressional Insurgents and the Party System.* Cambridge: Harvard University Press, 1967. 67-22866. 71

HOOGENBOOM, ARI. *Outlawing the Spoils: A History of the Civil Service Reform Movement, 1865-1883*. Urbana: University of Illinois Press, 1961. 61-6537. 17

———. and HOOGENBOOM, OLIVE, eds., *The Gilded Age*. Englewood Cliffs, N. J.: Prentice-Hall, 1967. 67-28392. 17

HOPKINS, CHARLES HOWARD. *The Rise of the Social Gospel in American Protestantism, 1865-1915*. New Haven: Yale University Press, 1940. 41-1101. 19

HOPPER, JAMES. *"9009."* New York: McClure, 1908. 8-27364. 45

HOUSE, EDWARD M. *Philip Dru: Administrator*. New York: B. W. Huebsch, 1912. 13-1612. 77

HOWE, E. W. *The Story of a Country Town*. Atchison, Kansas: Howe & Company, rev. 1883. 45-45006. 37

HOWE, FREDERIC C. *The City, The Hope of Democracy*. New York: Da Capo Press, 1905. 62

———. *Confessions of a Reformer*. New York: Scribner's, 1925. 25-23619. 61

———. *The Modern City and Its Problems*. New York: Scribner's, 1915. 15-2085. 36

———. *Wisconsin: An Experiment in Democracy*. New York: Scribner's, 1912. 12-10638. 62

HOWE, JULIA WARD. *Margaret Fuller (Marchesa Ossoli)*. Boston: Roberts, 1883. 12-34274. 12

HOWLAND, HAROLD. *Theodore Roosevelt and His Times*. New Haven: Yale University Press, 1921. 21-14811. 51

HUBBART, H. C. *The Older Middle West, 1840-1880*. New York: D. Appleton-Century, 1936. 36-11022. 36

HUBER, RICHARD M. *The American Idea of Success*. New York: McGraw-Hill, 1971. 76-167555. 73

HUBERMAN, LEO. *The Labor Spy Racket*. New York: Modern Age Books, 1937. 37-28669. 97

HUNTER, ROBERT. *Poverty*. New York: Macmillan, 1904. 4-32745. 56, 59

———. *Violence and the Labor Movement*. New York: Macmillan, 1914. 14-4908. 69

HURLEY, F. JACK. *Portrait of a Decade: Roy Stryker and the Development of Documentary Photography in the Thirties*. Baton Rouge: Louisiana State Univ. Press, 1972. 99

HUTCHINSON, WILLIAM T. *Cyrus Hall McCormick*. New York: Century, 1930-1935. 30-30678. 67

HUTCHISON, WILLIAM, R., ed. *American Protestant Thought: The Liberal Era*. New York: Harper & Row, 1968. 68-27286. 34

HUTHMACHER, J. JOSEPH. *A Nation of Newcomers*. New York: Dell, 1967. 68-1100. 57

———. *Senator Robert F. Wagner and the Rise of Urban Liberalism*. New York: Atheneum, 1968. 68-16869. 52

———, and SUSMAN, WARREN I., eds. *Herbert Hoover and the Crisis of American Capitalism*. Cambridge: Schenkman, 1974. 72-92264. 91

HUXLEY, THOMAS HENRY. *Evolution and Ethics, and other Essays*. New York: D. Appleton, 1896. 32-24604. 7

ICKES, HAROLD L. *The Autobiography of a Curmudgeon*. New York: Reynal & Hitchcock, 1943. 43-51100. 95

IRWIN, WILL. *The Making of a Reporter.* New York: G. P. Putnam's Sons, 1942. 42-25254. 44

_____. *Propaganda and the News.* New York: McGraw-Hill, 1936. 36-2389. 44

ISAAC, PAUL E. *Prohibition and Politics: Turbulent Decades in Tennessee 1885–1920.* Knoxville: University of Tennessee Press, 1965. 65-17347. 57

ISRAEL, JERRY. *Progressivism and the Open Door: America and China, 1905–1921.* Pittsburgh: University of Pittsburgh Press, 1971. 73-123095. 31

JACK, ROBERT J. *History of the National Association for the Advancement of Colored People.* Boston: Meador Pub. Co., 1943. 43-3386. 66

JACKSON, HELEN HUNT. *A Century of Dishonor: A Sketch of the United States Government's Dealings with Some of the Indian Tribes.* New York: Harper & Brothers, 1881. 2-15271. 15

_____. *Ramona; A Story.* Boston: Roberts Brothers, 1884. 1-1275. 15

JACKSON, KENNETH T. *The Ku Klux Klan in the City 1915–1930.* New York: Oxford Univ. Press, 1967. 55

JAMES, BERNARD J. *The Death of Progress.* New York: Knopf, 1973. 76-171154. 4, 115

JAMES, BESSIE R. *Anne Rogall's U.S.A.* New Brunswick, N.J.: Rutgers University Press, 1972. 72-1796. 39

_____, and WATERSTREET, MAY, comps. *Adlai's Almanac: The Wit and Wisdom of Stevenson.* New York: H. Schuman, 1952. 52-13990. 103

JAMES, EDWARD T., *et al.,* ed. *Notable American Women, 1607–1950; A Biographical Dictionary.* 3 vols. Cambridge, Mass.: Belknap Press. 1971. 76-152274. 11

JAMES, MARLISE. *The People's Lawyers.* New York: Holt, Rinehart and Winston, 1973. 74-182761. 111

JAMES, WILLIAM. *Essays on Faith and Morals.* New York: Longmans, Green, 1943. A44-680. 33

_____. *The Will to Believe and Other Essays in Popular Philosophy.* rev. ed. New York: Longmans, Green, 1937. 38-30375. 24

JAMESON, JOHN FRANKLIN. *The American Revolution Considered as a Social Movement.* Princeton: Princeton University Press, 1926. 26-10868. 3

JOHANNSEN, ROBERT WALTER. *Stephen A. Douglas.* New York: Oxford University Press, 1973. 72-92293. 8

JOHNPOLL, BERNARD K. *Pacifist's Progress: Norman Thomas and the Decline of American Socialism.* Chicago: Quadrangle Books, 1970. 70-116078. 94

JOHNSON, CLAUDIUS O. *Borah of Idaho.* New York: Longmans, Green, 1936. 36-8450. 61

JOHNSON, DONALD. *The Challenge to American Freedoms.* Lexington: University of Kentucky, 1963. 64-52222. 86

JOHNSON, DONALD B. *The Republican Party and Wendell Willkie.* Urbana: University of Illinois, 1960. 60-4021. 100

JOHNSON, OLIVER A. *Moral Knowledge.* The Hague: Martinus Nijhoff, 1966. 11

JOHNSON, ROGER T. *Robert M. La Follette, Jr., and the Decline of the Progressive Party in Wisconsin.* Hamden, Conn.: Archon Books, 1970. 70-113017. 62

JOHNSON, TOM L. *My Story.* New York: B. W. Huebsch, 1911. 11-35975. 36

JOHNSON, WALTER, ed. *Selected Letters of William Allen White 1899-1943.* New York: H. Holt, 1947. 44

_____. *William Allen White's America.* New York: H. Holt, 1947. 47-4962. 44

JOHNSTON, JOHANNA. *Mrs. Satan: The Incredible Saga of Victoria C. Woodhull.* New York: Putnam, 1967. 67-15111. 18

JONAS, MANFRED. *Isolationism in America, 1935-1941.* Ithaca, N.Y.: Cornell University Press, 1966. 66-16289. 31

JORDAN, DAVID STARR. *Footnotes to Evolution: A Series of Popular Addresses on the Evolution of Life with Supplementary Essays by Edwin Grant Conklin, Frank Mace McFarland, James Perrin Smith.* New York: D. Appleton, 1898. 98-1569. 7

_____. *Imperial Democracy: A Study of the Relation of Government by the People, Equality Before the Law, and Other Tenets of Democracy, to the Demands of a Vigorous Foreign Policy and Other Demands of Imperial Dominion.* New York: D. Appleton, 1899. 99-2549. 29

JOSEPHSON, MATTHEW. *The President Makers; The Culture of Politics and Leadership in an Age of Enlightenment, 1896-1919.* New York: Harcourt, Brace, 1940. 40-33441. 27

KAKAR, SUDHIR. *Frederick Taylor: A Study in Personality and Innovation.* Cambridge: MIT Press, 1970. 79-122260. 73

KAPLAN, JUSTIN. *Lincoln Steffens.* New York: Simon and Schuster, 1974. 73-15486. 44

KARIEL, HENRY. *The Decline of American Pluralism.* Stanford: Stanford University Press, 1961. 61-5505. 117

KARP, WALTER. *Indispensable Enemies: The Politics of Misrule in America.* New York: Saturday Review Press, 1973. 70-154261. 115

KARSNER, DAVID. *Talks with Debs in Terre Haute.* New York: New York Call, 1922. 23-1304. 68

KATCHER, LEO. *The Big Bankroll.* New York: Harper, 1959. 58-12452. 89

KATZMAN, DAVID M. *Before the Ghetto.* Urbana: University of Illinois Press, 1973. 72-76861. 109

KAZIN, ALFRED, and SHAPIRO, CHARLES, eds. *The Stature of Theodore Dreiser.* Bloomington: Indiana University Press, 1955. 55-8446. 48

KEEFER, TRUMAN FREDERICK. *Ernest Poole.* New York: Twayne, 1966. 66-24148. 45

KEFAUVER, ESTES. *Crime in America.* Garden City, N.Y.: Doubleday, 1951. 51-11582. 104

_____. *In a Few Hands: Monopoly Power in America.* New York: Pantheon, 1965. 64-18344. 104

_____. *A Twentieth-Century Congress.* New York: Duell, Sloan and Pearce, 1947. 47-3751. 104

KELLER, MORTON, ed. *Theodore Roosevelt: A Profile.* New York: Hill & Wang, 1967. 67-26854. 51

KELLOGG, CHARLES FLINT. *NAACP.* Baltimore: Johns Hopkins Press, 1967. 66-28507. 66

KENNEDY, DAVID M. *Birth Control in America.* New Haven: Yale University Press, 1970. 79-99827. 59

KENNEDY, JOHN F. *A Nation of Immigrants.* New York: Harper and Row, 1964. 64-7830. 104

KENT, FRANK R. *The Democratic Party.* New York: Century, 1928. 28-8482. 93

KEY, V. O., JR. *Southern Politics.* New York: Knopf, 1949. 49-10825. 66

_____. *Techniques of Political Graft in the United States.* Chicago: Private ed., 1936. 37-14018. 115

KING, JUDSON. *The Conservation Fight.* Washington: Public Affairs Press, 1959. 59-10226. 72

KINTON, JACK F. *American Ethnic Groups and the Revival of Cultural Pluralism: A Sourcebook for the 1970's,* 4th ed. Aurora, Ill.: Social Science & Sociological Resources, 1973. 74-171031. 16

KIRBY, JACK T. *Darkness at the Dawning.* Philadelphia: Lippincott, 1972. 77-161416. 109

KIRKLAND, EDWARD C. *Dream and Thought in the Business Community, 1860-1900.* Ithaca: Cornell University Press, 1956. 56-14414. 67

KIRWAN, ALBERT D. *The Revolt of the Rednecks: Mississippi Politics 1876-1925.* Lexington: University of Kentucky Press, 1951. 51-62000. 66

KNOLES, GEORGE H. *The Presidential Campaign and Election of 1892.* Stanford: Stanford University Press, 1942. 42-17328. 37

KOBLER, JOHN. *Capone: The Life and World of Al Capone.* New York: Putnam, 1971. 78-150267. 89

KOLKO, GABRIEL. *Railroads and Regulation.* Princeton: Princeton University Press, 1965. 65-10829. 73

_____. *The Triumph of Conservatism.* New York: Free Press of Glencoe, 1963. 63-16588. 70

KONVITZ, MILTON R., and ROSSITER, CLINTON, eds. *Aspects of Liberty.* New York: Johnson Reprint Corp., 1958. 59

KRAMER, DALE. *Heywood Broun.* New York: Current Books, 1949. 49-11638. 89

KRAUS, SIDNEY, ed. *The Great Debates.* Bloomington: Indiana University Press, 1962. 62-7487. 104

KREUTER, KENT, and GRETCHEN. *An American Dissenter. . .Algie Martin Simons 1870-1950.* Lexington: University of Kentucky Press, 1969. 68-55042. 85

KROUT, JOHN A. *The Origins of Prohibition.* New York: Knopf, 1925. 25-16666. 57

KUEHL, WARREN F. *Hamilton Holt: Journalist, Internationalist, Educator.* Gainesville: University of Florida Press, 1960. 60-15787. 30

KURLAND, GERALD. *Seth Low: The Reformer in an Urban and Industrial Age.* New York: Twayne, 1971. 76-125816. 17

LA FEBER, WALTER. *The New Empire: An Interpretation of American Expansion, 1860-1898.* Ithaca, N.Y.: Cornell University Press, 1963. 63-20868. 33

LA FOLLETTE, BELLE C., and FOLA. *Robert M. La Follette.* New York: Macmillan, 1953. 53-13106. 62

LA FOLLETTE, PHILIP F. *Adventure in Politics.* New York: Holt, Rinehart, and Winston, 1970. 78-84681. 62

LA FOLLETTE, ROBERT M. *Autobiography.* Madison, Wis.: Robert La Follette Co., 1913. 13-7510. 62

LANE, ANN J. *The Brownsville Affair: National Crisis and Black Reaction.* Port Washington, N.Y.: Kennikat Press, 1971. 73-139357. 28

LANE, HENRY HIGGINS. *Evolution and Christian Faith*. Princeton: Princeton University Press, 1923. 23-9124. 7

LANGFORD, GERALD. *The Richard Harding Davis Years*. New York: Holt, Rinehart and Winston, 1961. 61-5801. 42

LARSEN, CHARLES. *The Good Fight*. Chicago: Quadrangle Books, 1972. 78-152095. 58

LARSEN, WILLIAM E. *Montague of Virginia: The Making of a Southern Progressive*. Baton Rouge: Louisiana State University Press, 1965. 65-20299. 65

LARSON, ORVIN PRENTISS. *American Infidel: Robert G. Ingersoll, A Biography*. New York: Citadel Press, 1962. 62-10223. 20

LASCH, CHRISTOPHER. *The American Liberals and the Russian Revolution*. New York: Columbia University Press, 1962. 62-18617. 86

———. *The New Radicalism in America, 1889–1963; The Intellectual as a Social Type*. New York: Knopf, 1965. 65-11126. 27

LAUCK, WILLIAM JETT. *Political and Industrial Democracy, 1776–1926*. New York: Funk & Wagnalls, 1926. 26-22384. 4, 25

LAW, SYLVIA A. *Blue Cross: What Went Wrong?* New Haven: Yale University Press, 1974. 73-86907. 111

LAWSON, R. ALAN. *The Failure of Independent Liberalism 1930–1941*. New York: Putnam, 1971. 69-18186. 115

LAWSON, THOMAS W. *Frenzied Finance*. New York: Ridgway-Thayer, 1905, "Volume I" [no further volumes]. 5-40043. 44

LAZARUS, SIMON. *The Genteel Populists*. New York: Holt, Rinehart and Winston, 1974. 76-182767. 37

LEE, IVY. *Human Nature and Railroads*. Philadelphia: E. S. Nash, 1915. 15-11692. 68

LEECH, MARGARET. *In the Days of McKinley*. New York: Harper, 1959. 59-6310. 35

LEISERSON, WILLIAM L. *Right and Wrong in Labor Relations*. Berkeley: University of California Press, 1938. 38-16075. 96

LENS, SIDNEY. *The Labor Wars: From the Molly Maguires to the Sitdowns*. Garden City, N.Y.: Doubleday, 1973. 72-84926. 69

LEOPOLD, RICHARD WILLIAM. *Elihu Root and the Conservative Tradition*. Boston: Little, Brown, 1954. 54-6870. 28

LERNER, GERDA. *The Grimké Sisters from South Carolina: Rebels Against Slavery*. Boston: Houghton Mifflin, 1967. 67-25218. 13

LERNER, MAX, ed. *The Mind and Faith of Justice Holmes*. Boston: Little, Brown, 1943. 43-6772. 98

LESTER, JULIUS, ed. *The Seventh Son: The Thought and Writings of W. E. B. Du Bois*. 2 vols. New York: Random House, 1971. 77-140716. 65

LEUCHTENBERG, WILLIAM E. *Franklin D. Roosevelt and the New Deal*. New York: Harper & Row, 1963. 63-12053. 94

LEVIN, N. GORDON. *Woodrow Wilson and World Politics*. New York: Oxford University Press, 1968. 68-15893. 83

LEVINE, DANIEL. *Jane Addams and the Liberal Tradition*. Madison: State Historical Society of Wisconsin, 1971. 70-634145. 54

_____. *Varieties of Reform Thought*. Madison: State Historical Society of Wisconsin, 1964. 64-63188. 25

LEWIS, SINCLAIR. *It Can't Happen Here*. New York: Doran, 1935. 35-19689. 97

LINDSEY, ALMONT. *The Pullman Strike*. Chicago: University of Chicago Press, 1942. 42-50022. 35

LINDSEY, BEN. *The Beast*. New York: Doubleday, Page & Co., 1910. 10-10595. 45

LINK, ARTHUR S. *Woodrow Wilson*. Cleveland: World Pub. Co., 1963. 63-8980. 77

_____. *Woodrow Wilson and the Progressive Era, 1910–1917*. New York: Harper, 1954. 53-11849. 24

_____. et al. *The Papers of Woodrow Wilson*. Princeton: Princeton University Press, 1966. 66-10880. 77

_____, and LEARY, WILLIAM M., JR. *The Progressive Era and the Great War, 1896–1920*. New York: Appleton-Century-Crofts, 1969. 70-75036. 23

LIPPMAN, LEOPOLD and GOLDBERG, I. IGNACY. *Right to Education*. New York: Teachers College Press, 1973. 73-78038. 111

LIPPMANN, WALTER. *A Preface to Morals*. New York: Macmillan, 1929. 29-10228. 89

LITWACK, LEON F. *North of Slavery: The Negro in the Free States, 1790–1860*. Chicago: University of Chicago Press, 1961. 61-10869. 14

LIVERMORE, MARY ASHTON. *The Story of My Life: or, The Sunshine and Shadow of Seventy Years*. Hartford: A. D. Worthington & Co., 1899. 17-18747. 12

LLOYD, CAROLINE AUGUSTA. *Henry Demarest Lloyd, 1847–1903, a Biography*. New York: G. P. Putnam's Sons, 1912. 12-10840. 69

LLOYD, HENRY DEMAREST. *Wealth against Commonwealth*. New York: Harper & Brothers, 1894. 4-3852. 41, 69

LOEWENBERG, BERT JAMES, ed. *Darwinism, Reaction or Reform?* New York: Rinehart, 1957. 57-59038. 7

LOGAN, ANDY. *The Man Who Robbed the Robber Barons*. New York: W. W. Norton, 1965. 65-13031. 44

LONDON, JACK. *The Iron Heel*. New York: Macmillan, 1907. 7-3084. 7

_____. *Martin Eden*. New York: Macmillan, 1909. 9-22752. 7

_____. *The People of the Abyss*. Boston: Gregg, 1970 (repr. of 1903 ed.). 45

LOVEJOY, A. T. *La Follette and the Establishment of the Direct Primary in Wisconsin*. New Haven: Yale University Press, 1941. 42-2880. 62

LOVETT, ROBERT MORSS. *All Our Years*. New York: Viking Press, 1948. 48-6986. 97

LOWELL, JOSEPHINE SHAW, comp. *Industrial Arbitration and Conciliation; Some Chapters from the Industrial History of the Past Thirty Years*. New York: G. P. Putnam's Sons, 1893. 2-19648. 17

_____. *The Philanthropic Work of Josephine Shaw Lowell*, collected and arranged for publication by William Stewart Rhinelander. New York: Macmillan, 1911. 11-28795. 17

_____. *Public Relief and Private Charity*. New York: G. P. Putnam's Sons, 1884. 9-4993. 17

LOWI, THEODORE. *The End of Liberalism*. New York: Norton, 1969. 69-14704. 117

LOWITT, RICHARD. *George W. Norris: The Making of a Progressive 1861–1912.* Syracuse: N.Y.: Syracuse University Press, 1963. 63-19724. 61

LUBOVE, ROY. *The Professional Altruist.* Cambridge: Harvard University Press, 1965. 65-12786. 55

———. *The Progressives and the Slums: Tenement House Reform in New York City, 1890–1917.* Pittsburgh: University of Pittsburgh Press, 1962. 62-14380. 51

LUNDBERG, FERDINAND. *Imperial Hearst: A Social Biography.* New York: Equinox Cooperative Press, 1936. 36-8695. 5

LUSKIN, JOHN. *Lippmann, Liberty, and the Press.* University: University of Alabama Press, 1972. 72-4060. 77

LUTHIN, REINHARD H. *American Demagogues: Twentieth Century.* Boston: Beacon Press, 1954. 54-8428. 53, 66

LYNCH, DENIS T. *Criminals and Politicians.* New York: Macmillan, 1932. 32-33381. 96

LYON, PETER. *Success Story: The Life and Times of S. S. McClure.* New York: Scribner, 1963. 63-16757. 42

LYONS, LOUIS MARTIN. *Newspaper Story: One Hundred Years of the Boston Globe.* Cambridge: Belknap Press of Harvard University Press, 1971. 74-152697. 39

McCARTHY, CHARLES. *The Wisconsin Idea.* New York: Macmillan, 1912. 12-7674. 62

McCARTHY, EUGENE J. *The Limits of Power.* New York: Holt, Rinehart and Winston, 1967. 68-10052. 106

McCLURE, S. S. *My Autobiography.* New York: Frederick A. Stokes, 1914. 14-15200. 44

McCONAUGHY, JOHN. *Who Rules America?* New York: Longmans, Green, 1934. 34-4691. 96

MacDOUGALL, C. D. *Gideon's Army.* New York: Marzani & Munsell, 1965. 65-18683. 101

McGEARY, M. NELSON. *Gifford Pinchot, Forester Politician.* Princeton, N.J.: Princeton University Press, 1960. 60-12232. 72

McGINNISS, JOE. *The Selling of the President.* New York: Trident Press, 1969. 77-92157. 110

McKAY, KENNETH C. *The Progressive Movement of 1924.* New York: Columbia University Press, 1947. 47-3855. 92

McKEAN, DAYTON DAVID. *The Boss: The Hagne Machine in Action.* Boston: Houghton Mifflin, 1940. 40-32284. 54

McKELVEY, BLAKE. *The Urbanization of America.* New Brunswick, N.J.: Rutgers University Press, 1963. 62-21248. 35

McKELWAY, ST. CLAIR. *Gossip: The Life and Times of Walter Winchell.* New York: Viking Press, 1940. 40-32480. 5

McKENNA, MARIAN C. *Borah.* Ann Arbor: University of Michigan Press, 1961. 60-15771. 61

McKENNEY, THOMAS LORAINE. *Memoirs, Official and Personal; with Sketches of Travels Among the Northern and Southern Indians; Embracing a War Excursion and Descriptions of Scenes Along the Western Borders.* New York: Paine and Burgess, 1846. 2-15067. 15

MACKENZIE, WILLIAM LYON. *The Lives and Opinions of Benjamin Franklin Butler, United States District Attorney for the Southern District of New York, and Jesse Hoyt, Counsellor at Law, Formerly Collector of Customs for the Port of New York: with Anecdotes or Biographical Sketches of Stephen Allen; George P. Barker* [*etc.*]. Boston: Cook & Co., 1845. 3-33150. 39

McMURRY, DONALD L. *Coxey's Army: A Study of the Industrial Army Movement of 1894.* Boston: Little, Brown, 1929. 29-23512. 35, 38

McWHINEY, GRADY. *Southerners and other Americans.* New York: Basic Books, 1973. 72-98003. 15

MAGNUSON, WARREN G., and SEGAL, ELLIOT A. *How Much for Health?* Washington: R. B. Luce, 1974. 74-7834. 110

MALIN, JAMES C. *The United States after the War.* Boston: Ginn, 1930. 30-20107. 90

MANDEL, BERNARD. *Samuel Gompers.* Yellow Springs, O.: Antioch Press, 1963. 63-14380. 70

MANDELBAUM, SEYMOUR J. *Boss Tweed's New York.* New York: J. Wiley, 1965. 65-16417. 18

MANN, ARTHUR. *La Guardia.* Philadelphia: Lippincott, 1959. 59-13077. 75

_____, ed. *The Progressive Era: Liberal Renaissance or Liberal Failure?* Holt, 1963. 63-15138. 26

_____. *Yankee Reformers in the Urban Age.* Cambridge: Belknap Press of Harvard University Press, 1954. 54-5020. 34

MANN, HORACE. *Horace Mann on the Crisis in Education.* Edited with an Introd. by Louis Filler. Yellow Springs, Ohio: Antioch Press, 1965. 65-18902. 8

MARBERRY, M. MARION. *Vicky: A Biography of Victoria C. Woodhull.* New York: Funk & Wagnalls, 1967. 67-16224. 18

MARDOCK, ROBERT WINSTON. *The Reformers and the American Indian.* Columbia: University of Missouri Press, 1971. 79-113815. 16

MARGULIES, HERBERT T. *Decline of the Progressive Movement in Wisconson 1890–1920.* Madison: State Historical Society of Wisconsin, 1968. 68-63073. 62

MARTIN, ALBRO. *Enterprise Denied.* New York: Columbia University Press, 1971. 71-159673. 73

MARTIN, RALPH G. *The Bosses.* New York: Putnam, 1964. 64-18010. 52

MASON, ALPHEUS T. *Brandeis.* New York: Viking Press, 1946. 46-25268. 58

_____. *Bureaucracy Convicts Itself.* New York: Viking Press, 1941. 41-1997. 72

MASOTTI, LOUIS H. and HADDEN, JEFFREY K., eds. *The Urbanization of the Suburbs.* Beverly Hills: Sage Publications, 1973. 72-98038. 111

MATHEWSON, JOE. *Up Against Daley.* La Salle, Ill.: Open Court, 1974. 74-13055. 54

MATTHEWS, WILLIAM H. *Adventure in Giving.* New York: Dodd, Mead, 1939. 39-12305. 56

MATUSOW, ALLEN J., ed. *Joseph R. McCarthy.* Englewood Cliffs, N.J.: Prentice-Hall, 1970. 73-104846. 102

MAXWELL, ROBERT S., ed. *La Follette.* Englewood Cliffs, N.J.: Prentice-Hall, 1969. 69-15341. 63

———. *La Follette and the Rise of the Progressives in Wisconsin.* Madison: State Historical Society of Wisconsin, 1956. 59-62973. 63

MAY, ERNEST R. *Imperial Democracy: The Emergence of America as a Great Power.* New York: Harcourt, Brace & World, 1961. 61-13354. 33

MAY, HENRY FARNHAM. *Protestant Churches and Industrial America.* New York: Harper, 1949. 49-8159. 19

MENZEL, PAUL T., ed. *Moral Argument and the War in Vietnam: A Collection of Essays.* Nashville: Aurora, 1971. 79-143721. 10

MERRIAM, CHARLES EDWARD. *American Political Ideas.* New York: Macmillan, 1920. 20-18416. 60

MIDDLETON, NEIL, ed. *The I.F. Stone Weekly Reader.* New York: Random House, 1973. 73-5030. 111

MILLER, ARTHUR. *Death of a Salesman.* New York: Viking Press, 1949. 49-8817. 6

MILLER, HUGH. *The Foot-prints of the Creator: Or the Asterolepis of Stromness.* From the 3rd London ed. With a memoir of the author by Louis Agassiz. Boston: Gould and Lincoln, 1869. 17-11045. 7

MILLER, KELLY. *The Everlasting Stain.* Washington: Associated Publishers, 1924. 25-2354. 65

———. *Race Adjustment.* New York: Neale Pub. Co., 1908. 8-24845. 65

———, and GAY, J. R. *Progress and Achievements of the Colored People.* Washington: Austin Jenkins Co., 1917. 64

MILLER, SALLY M. *Victor Berger and the Promise of Constructive Socialism 1910-1920.* Westport, Conn.: Greenwood Press, 1973. 72-175609. 59

MILLER, WILLIAM D. *Memphis During the Progressive Era, 1900-1917.* Memphis: Memphis State University Press, 1957. 58-21437. 66

MILLER, ZANE L. *Boss Cox's Cincinnati: Urban Politics in the Progressive Era.* New York: Oxford University Press, 1968. 68-29722. 18, 52

MILLIS, WALTER. *The Martial Spirit: A Study of Our War with Spain.* Boston: Houghton Mifflin, 1931. 31-27021. 29

———. *The Road to War; America, 1914-1917.* Boston: Houghton Mifflin, 1935. 35-6576. 29

MILLS, C. WRIGHT. *Listen Yankee.* New York: McGraw-Hill, 1960. 60-8989. 105

———. *The Power Elite.* New York: Oxford University Press, 1956. 56-5427. 105

———. *White Collar: The American Middle Classes.* New York: Oxford University Press, 1951. 51-5298. 105

MILLSPAUGH, ARTHUR. *Haiti under American Control 1915-1930.* 83

MINER, DWIGHT CARROL. *The Fight for the Panama Route: The Story of the Spooner Act and the Hay-Herrán Treaty.* New York: Columbia University Press, 1940. 40-11864. 28

MITCHELL, JOHN. *Organized Labor.* Philadelphia: American Book and Bible House, 1903. 3-27926. 69

_____. *The Wage Earner and His Problems*. Washington: P. S. Ridsdale, 1913. 13-11016. 69

MOCK, JAMES R., and LARSON, CEDRIC. *Words that Won the War*. Princeton: Princeton University Press, 1939. 39-27871. 84

Modern Language Association. *American Literary Manuscripts*. Austin: University of Texas Press, 1960. 60-10356. 49

MOODY, JOHN. *The Long Road Home*. New York: Macmillan, 1933. 33-10961. 67

_____. *The Masters of Capital*. New Haven: Yale University Press, 1919. 19-19139. 67

MORGAN, ARTHUR ERNEST. *Edward Bellamy*. New York: Columbia University Press, 1944. A44-5392. 19

_____. *Nowhere Was Somewhere: How History Makes Utopias and How Utopias Make History*. Chapel Hill: University of North Carolina Press, 1946. 46-25233. 23

MORGAN, HOWARD WAYNE. *America's Road to Empire: The War with Spain and Overseas Expansion*. New York: Wiley, 1965. 64-8714. 31

MORLAN, ROBERT L. *Political Prairie Fire, the Non-Partisan League 1915-1922*. Minneapolis: University of Minnesota Press, 1955. 55-8488. 72

MORRIS, CHARLES E. *The Progressive Democracy of James M. Cox*. Indianapolis: Bobbs-Merrill, 1920. 20-20624. 90

MORRIS, LLOYD R. *Not So Long Ago*. New York: Random House, 1949. 49-11404. 25

_____. *Postscript to Yesterday; America: The Last Fifty Years*. New York: Random House, 1947. 47-11260. 25

MOSCOW, WARREN. *The Last of the Big-Time Bosses*. New York: Stein and Day, 1971. 79-160351. 111

MOTT, FRANK LUTHER. *American Journalism: A History, 1690-1960*. 3rd ed. New York: Macmillan, 1962. 62-7157. 26

_____. *A History of American Magazines*. Cambridge: Harvard University Press, 1938-1968. 5 v. 39-2823. 26

MOWRY, GEORGE E. *The California Progressives*. Berkeley: University of California Press, 1951. 51-63048. 61

_____. *The Era of Theodore Roosevelt 1900-1912*. New York: Harper, 1958. 58-8835. 24

_____. *The Progressive Movement, 1900-1920: Recent Ideas and New Literature*. Washington: Service Center for Teachers of History, 1958. 58-6045. 23

_____. *Theodore Roosevelt and the Progressive Movement*. Madison: University of Wisconsin Press, 1946. 46-25103. 27

"MUL." [WILLIAM H. MULDOON]. *Mark Hanna's "Moral Cranks" and—Others*, rev. ed. Brooklyn: G. F. Spinney Co., 1900. 0-3721. 36

MULLER, HERBERT J. *Adlai Stevenson: A Study in Values*. New York: Harper and Row, 1967. 67-22503. 103

MUMFORD, LEWIS. *The Story of Utopias*. New York: Boni and Liveright, 1922. 22-23191. 91

MUNRO, DANA G. *Intervention and Dollar Diplomacy in the Caribbean, 1900-1921*. Princeton: Princeton University Press, 1964. 63-18647. 83

MURPHY, EDGAR GARDNER. *The Basis of Ascendency*. New York: Longmans, Green, 1910. 36-4092. 66

——. *Problems of the Present South.* New York: Longmans, Green, 1909. 9-13280. 66

MURRAY, ROBERT K. *Red Scare: A Study in National Hysteria 1919–1920.* Minneapolis: University of Minnesota Press, 1955. 55-7034. 86

MUSHKAT, JEROME. *Tammany.* Syracuse: Syracuse University Press, 1971. 78-150346. 53

MYERS, GUSTAVUS. *A History of Bigotry in the United States.* New York: Random House, 1943. 43-9842. 92

NADER, RALPH. *Unsafe at Any Speed.* New York: Grossman, 1965. 65-16856. 112

NADWORNY, MILTON J. *Scientific Management and the Unions, 1900–1932.* Cambridge: Harvard University Press, 1955. 55-11606. 73

NAMMACK, GEORGIANA C. *Fraud, Politics, and the Dispossession of the Indians: The Iroquois Land Frontier in the Colonial Period.* Norman: University of Oklahoma Press, 1969. 69-16722. 16

NEARING, SCOTT. *The Making of a Radical.* New York: Harper & Row, 1972. 78-180725. 59

NEVINS, ALLAN. *Abram S. Hewitt: With Some Account of Peter Cooper.* New York: Harper & Brothers, 1935. 35-30046. 17

——, ed. *The Burden and the Glory.* New York: Harper and Row, 1964. 64-12673. 105

——. *Ford, the Times, the Man, the Company.* New York: Scribner's, 1954. 54-6305. 91

——. *Herbert Lehman and His Era.* New York: Scribner's, 1963. 63-8464. 94

——. *Study in Power, John D. Rockefeller, Industrialist and Philanthropist.* New York: Scribner's, 1953. 53-9394. 69

NICHOLLS, WILLIAM HORD. *Southern Tradition and Regional Progress.* Chapel Hill: University of North Carolina Press, 1960. 60-10535. 15

NIEBUHR, REINHOLD. *Moral Man and Immoral Society: A Study in Ethics and Politics.* New York and London: C. Scribner's Sons, 1932. 33-1231. 11

NIXON, RAYMOND B. *Henry W. Grady: Spokesman of the New South.* New York: A. A. Knopf, 1943. 43-15890. 64

NOBLE, DAVID W. *The Paradox of Progressive Thought.* Minneapolis: University of Minnesota, 1958. 58-8765. 25

NOBLE, RANSOM E., JR. *New Jersey Progressivism before Wilson.* Princeton: Princeton University Press, 1946. A46-5138. 61

NOCK, A. J. *The Myth of a Guilty Nation.* New York: B. W. Huebsch, 1922, 22-14207. 85

NOGGLE, BURL. *Teapot Dome.* Baton Rouge: Louisiana State University Press, 1962. 62-15031. 93

NORRIS, FRANK. *The Pit.* New York: Doubleday, Page & Co., 1903. 3-1580. 68

——. *The Octopus.* New York: Doubleday, Page & Co., 1901. 1-31483. 68

NORRIS, GEORGE W. *Fighting Liberal.* New York: Macmillan, 1945. 45-3790. 61

NORTHROP, WILLIAM B., and JOHN B. *The Insolence of Office.* New York: G. P. Putnam's, 1932. 32-27068. 96

NUGENT, WALTER T. K. *The Tolerant Populists: Kansas, Populism and Nativism.* Chicago: University of Chicago Press, 1963. 63-13069. 38

NYE, RUSSEL B. *Midwestern Progressive Politics. . .Its Origins and Development.* East Lansing: Michigan State College Press, 1951. 51-11144. 37

O'BRIEN, FRANK MICHAEL. *The Story of the Sun, New York, 1833–1918.* New York: George H. Doran Company, 1918. 18-20662. 39

O'CONNOR, EDWIN. *The Last Hurrah.* Boston: Little, Brown, 1956. 55-11224. 53, 95

O'CONNOR, HARVEY. *Mellon's Millions.* New York: John Day, 1933. 33-22292. 115

ODEGARD, PETER H. *Pressure Politics: The Story of the Anti-Saloon League.* New York: Columbia University Press, 1928. 28-22933. 57

O'GARA, GORDAN CARPENTER. *Theodore Roosevelt and the Rise of the Modern Navy.* Princeton, N.J.: Princeton University Press, 1943. A 43-1236. 30

OLDER, CORA MIRANDA. *William Randolph Hearst, American.* New York: D. Appleton-Century, 1936. 36-3848. 5, 40

OLDER, FREMONT. *My Own Story.* San Francisco: Call Publishing Co., 1919. 19-1807. 40

OLIN, SPENCER C. *California's Prodigal Sons: Hiram Johnson and Progressivism 1911–1917.* Berkeley: University of California Press, 1968. 68-11968. 61

O'NEILL, WILLIAM L. *Divorces in the Progressive Era.* New Haven: Yale University Press, 1967. 67-24507. 59

OPPENHEIM, FELIX E. *Moral Principles in Political Philosophy.* New York: Random House, 1968. 68-16369. 11

ORTH, SAMUEL P. *The Boss and the Machine.* New Haven: Yale University Press, 1919. 19-3705. 52

——. *Our Foreigners.* New Haven: Yale University Press, 1920. A23-877. 57, 63

OSBORNE, THOMAS MOTT. *Society and Prisons.* New Haven: Yale University Press, 1916. 16-14890. 58

——. *Within Prison Walls.* New York: D. Appleton, 1914. 14-10204. 58

OSGOOD, ROBERT E. *Ideals and Self-Interest in American Foreign Relations.* Chicago: University of Chicago Press, 1953. 53-10532. 83

OSSOLI, SARAH, and FULLER, MARGARET. *Woman in the Nineteenth Century.* New York: Greeley & McElrath, 1845. 28-22266. 12

OSTRANDER, GILMAN M. *The Prohibition Movement in California.* Berkeley: University of California Press, rev. 1957. A58-9056. 87

OVERACKER, LOUISE. *Money in Elections.* New York: Macmillan, 1932. 32-29858. 115

OVINGTON, MARY W. *The Walls Came Tumbling Down.* New York: Harcourt, Brace, 1947. 47-30961. 56

PADOVER, SAUL K., ed. *Wilson's Ideals.* Washington: American Council on Public Affairs, 1943. 43-51126. 78

PARK, ROBERT E. *The Immigrant Press and Its Control.* New York: Harper & Brothers, 1922. 22-2469. 16

PARKHURST, CHARLES H. *Our Fight with Tammany.* New York: C. Scribner's Sons, 1895. 9-32837. 35

PARRINGTON, VERNON LOUIS. *Main Currents in American Thought: Literature from the Beginnings to 1920.* New York: Harcourt, Brace, 1927–1930. 27-8440. 26

PARSONS, FRANK. *The City for the People*. Philadelphia: C. F. Taylor, 1900. 10-8504. 71

———. *Railroads, the Trusts and the People*. Philadelphia: C. F. Taylor, 1905. 6-46268. 71

———. *The Telegraph Monopoly*. Philadelphia: C. F. Taylor, 1899. 6-15085. 71

PARSONS, STANLEY B. *The Populist Context: Rural versus Urban Power on a Great Plains Frontier*. Westport, Conn.: Greenwood Press, 1973. 72-824. 38

PATTON, CLIFFORD WHEELER. *The Battle for Municipal Reform: Mobilization and Attack, 1875–1900*. Washington, D.C.: American Council on Public Affairs, 1940. 41-3544. 18

PAYNE, DANIEL ALEXANDER. *Recollections of Seventy Years*. Nashville, Tenn.: A.M.E. Sunday School Union, 1888. 14-12737. 14, 64

PEABODY, FRANCIS GREENWOOD, ed. *The Liquor Problem: A Summary of Investigations 1893–1903*. Boston: Houghton Mifflin, 1905. 5-28396. 87

PEARSON, DREW. *Diaries, 1949–1959*. Edited by Tyler Abell. New York: Holt, Rinehart and Winston, 1974. 72-78142. 5

———, and ALLEN, ROBERT S. *Washington Merry-Go-Round*. New York: United Feature Syndicate, 1935. 35-12484. 94

———, and ANDERSON, JACK. *The Case Against Congress*. New York: Simon and Schuster, 1968. 70-72033. 111

PEASE, WILLIAM HENRY and PEASE, JANE H. *Black Utopia: Negro Communal Experiments in America*. Madison: State Historical Society of Wisconsin, 1963. 63-64494. 14

PEEL, R. V., and DONNELLY, T. C. *The 1928 Campaign*. New York: R. R. Smith, 1931. 31-15620. 93

———, and DONNELLY, T. C. *The 1932 Campaign*. New York: Farrar & Rinehart, 1935. 35-7208. 94

PELLS, RICHARD H. *Radical Visions and American Dreams*. New York: Harper & Row, 1973. 72-85471. 97

PENICK, JAMES, JR. *Progressive Politics and Conservation*. Chicago: University of Chicago Press, 1968. 68-15798. 72

The Pentagon Papers. New York: Quadrangle Books, 1971. 75-173846. 6

PERCY, CHARLES H. *Growing Old in the Country of the Young*. New York: McGraw-Hill, 1974. 74-13940. 110

PERKINS, FRANCES. *People at Work*. New York: John Day, 1934. 34-14217. 95

———. *The Roosevelt I Knew*. New York: Viking Press, 1946. 46-11961. 94

PERSONS, STOW. *The Decline of American Gentility*. New York: Columbia University Press, 1973. 73-534. 18

———, ed. *Evolutionary Thought in America*. New York: George Braziller, 1956. 50-10345. 8

PESSEN, EDWARD. *Jacksonian America; Society, Personality, and Politics*. Ill.: Dorsey Press, 1969. 68-56870. 9

———. *Most Uncommon Jacksonians: The Radical Leaders of the Early Labor Movement*. Albany: State University of New York Press, 1967. 67-63761. 9

PETERS, CHARLES, and BRANCH, TAYLOR, eds. *Blowing the Whistle: Dissent in the Public Interest*. New York: Praeger, 1972. 72-185768. 113

PETERSON, F. ROSS. *Prophet without Honor: Glen Taylor*. Lexington: University Press of Kentucky, 1974. 72-91668. 101

PETERSON, HORACE C., and FITE, GILBERT C. *Opponents of War 1917–1918*. Madison: University of Wisconsin Press, 1957. 57-5239. 86

Philanthropy and Social Progress. New York: T. Y. Crowell, 1893.

PHILLIPS, DAVID GRAHAM. *The Grain of Dust*. New York: D. Appleton, 1911. 11-7868. 49

———. *The Hungry Heart*. New York: D. Appleton, 1909. 9-22750. 49

———. *The Husband's Story*. New York: D. Appleton, 1910. 10-20846. 49

———. *Light Fingered Gentry*. New York: D. Appleton, 1907. 7-30833. 49

———. *Old Wives for New*. New York: D. Appleton, 1908. 8-8091. 49

———. *The Plum Tree*. Indianapolis: Bobbs-Merrill, 1905. 5-7622. 49

———. *The Price She Paid*. New York: D. Appleton, 1912. 12-14456. 49

———. *Susan Lenox: Her Fall and Rise*. D. Appleton, 1917. 17-6327. 48

———. *The Treason of the Senate*. Chicago: Quadrangle Books, 1964. 64-21838. 49

PIKE, FREDERICK B. *Chile and the United States, 1880–1962: The Emergence of Chile's Social Crisis and the Challenge to United States Diplomacy*. Notre Dame, Ind.: University of Notre Dame Press, 1963. 63-9097. 29

PILAT, OLIVER RAMSEY. *Drew Pearson: An Unauthorized Biography*. New York: Harper's Magazine Press, 1973. 72-79719. 5

PILISUK, MARC and PHYLLIS, eds. *Poor Americans: How the White Poor Live*. Chicago: Aldine, 1971. 79-133309. 116

PINCHOT, AMOS R. E. *History of the Progressive Party, 1912–1916*. New York: New York University Press, 1958. 57-10135. 83

PINCHOT, GIFFORD. *Breaking New Ground*. New York: Harcourt, Brace, 1947. 47-11529. 72

PIVAR, DAVID J. *Purity Crusade: Sexual Morality and Social Control, 1868–1900*. Westport, Conn.: Greenwood Press, 1973. 70-179650. 18, 59

PLATT, CHESTER C. *What La Follette's State Is Doing*. Batavia, N.Y.: Batavia Times Press, 1924. 24-18645. 62

PLESUR, MILTON. *America's Outward Thrust: Approaches to Foreign Affairs, 1865–1890*. DeKalb: Northern Illinois University Press, 1971. 76-137882. 32

———, ed. *Intellectual Alienation in the 1920's*. Lexington: Heath, 1970. 72-134279. 89

PLETCHER, DAVID M. *The Awkward Years: American Foreign Relations under Garfield and Arthur*. Columbia: University of Missouri Press, 1962. 62-15589. 31

POLLACK, NORMAN. *The Populist Response to Industrial America: Midwestern Populist Thought*. Cambridge: Harvard University Press, 1962. 62-20249. 38

POOLE, ERNEST. *The Bridge*. New York: Macmillan, 1940. 40-30230. 45

———. *The Harbor*. New York: Macmillan, 1915. 15-2844. 45

PRATT, JULIUS W. *America and World Leadership, 1900–1921*. London: Collier-Macmillan, 1967. 7206280. 83

———. *America's Colonial Experiment: How the United States Gained, Governed, and in Part Gave Away a Colonial Empire*. New York: Prentice-Hall, 1950. 50-11728. 32

_____. *Expansionists of 1898: The Acquisition of Hawaii and the Spanish Islands*. Baltimore: Johns Hopkins Press, 1936. 37-175. 30

PRESTON, WILLIAM J. *Aliens and Dissenters*. Cambridge: Harvard University Press, 1963. 63-10873. 85

PRIEST, LORING BENSON, *Uncle Sam's Stepchildren: The Reformation of United States Indian Policy, 1865-1887*. New Brunswick, N.J.: Rutgers University Press, 1942. 42-8373. 16

PRINGLE, HENRY FOWLES. *Alfred E. Smith: A Critical Study*. New York: Macy-Masius, 1927. 29-2116. 93

_____. *The Life and Times of William Howard Taft: A Biography*. New York: Farrar & Rinehart, 1939. 39-27878. 27

_____. *Theodore Roosevelt, a Biography*. New York: Harcourt, Brace, 1931. 31-31893. 27

PRUCHA, FRANCIS PAUL, comp. & ed. *Americanizing the American Indians: Writings by the "Friends of the Indian," 1880-1900*. Cambridge, Mass.: Harvard University Press, 1973. 72-92132. 16

PULESTON, WILLIAM DILWORTH. *Mahan; The Life and Work of Captain Alfred Thayer Mahan*. New Haven: Yale University Press, 1939. 39-10963. 30

PULLEN, JOHN J. *Patriotism in America: A Study of Changing Devotions, 1770-1970*. New York: American Heritage Press, 1971. 78-142981. 29

PUSEY, MERLE J. *Charles Evans Hughes*. New York: Macmillan, 1951. 51-7851. 58

PUTNAM, CARLETON. *Theodore Roosevelt, a Biography*. New York, Scribner, 1958. 58-6735. 27

PYLE, JOSEPH G. *The Life of James J. Hill*. Garden City, N.Y.: Doubleday, Page & Co., 1917. 17-15184. 67

QUARLES, BENJAMIN. *Black Abolitionists*. New York: Oxford University Press, 1969. 69-17766. 14

QUIRK, ROBERT E. *An Affair of Honor*. Lexington: University of Kentucky Press, 1962. 62-13972. 84

RADER, BENJAMIN G. *The Academic Mind and Reform: The Influence of Richard T. Ely in American Life*. Lexington: University of Kentucky Press, 1966. 66-26694. 18

RANDALL, JAMES GARFIELD. *Lincoln, the Liberal Statesman*. New York: Dodd, Mead, 1947. 47-4344. 9

RANDALL, MERCEDES M. *Improper Bostonian: Emile Green Balch*. New York: Twayne, 1964. 64-25058. 56

RANEY, W. F. *Wisconsin, A Story of Its Progress*. New York: Prentice-Hall, 1940. 40-7607. 62

RAPPORT, GEORGE C. *The Statesman and the Boss*. New York: Vantage Press, 1961. 61-14971. 54

RATNER, SIDNEY. *American Taxation*. New York: W. W. Norton, 1942. 42-6329. 74

RAVAGE, M. E. *An American in the Making*. New York: Harper & Brothers, 1917. 17-28804. 57

RAVITZ, ABE C. *Clarence Darrow and the American Literary Tradition*. Cleveland: Press of Western Reserve University, 1962. 62-17760. 46

RESEK, CARL., ed. *The Progressives*. Indianapolis: Bobbs-Merrill, 1967. 66-16754. 26

RICE, STUART A. *Farmers and Workers in American Politics*. New York: Columbia University Press, 1924. 24-29312. 69

RICHARDSON, ELMO R. *The Politics of Conservation*. Berkeley: University of California Press, 1962. 62-64234. 72

RICHBERG, DONALD R. *Tents of the Mighty*. New York: Willett, Clark & Colby, 1930. 30-19070. 90

RICHMOND, MARY ELLEN. *The Good Neighbor in the Modern City*. Philadelphia: J. B. Lippincott, 1907. 7-39066. 17

———. *What Is Social Case Work?* New York: Russell Sage Foundation, 1922. 22-5436. 17

RIDGE, MARTIN. *Ignatius Donnelly: The Portrait of a Politician*. Chicago: University of Chicago Press, 1962. 62-19937. 37

RIENOW, ROBERT, and RIENOW, LEONA TRAIN. *Of Snuff, Sin, and the Senate*. Chicago: Follett, 1965. 65-13267. 74

RIESMAN, DAVID. *Thorstein Veblen: A Critical Interpretation*. New York: Scribner, 1960. 61-851. 25

RIIS, JACOB. *How the Other Half Lives*. New York: C. Scribner's, 1890. 4-11775. 52

RING, ELIZABETH. *Progressive Movement of 1912 and Third Party Movement of 1924 in Maine*. Orono: University of Maine Press, 1933. 33-27764. 92

RINGENBACH, PAUL T. *Tramps and Reformers 1873–1916*. Westport, Conn.: Greenwood Press, 1973. 77-175610. 55

RIORDAN, WILLIAM L. *Plunkitt of Tammany Hall: A Series of Very Plain Talks on Very Practical Politics, Delivered by Ex-senator George Washington Plunkitt*. New York, McClure, Phillips, 1905. 5-33226. 18

RIPLEY, WILLIAM Z. *Railroads: Rates and Regulation*. New York: Longmans, Green, 1912. 12-26396. 73

ROGIN, MICHAEL P. *The Intellectuals and McCarthy*. Cambridge: MIT Press, 1967. 67-16489. 102

ROOSEVELT, THEODORE. *Letters*, selected and edited by Elting E. Morison; John M. Blum, associate editor, John J. Buckley, copy editor. Cambridge: Harvard University Press, 1951–54. 8 volumes. 51-10037. 27

———. *The Rough Riders*. New York: C. Scribner's, 1899. 99-2686. 34

———. *Theodore Roosevelt; An Autobiography*. New York: Macmillan, 1913. 13-24840. 27

———. *The Works of Theodore Roosevelt*. New York: C. Scribner's, 1923–1926. 20 volumes. 23-17884. 28

ROSEWATER, VICTOR. *Backstage in 1912*. Philadelphia: Dorrance, 1932. 32-28816. 78

ROSS, B. JOYCE. *J. E. Spingarn and the Rise of the NAACP, 1911–1939*. New York: Atheneum, 1972. 78-139326. 66

ROSS, EDWARD A. *Seventy Years of It*. New York: D. Appleton-Century, 1936. 36-27416. 61

———. *Sin and Society*. Boston: Houghton, Mifflin, 1907. 7-36978. 61

ROSS, ISHBEL. *Angel of the Battlefield: The Life of Clara Barton*. New York: Harper, 1956. 56-6033. 11

ROSSITER, CLINTON, and LARE, JAMES, eds. *The Essential Lippmann.* New York: Random House, 1963. 63-11623. 76

ROYALL, ANNE NEWPORT. *Letters from Alabama 1817-1822.* University: University of Alabama Press, 1969. 70-76584. 39

ROZWENC, EDWIN CHARLES, ed. *The New Deal: Revolution or Evolution?*, rev. ed. Boston: Heath, 1959. 59-1861. 3

RUGG, HAROLD. *Foundations for American Education.* Yonkers-on-Hudson, N.Y.: World Book Co., 1947. 47-6877. 96

_____. *That Men May Understand.* New York: Doubleday, Doran, 1941. 41-4889. 89

RUSK, RALPH L. *The Literature of the Middle Western Frontier.* New York: Columbia University Press, 1925. 25-11215. 37

RUSSELL, CHARLES EDWARD. *Bare Hands and Stone Walls.* New York: C. Scribner's Sons, 1938. 33-29774. 43

_____. *Business.* New York: John Lane Co., 1911. 11-17831. 70

_____. *The Story of the Nonpartisan League.* New York: Harper & Bros., 1920. 20-11024. 92

_____. *These Shifting Scenes.* New York: Hodder & Stoughton, 1914. 14-7492. 41

_____, and RODRIQUEZ, E. B. *The Hero of the Filipinos: The Story of José Rizal, Poet, Patriot and Martyr.* New York: Century, 1923. 23-13074. 31

RUTLAND, ROBERT ALLEN. *The Newsmongers: Journalism in the Life of the Nation 1690-1972.* New York: Dial Press, 1973. 72-10757. 27

RYAN, JOHN A. *The Catholic Church and the Citizen.* New York: Macmillan, 1928. 28-11115. 92

_____. *Questions of the Day.* Boston: Stratford, 1931. 31-9845. 92

SALISBURY, WILLIAM. *The Career of a Journalist.* New York: B. W. Dodge, 1908. 8-9151. 42

SALOUTOS, THEODORE, ed. *Populism: Reaction or Reform?* New York: Holt, Rinehart & Winston, 1968. 68-54044. 35

_____, and HICKS, JOHN D. *Agricultural Discontent in the Middle West, 1900-1939.* Madison: University of Wisconsin Press, 1951. 51-4287. 37

SAMPSON, ANTHONY. *The Sovereign State of ITT.* New York: Stein & Day, 1973. 72-96745. 116

SANGER, ELLIOTT M. *Rebel in Radio: The Story of WQXR.* New York: Hastings House, 1973. 72-13094. 110

SANGER, MARGARET. *My Fight for Birth Control.* New York: Farrar & Rinehart, 1931. 31-28223. 26

SCHAPMEIER, L. L., and F. H. *Walter Lippmann, Philosopher-Journalist.* Washington: Public Affairs Press, 1969. 70-96032. 76

SCHLESINGER, ARTHUR MEIER, JR. *The Age of Jackson.* Boston: Little, Brown, 1945. 45-8340. 3, 4

_____. *The Rise of the City 1878-1898.* New York: Macmillan, 1933. 33-2887. 35

SCHMIDT, KARL M. *Henry Wallace.* Syracuse: Syracuse University Press, 1960. 60-16440. 101

SCHOOLCRAFT, HENRY ROWE. *Notes on the Iroquois; or, Contributions to American History, Antiquities, and General Ethnology*. Albany: E. H. Pease, 1847. 2-18177. 15

———. *Personal Memories of a Residence of Thirty Years with the Indian Tribes on the American Frontiers*. Philadelphia: Lippincott, Grambo, 1851. 2-15006. 15

SCHRAG, PETER. *The Decline of the WASP*. New York: Simon and Schuster, 1971. 73-163495. 18

SCHRIFTGIESSER, KARL. *The Gentleman from Massachusetts*. Boston: Little, Brown, 1944. 44-7415. 88

SCHROEDER, THEODORE. *Free Speech Anthology*. New York: Free Speech League and Truth Seeker Pub. Co., 1909. 10-2935. 59

———. *"Obscene" Literature and Constitutional Law: A Forensic Defense of Freedom of the Press*. New York: Priv. Printed, 1911. 11-10111. 59

SCHURZ, CARL. *The Reminiscences of Carl Schurz*. 3 volumes. New York: McClure, 1907–1908. 7-36232. 33

———. *Speeches, Correspondence and Political Papers of Carl Schurz*. Selected and ed. by Frederic Bancroft. New York: G. P. Putnam's, 1913. 13-13552. 33

SCOTT, JAMES C. *Comparative Political Corruption*. Englewood Cliffs, N.J.: Prentice-Hall, 1972. 75-161461. 116

SCRIPPS, EDWARD WYLLIS. *I Protest. . .*edited and with a biographical introd. by Oliver Knight. Madison: University of Wisconsin Press, 1966. 66-11806. 40

SCUDDER, VIDA. *On Journey*. New York: Dutton, 1937. 37-27231. 56

SEABROOK, ISAAC DUBOSE. *Before and After; or, the Relations of the Races at the South*. Baton Rouge: Louisiana State University Press, 1967. 67-13893. 15

SEIDLER, MURRAY B. *Norman Thomas, Respectable Rebel*. Syracuse: Syracuse University Press, 1967. 67-15881. 96

SEIDMAN, HAROLD. *Labor Czars*. New York: Liveright, 1938. 38-9949. 97

SEITZ, DON CARLOS. *Joseph Pulitzer: His Life and Letters*. New York: Simon & Schuster, 1924. 24-30178. 40

SELDES, GEORGE. *Freedom of the Press*. Indianapolis: Bobbs-Merrill, 1935. 35-15779. 97

———. *Iron, Blood and Profits*. New York: Harper & Bros., 1934. 34-10357. 97

———. *Lords of the Press*. New York: J. Messner, 1938. 38-28990. 94, 97

———. *Tell the Truth and Run*. New York: Greenberg, 1953. 53-10452. 104

———. *Witch Hunt*. New York: Modern Age, 1940. 40-27853. 97

SELLERS, CHARLES GRIER, JR., ed. *The Southerner as American* [By] John Hope Franklin [and others]. Chapel Hill: University of North Carolina Press, 1960. 60-4104. 15, 64

SEMMEL, BERNARD. *Imperialism and Social Reform, English Social-Imperial Thought 1895–1914*. Cambridge: Harvard University Press, 1960. 60-4234. 32.

SEMOUCHE, JOHN E. *Ray Stannard Baker: A Quest for Democracy in Modern America 1870–1918*. Chapel Hill: University of North Carolina Press, 1969. 69-16215. 44

SEYMOUR, CHARLES, ed. *The Intimate Papers of Colonel House*. Boston: Houghton Mifflin, 1930, 30-22524. 77

SHANNON, DAVID. *The Decline of American Communism*. New York: Harcourt, Brace, 1959. 59-11770. 102

SHANNON, FRED A. *The Farmer's Last Frontier, 1860–1897.* New York: Farrar & Rinehart, 1945. 45-35139. 37

SHANNON, WILLIAM VINCENT. *The American Irish.* New York: Macmillan, rev. ed., 1966. 66-2047. 14

———. and TRETICK, STANLEY. *They Could Not Trust the King.* New York: Macmillan, 1974. 114 9

SHAPIRO, CHARLES. *Theodore Dreiser: Our Bitter Patriot.* Carbondale: Southern Illinois University Press, 1962. 62-16696. 48

SILVERMAN, MILTON, and LEE, PHILIP R. *Pills, Profits & Politics.* Berkeley: University of California Press, 1974. 73-89166. 110

SIMKHOVITCH, MARY M. *Here Is God's Plenty.* New York: Harper, 1949. 49-48097. 56

———. *My Story of Greenwich House.* New York: Norton, 1938. 38-27282. 56

SIMKINS, FRANCIS B. *Pitchfork Ben Tillman.* Baton Rouge: Louisiana State University Press, 1944. 44-9640. 66

SIMMONS, WILLIAM J. *Men of Mark.* Cleveland: G. M. Rewell, 1887. 6-5585. 63

SIMONS, A. M. *Class Struggles in America.* Chicago: C. H. Kerr, 1903. 3-13354. 69, 85

———. *Personnel Relations in Industry.* New York: Ronald Press, 1921. 21-8298. 85

———. *Social Forces in American History.* New York: Macmillan, 1911. 11-27123. 85

———. *The Vision for Which We Fought: A Study of Reconstruction.* New York: Macmillan, 1919. 19-2070. 85

SINCLAIR, UPTON. *American Outpost.* New York: Farrar & Rinehart, 1932. 32-26373. 46

———. *Autobiography.* New York: Harcourt, Brace, & World, 1962. 62-19592. 46

———. *Boston.* New York: A. & C. Boni, 1928. 29-26043. 47

———. *The Brass Check.* Pasadena, Calif.: The Author, 1919. 20-11913. 47

———. *The Cup of Fury.* Great Neck, N.Y.: Channel Press, 1956. 56-13860. 47

———. *Good Health and How We Won It.* New York: F. A. Stokes, 1909. 9-2074. 46

———. *The Goose-Step.* Pasadena, Calif.: The Author, 1923. 23-8213. 47

———. *The Goslings.* Pasadena, Calif.: The Author, 1924. 24-5791. 47

———. *The Industrial Republic.* New York: Doubleday, Page & Co., 1907. 7-18298. 46

———. *Jimmie Higgins.* New York: Boni & Liveright, 1919. 19-8807. 47

———. *The Journal of Arthur Stirling.* New York: D. Appleton, 1903. 3-2703. 46

———. *The Jungle.* New York: Doubleday, Page & Company, 1906. 6-6264. 43, 46, 61, 113

———. *Love's Pilgrimage.* New York: M. Kennerley, 1911. 11-5410. 47

———. *Mammonart.* Pasadena, Calif.: The Author, 1925. 25-7504. 47

———. *Money Writes!* New York: A. & C. Boni, 1927. 27-24135. 47

———. *My Lifetime in Letters.* Columbia: University of Missouri Press, 1960. 46

———. *Oil!* New York: A. & C. Boni, 1927. 27-7669. 47

———. *100 %: The Story of a Patriot.* Pasadena, Calif.: The Author, 1920, 21-1179. 47

———. *The Profits of Religion.* Pasadena, Calif.: The Author, 1918. 18-22885. 47

———. *Samuel the Seeker.* New York: B. W. Dodge, 1910. 11-19643. 47

_____. *Singing Jailbirds*. Pasadena, Calif.: The Author, 1924. 24-32213. 47

_____. *Upton Sinclair Presents William Fox*. Los Angeles, Calif.: The Author, 1933. 33-4946. 47

_____. *The Wet Parade*. New York: Farrar & Rinehart, 1931. 31-23681. 47

SLOAN, ALFRED P., JR. *My Life with General Motors*. Garden City, N.Y.: Doubleday, 1963. 64-11306. 91

SMITH, A. D. H. *The Real Colonel House*. New York: George H. Doran, 1918. 18-12108. 78

SMITH, ALFRED E. *Progressive Democracy*. New York: Harcourt, Brace, 1928. 28-13918. 93

SMITH, HENRY NASH. *Virgin Land*. Cambridge: Harvard University Press, 1950. 50-6230. 34

SMITH, J. ALLEN. *The Spirit of American Government*. New York: Macmillan, 1907. 7-16497. 60

SMITH, MORTIMER. *William Jay Gaynor, Mayor of New York*. Chicago: H. Regnery, 1951. 51-12724. 53

SMITH, RIXEY, and BEASLEY, NORMAN. *Carter Glass*. New York: Longmans, Green, 1939. 39-10859. 74

SMITH, STEPHEN. *The City that Was*. New York: F. Allaben, 1911. 12-17209. 35

SOUTHERN, DAVID W. *Malignant Heritage: Yankee Progressives and the Negro Question*. Chicago: Loyola University Press, 1968. 68-20410. 64

SPARGO, JOHN. *The Bitter Cry of the Children*. New York: Macmillan, 1906. 6-5679. 56, 59

_____. *Syndicalism, Industrial Unionism, and Socialism*. New York: B. W. Huebsch, 1913. 13-9157. 69

SPIVAK, JOHN L. *A Man in His Time*. New York: Horizon Press, 1967. 67-17783. 97

SPROAT, JOHN G. *"The Best Men": Liberal Reformers in the Gilded Age*. New York: Oxford University Press, 1968. 68-8413. 16, 18

STANTON, ELIZABETH CADY, ANTHONY, SUSAN B. and GAGE, MATILDA JOSLYN, eds. *History of Woman Suffrage*. New York: Fowler and Wells, 1881-1922, 6 volumes. 3-16908. 11

STAVE, BRUCE M. *The New Deal and the Last Hurrah*. Pittsburgh: University of Pittsburgh Press, 1970. 78-93863. 94

STEAD, WILLIAM T. *The Americanization of the World; or, the Trend of the Twentieth Century*. New York and London: H. Markley, 1901. 2-1813. 32

STEARNS, HAROLD. *Liberalism in America*. New York: Boni and Liveright, 1919. 20-1878. 86

STEFFENS, LINCOLN. *Autobiography*. New York: Harcourt, Brace, 1931. 31-28251. 43, 116

_____. *The Shame of the Cities*. New York: McClure, Phillips, 1904. 4-7545. 43

_____. *Upbuilders*. New York: Doubleday, Page & Co., 1909. 9-26002. 50, 60, 87

STEIN, LEON. *The Triangle Fire*. Philadelphia: Lippincott, 1962. 62-10546. 75

STEINBERG, ALFRED. *The Bosses*. New York: Macmillan, 1972. 73-190158. 111

STEPHENSON, GEORGE M. *A History of American Immigration*. Boston: Ginn, 1926. 26-4956. 56

STERN, MADELEINE B. *The Pantarch: A Biography of Stephen Pearl Andrews.* Austin: University of Texas Press, 1968. 68-18386. 50

———. *Queen of Publishers' Row.* New York: J. Messner, 1965. 65-21605. 43

STERNSHER, BERNARD. *Rexford Tugwell and the New Deal.* New Brunswick, N.J.: Rutgers University Press, 1964. 63-15522. 94

STEVENS, SYLVESTER KIRBY. *American Expansion in Hawaii, 1842-1898.* Harrisburg: Archives Publishing Co. of Pennsylvania, 1945. 46-3402. 33

STEVENS, WILLIAM H. S. *Unfair Competition,* rev. ed. New York: Ginn, 1914. 14-17997. 90

STEVENSON, ADLAI. *The New America.* New York: Harper, 1957. 57-10250. 103

STEWART, FRANK M. *A Half-Century of Municipal Reform.* Berkeley: University of California Press, 1950. 50-10845. 60

STEWART, WILLIAM RHINELANDER, ed. *The Philanthropic Work of Josephine Shaw Lowell.* Montclair, N.J.: Patterson Smith, 1973 (repr. of 1911 ed.). 17

STINCHCOMBE, JEAN L. *City Politics in Toledo.* Belmont, Calif.: Wadsworth, 1968. 68-20741. 36

STIRN, ERNEST W. *An Annotated Bibliography of Robert M. La Follette.* Chicago: University of Chicago Press, 1937. 37-22204. 62

STODDARD, LOTHROP. *Master of Manhattan: The Life of Richard Croker.* New York: Longmans, Green, 1931. 31-6849. 53

———. *The Rising Tide of Color.* New York: Scribner, 1920. 20-7502. 53

STONE, HAROLD A., et al. *City Manager Government in the United States.* Chicago: Public Administration Service, 1939. 40-3902. 72

STONE, I. F. *The Hidden History of the Korea War.* New York: Monthly Review Press, 1952. 52-9751. 104

———. *The Truman Era.* New York: Monthly Review Press, 1953. 53-7505. 104

STOWE, HARRIET BEECHER. *Uncle Tom's Cabin; or Life Among the Lowly.* Boston: John P. Jewett, 1852. 16-3413. 10, 46

STRAUSS, A. L., ed. *The American City.* Chicago: Aldine, 1968. 67-17610. 52

STRONG, JOSIAH. *Expansion under New World Conditions.* New York: Baker and Taylor, 1900. 0-5589. 30

———. *Our Country: Its Possible Future and Its Present Crisis.* New York: Baker & Taylor, 1885. 11-33697. 30

———. *The Twentieth Century City.* New York: Baker and Taylor, 1898. 9-33917. 35

SUGGS, GEORGE G., JR. *Colorado's War on Militant Unionism.* Detroit: Wayne State University Press, 1972. 70-39624. 69

SUHL, YURI. *Ernestine L. Rose and the Battle for Human Rights.* New York: Reynal, 1959. 59-8324. 13

SULLIVAN, MARK. *The Education of an American.* New York: Doubleday, Doran & Co., 1938. 38-28922. 43

———. *Our Times: The United States, 1900-1925.* 6 vols. New York: Scribner's, 1928-1935. 30-30496. 23

SUMMERS, FESTUS. P. *William L. Wilson and Tariff Reform.* New Brunswick, N.J.: Rutgers University Press, 1953. 53-8214. 75

SUMNER, WILLIAM GRAHAM. *War and Other Essays.* New Haven: Yale University Press, 1911. 11-30802. 7

———. *What Social Classes Owe to Each Other.* New York: Harper & Brothers, 1883. 4-10427. 7

SWANBERG, W. A. *Citizen Hearst: A Biography of William Randolph Hearst.* New York: Scribner, 1961. 61-7220. 5

———. *Pulitzer.* New York: Scribner, 1967. 67-23695. 40

SWARD, KEITH T. *The Legend of Henry Ford.* New York: Rinehart, 1948. 48-2546. 91

SWARTZ, EDWARD M. *Toys that Don't Care.* Boston: Gambit, 1971. 70-140966. 110

SWING, RAYMOND GRAM. *Forerunners of American Fascism.* New York: J. Messner, 1935, 2nd printing. 35-27182. 5

SWISSHELM, JANE GREY. *Half a Century.* Chicago: J. G. Swisshelm, 1880. 10-7633. 13

SYMES, LILLIAN, and CLEMENT, TRAVERS. *Rebel America.* New York: Harper & Bros., 1934. 34-5886. 79

SYRETT, HAROLD C., ed. *The Gentleman and the Tiger: The Autobiography of George B. McClellan, Jr.* Philadelphia: Lippincott, 1956. 56-5859. 53

TAFT, WILLIAM HOWARD. *Present-Day Problems.* New York: Dodd, Mead, 1908. 8-19618. 70

TAGER, JACK. *The Intellectual as Urban Reformer: Brand Whitlock and the Progressive Movement.* Cleveland: Press of Case Western Reserve University, 1968. 67-27798. 44

TALESE, GAY. *The Kingdom and the Power.* New York: World, 1969. 73-81757. 40

TARBELL, IDA M. *All in the Day's Work.* New York: Macmillan, 1939. 39-27284. 42

———. *The Business of Being a Woman.* New York: Macmillan, 1912. 12-24007. 59

———. *The History of the Standard Oil Company.* New York: McClure, Phillips, 1904. 4-35331. 43

———. *The Life of Elbert H. Gary.* New York: D. Appleton, 1925. 25-22357. 91

TARR, JOEL ARTHUR. *A Study in Boss Politics: William Lorimer of Chicago.* Urbana: University of Illinois Press, 1971. 72-133945. 52

TAUSSIG, FRANK W. *Tariff History of the United States.* New York: G. P. Putnam's, 1931. 31-27019. 75

TAYLOR, A. ELIZABETH. *The Woman Suffrage Movement in Tennessee.* New York: Bookman Associates, 1957. 57-2117. 59

TAYLOR, FREDERICK. *Principles of Scientific Management.* New York: Harper & Bros., 1911. 11-10339. 72

TAYLOR, GRAHAM R. *Chicago Commons through Forty Years.* Chicago: Chicago Commons Association, 1936. 27094. 56

———. *Pioneering on Social Frontiers.* Chicago: University of Chicago Press, 1930. 30-18133. 56

———. *Satellite Cities: A Study of Industrial Suburbs.* New York: D. Appleton, 1915. 15-21654. 75

TAYLOR, RONALD B. *Sweatshops in the Sun: Child Labor on the Farm.* Boston: Beacon Press, 1973. 72-6233. 111

TEBBEL, JOHN. *The American Magazine.* New York: Hawthorn Books, 1969. 73-87864. 42.

———. *George Horace Lorimer and the Saturday Evening Post.* Garden City, N.J.: Doubleday, 1948. 48-6490. 43

———. *The Life and Good Times of William Randolph Hearst.* New York: Dutton, 1952. 52-8258. 5

THARP, LOUISE HALL. *The Peabody Sisters of Salem.* Boston: Little, Brown, 1950. 49-49265. 11

THELEN, DAVID P. *The Early Life of Robert M. La Follette 1855-1884.* Chicago: Loyola University Press, 1966. 66-11931. 63

———. *The New Citizenship.* Columbia: University of Missouri Press, 1972. 79-158075. 63

THOMAS, LATELY. *A Debonair Scoundrel.* New York: Holt, Rinehart and Winston, 1962. 62-12137. 51

THOMAS, BOB. *Winchell.* New York: Berkley Pub., 1972. 5

———. *The Mayor Who Mastered New York.* New York: Morrow, 1969. 70-83690. 53

THOMAS, NORMAN. *The Conscientious Objector in America.* New York: B. W. Huebsch, 1923. 24-4026. 85

———. *Socialism on the Defensive.* New York: Harper and Bros., 1938. 38-27972. 96

THOMPSON, KENNETH W. *The Moral Issue in Statecraft; Twentieth Century Approaches and Problems.* Baton Rouge: Louisiana State University Press, 1966. 66-21758. 11

THORNBOROUGH, EMMA LOU. *T. Thomas Fortune: Militant Journalist.* Chicago: University of Chicago Press, 1972. 73-175305. 65

THORELLI, HANS B. *The Federal Antitrust Policy.* Baltimore: Johns Hopkins Press, 1954. 55-2266. 73

TIFFANY, FRANCIS. *Life of Dorothea Lynde Dix.* Boston and New York: Houghton, Mifflin, 1890. 5-2597. 11

TIMBERLAKE, JAMES H. *Prohibition and the Progressive Movement 1900-1920.* Cambridge: Harvard University Press, 1963. 63-9564. 57

TINDALL, GEORGE B. *The Emergence of the New South.* Baton Rouge: Louisiana State University Press, 1967. 67-24551. 77

———, ed. *A Populist Reader.* New York: Harper & Row, 1966. 66-10531. 35

TODD, ALDEN L. *Justice on Trial: The Case of Louis D. Brandeis.* New York: McGraw-Hill, 1964. 64-16300. 58

TOLMAN, WILLIAM HOWE. *Municipal Reform Movements in the United States.* New York: Fleming H. Revell, 1895. 12-5013. 18

TOMSICH, JOHN. *A Genteel Endeavor; American Culture and Politics in the Gilded Age.* Stanford, Calif.: Stanford University Press, 1971. 75-119503. 18

TORELLE, ELLEN, comp. *The Political Philosophy of Robert M. La Follette.* Madison, Wis.: Robert M. La Follette Co., 1920. 20-15383. 62

TRACHTENBERG, ALEXANDER, ed. *The American Socialists and the War.* New York: Rand School of Social Science, 1917. 17-20005. 86

[TRAIN, ARTHUR.] *Yankee Lawyer: The Autobiography of Ephraim Tutt.* New York: C. Scribner's, 1943. 43-12455. 51

TRATTNER, WALTER I. *Crusade for the Children.* Chicago: Quadrangle Books, 1970. 76-116090. 58

——. *Homer Folks: Pioneer in Social Welfare.* New York: Columbia University Press, 1968. 67-29169. 55

TUCHMAN, BARBARA. *The Proud Tower; A Portrait of the World Before the War, 1890–1914.* New York: Macmillan, 1966. 65-23074. 32

TUGWELL, REXFORD G. *The Economic Basis of Public Interest.* Menasha, Wis.: George Banta Pub. Co., 1922. 22-20913. 95

TYLER, ALICE FELT. *Freedom's Ferment; Phases of American Social History to 1860* Minneapolis: University of Minnesota Press, 1944. A44-463. 8

UNGAR, SANFORD J. *The Papers and the Papers.* New York: Dutton, 1972. 77-190699. 6

U. S. Senate Committee on Education and Labor. *Violations of Free Speech and Assembly and Interference with the Rights of Labor.* Washington: Government Printing Office, 1936. 36-26473. 96

UNTERMYER, SAMUEL. *Who Is Entitled to the Credit for the Federal Reserve Act?* New York, 1927. 28-7808. 74

UROFSKY, MELVIN I. *A Mind of One Piece: Brandeis and American Reform.* New York: Scribner, 1971. 74-143945. 58

——, and LEVY, DAVID W. *The Letters of Louis D. Brandeis.* Albany: State Univ. of New York Press, 1971–1973. 73-129640. 58

USHER, ELLIS BAKER. *The Greenback Movement of 1875–1884 and Wisconsin's Part in It.* Milwaukee: E. B. Usher, 1911. 11-24408. 37

VAN DENSEN, GLYNDON G. *Horace Greeley.* Philadelphia: University of Pennsylvania Press, 1953. 39

VARE, WILLIAM S. *My Forty Years in Politics.* Philadelphia: Roland Swain, 1933. 33-15787. 54

VEBLEN, THORSTEIN. *Essays, Reviews, and Reports; Previously Uncollected Writings.* Edited with an introd., *New Light on Veblen,* by Joseph Dorfman. Clifton, N.J.: A. M. Kelley, 1973. 72-13590. 19

——. *The Theory of the Leisure Class: An Economic Study of Institutions.* New York: Macmillan, 1899. 90-1220. 25

VIERECK, GEORGE SYLVESTER. *Spreading Germs of Hate.* New York: Liveright, 1930. 30-17303. 85

VILLARD, OSWALD GARRISON. *Fighting Years; Memoirs of a Liberal Editor.* New York: Harcourt, Brace, 1939. 39-27286. 30

——. *Prophets True and False.* New York: Knopf, 1928. 28-15599. 91

——. *Some Newspapers and Newspapermen,* rev. ed. New York: Knopf, 1926. 26-17793. 40

WADE, LOUISE C. *Graham Taylor: Pioneer for Social Justice.* Chicago: University of Chicago Press, 1964. 64-24976. 56

WADE, MASON. *Margaret Fuller, Whetstone of Genius.* New York: Viking Press, 1940. 40-6649. 12

WALCUTT, CHARLES CHILD. *American Literary Naturalism, a Divided Stream.* Minneapolis: University of Minnesota Press, 1956. 56-12465. 40

WALD, LILLIAN. *The House on Henry Street.* New York: Holt, 1915. 15-25238. 55

——. *Windows on Henry Street.* Boston: Little, Brown, 1934. 34-5571. 55

WALLAS, GRAHAM. *The Great Society, a Psychological Analysis.* New York: Macmillan, 1914. 14-11250. 76

——. *Human Nature in Politics.* London: A. Constable, 1908. 9-35520. 76

WALLING, WILLIAM ENGLISH. *American Labor and American Democracy.* New York: Harper & Bros., 1926. 26-21991. 69

——. *Progressivism and After.* New York: Macmillan, 1914. 14-5321. 71

WALSH, LOUIS J. *John Mitchel.* Dublin and Cork: Talbot Press, 1934. 35-12632. 14

WALSH, THOMAS J. *Three Years of the New Freedom.* Washington: Government Printing Office, 1916. 16-26381. 83

WALTON, RICHARD J. *The Remnants of Power: The Tragic Last Years of Adlai Stevenson.* New York: Coward, 1968. 68-23373. 103

WARNER, HOYT L. *Progressivism in Ohio 1897–1917.* Columbus: Ohio State University Press, 1964. 65-11267. 60

WARNER, SAMUEL B., JR. *Streetcar Suburbs: The Process of Growth in Boston, 1870–1900.* Cambridge: Harvard University Press, 1962. 62-17228. 36

WARREN, FRANK A., III. *Liberals and Communism.* Bloomington: Indiana University Press, 1966. 66-12735. 97

WASHINGTON, BOOKER T. *The Future of the American Negro.* Boston: Small, Maynard, 1899. 0-2908. 65

——. *The Negro in Business.* Boston: Hertel, Jenkins, 1907. 7-37616. 65

WATSON, FRANK DEKKER. *The Charity Organization Movement in the United States: A Study in American Philanthropy.* New York: Macmillan, 1922. 22-23080. 17

WEATHERFORD, WILLIS D., and JOHNSON, CHARLES S. *Race Relations: Adjustment of Whites and Negroes in the United States.* Boston: D. C. Heath, 1934. 34-36788. 65

WEAVER, JOHN DOWNING. *The Brownsville Raid.* New York: W. W. Norton, 1970. 73-119697. 28

WECTER, DIXON. *The Age of the Great Depression.* New York: Macmillan, 1948. 48-10172. 94

WEINBERG, ARTHUR, and LILA, eds. *Clarence Darrow's Verdicts Out of Court.* Chicago: Quadrangle Books, 1963. 63-18472. 68

——, eds. *The Muckrakers.* rev. New York: Simon & Schuster, 1961. 61-16557. 44

WEINER, EDWARD HORACE. *Let's Go to Press: A Biography of Walter Winchell.* New York: Putnam, 1955. 55-12041. 5

WEINGAST, DAVID. *Walter Lippmann, a Study in Personal Journalism.* New Brunswick, N.J.: Rutgers University Press, 1949. 49-50334 rev. 76, 90

WEINSTEIN, GREGORY. *Reminiscences of an Interesting Decade: The Ardent Eighties.* New York: The International Press, 1928. 28-29977. 56

WEINSTEIN, JAMES. *The Corporate Ideal in the Liberal State.* Boston: Beacon Press, 1968. 68-12846. 69

_____, and EAKINS, DAVID W., eds. *For a New America; Essays in History and Politics from Studies on the Left, 1959–1967.* New York: Random House, 1970. 73-85618. 31

WEINTRAUB, HYMAN. *Andrew Furuseth, Emancipator of Seamen.* Berkeley: University of California Press, 1939. 59-5747. 74

WEISBERGER, BERNARD A. *The American Newspaperman.* Chicago: University of Chicago Press, 1961. 61-8647. 39

WEISS, NANCY J. *Charles Francis Murphy. . .in Tammany Politics.* Northampton, Mass.: Smith College, 1968. 67-21037. 52

WELLES, SUMNER. *Naboth's Vineyard, The Dominican Republic 1844–1924.* New York: Payson & Clarke, 1928. 28-21952. 83

WELLS, EVELYN. *Fremont Older.* New York and London: D. Appleton-Century, 1936. 36-25254. 40

WERNER, M. R. *Privileged Characters.* New York: R. M. McBride, 1935. 35-27184. 96

_____. *Tammany Hall.* Garden City, N.Y.: Doubleday, Doran & Co., 1928. 28-12991. 53

WERTENBAKER, THOMAS JEFFERSON. *Torchbearer of the Revolution, the Story of Bacon's Rebellion and Its Leader.* Princeton, N.J.: Princeton University Press, 1940. 40-34256. 3

WESLEY, CHARLES HARRIS. *Neglected History; Essays in Negro History by a College President: Charles H. Wesley.* Wilberforce, Ohio: Central State College Press, 1965. 65-5958. 14

WESSER, ROBERT F. *Charles Evans Hughes and Politics and Reform in New York 1905–1910.* Ithaca, N.Y.: Cornell University Press, 1967. 67-19029. 53

WESTON, RUBIN FRANCIS. *Racism in U.S. Imperialism: The Influence of Racial Assumptions on American Foreign Policy, 1893–1946.* Columbia: University of South Carolina Press, 1972. 70-144803. 29

WEYL, WALTER. *Tired Radicals and Other Papers.* New York: B. W. Huebsch, 1921. 21-15181. 89

WHARTON, EDITH. *The Horse of Mirth.* New York: Scribner's, 1905. 5-33501. 45

WHEELER, JOHN. *I've Got News for You.* New York: Dutton, 1961. 61-6015. 5

WHITE, LEONARD D. *The City Manager.* Chicago: University of Chicago Press, 1927. 27-23675. 54

WHITE, MORTON GABRIEL. *Social Thought in America: The Revolt against Formalism.* Boston: Beacon Press, 1957. 57-2119. 25

WHITE, WALTER. *Rope and Fagot.* New York: Knopf, 1929. 29-10015. 92

WHITE, WILLIAM ALLEN. *Autobiography.* New York: Macmillan, 1946. 46-1656. 43, 44

_____. *Woodrow Wilson.* Boston: Houghton Mifflin, 1924. 24-27886. 78

WHITESIDE, THOMAS. *The Investigation of Ralph Nader.* New York: Arbor House, 1972. 72-79452. 113

WHITLOCK, BRAND. *Forty Years of It,* 2nd ed. Cleveland: Press of Case Western Reserve University, 1970. 71-99230. 26, 43

_____. *Letters and Journal,* ed. by Allen Nevins. New York: D. Appleton-Century, 1936. 36-29810. 60

WHYTE, FREDERIC. *The Life of W. T. Stead.* New York: Houghton Mifflin, 1925. 26-1965. 41

WIEBE, ROBERT. *Businessmen and Reform.* Cambridge: Harvard University Press, 1962. 62-18718. 67

———. *The Search for Order, 1877–1920.* New York: Hill and Wang, 1967. 66-27609. 24

WILKERSON, MARCUS N. *Public Opinion and the Spanish-American War, a Study of War Propaganda.* Baton Rouge: Louisiana State University Press, 1932. 33-7362. 30

WILLIAMS, WILLIAM APPLEMAN. *The Contours of American History.* Cleveland: World, 1961. 61-5811. 31

WILLKIE, WENDELL. *An American Program.* New York: Simon & Schuster, 1944. 44-40191. 100

———. *One World.* New York: Simon & Schuster, 1943. 43-51091. 100

WILLS, HENRY T. *Scientific Tariff Making.* New York: Blanchard Press, 1913. 13-18479. 75

WILSON, EDITH BOLLING. *My Memoir.* Indianapolis: Bobbs-Merrill, 1939. 39-27215. 78

WILSON, HOWARD E. *Mary McDowell: Neighbor.* Chicago: University of Chicago Press, 1928. 29-3139. 56

WILSON, JOAN HOFF. *Herbert Hoover: Forgotten Progressive.* Boston: Little, Brown, 1975. 74-25676. 94

WILSON, RAYMOND JACKSON, ed. *Darwinism and the American Intellectual: A Book of Readings.* Homewood, Ill.: Dorsey Press, 1967. 67-23773. 20

WILSON, WOODROW. *Mere Literature and Other Essays.* Boston: Houghton Mifflin, 1896. 4-13867. 78

WINGATE, CHARLES FREDERICK, ed. *Views and Interviews on Journalism.* New York: F. B. Patterson, 1875. 11-26348. 39

WINTER-BERGER, ROBERT N. *The Washington Pay-Off.* New York: Lyle Stuart, 1972. 73-185421. 116

WIRT, WILLIAM ALBERT. *Newer Ideals in Education: The Complete Use of the School Plant.* Philadelphia: Public Education Association of Philadelphia, 1912. 16-16583. 25

WISAN, JOSEPH EZRA. *The Cuban Crisis as Reflected in the New York Press, 1895–1898.* New York: Columbia University Press, 1934. 35-835. 30

WITTKE, CARL FREDERICK. *The Irish in America.* Baton Rouge: Louisiana State University Press, 1956. 56-6199. 14

WOLF, HAZEL CATHERINE. *On Freedom's Altar: The Martyr Complex in the Abolition Movement.* Madison: University of Wisconsin Press, 1952. 52-13402. 9

WOLFE, TOM, and JOHNSON, E. W., eds. *The New Journalism.* New York: Harper & Row, 1973. 71-123972. 111

WOLFF, ROBERT P. *The Poverty of Liberalism.* Boston: Beacon Press, 1968. 68-29314. 117

WOOD, STEPHEN B. *Constitutional Politics in the Progressive Era.* Chicago: University of Chicago Press, 1968. 67-25525. 58

WOODS, ROBERT A., and KENNEDY, ALBERT J. *The Settlement Horizon: A National Estimate.* New York: Russell Sage Foundation, 1922. 22-16249. 55

———, and KENNEDY, ALBERT J. *The Zone of Emergence.* Cambridge: Harvard University Press, 1962. 62-20200. 55

WOODSON, CARTER GODWIN, ed. *The Mind of the Negro as Reflected by Letters Written During the Crisis, 1800–1860.* Washington, D.C.: Association for the Study of Negro Life and History, 1926. 26-14304. 14

———. *Negro Orators and Their Orations.* Washington, D.C.: Associated Publishers, 1925. 25-20434. 14

———, and WESLEY, CHARLES H. *The Negro in Our History,* 10th ed. Washington, D.C.: Associated Publishers, 1962. 62-3979. 14, 63

WOODWARD, C. VANN. *Origins of the New South.* Baton Rouge: Louisiana State University Press, 1951. 51-28703. 66, 72, 77, 87

———. *Tom Watson.* New York: Macmillan, 1938. 38-8354. 38, 65

WOODWARD, HELEN BEAL. *The Bold Women.* New York: Farrar, Straus and Young, 1953. 53-7084. 13

WRESZIN, MICHAEL. *Oswald Garrison Villard.* Bloomington: Indiana University Press, 1955. 65-11795. 92

WRIGHT, RICHARD. "I Tried to Be a Communist," *Atlantic* 174 (1944), Aug. (61–70), Sept. (48–56). 98

WYATT-BROWN, BERTRAM. *Lewis Tappan and the Evangelical War against Slavery.* Cleveland: Press of Case Western Reserve University, 1969. 68-19228. 9

WYLLIE, IRVIN G. *The Self-Made Man in America.* New Brunswick, N.J.: Rutgers University Press, 1954. 54-10602. 34

WYNES, CHARLES E., ed. *Forgotten Voices; Dissenting Southerners in an Age of Conformity.* Baton Rouge: Louisiana State University Press, 1967. 67-11685. 15, 65

YARNELL, ALLEN. *Democrats and Progressives: The 1948 Presidential Election.* Berkeley: University of California Press, 1974. 73-83060. 101

YELLOWITZ, IRWIN. *Labor and the Progressive Movement in New York State 1897–1916.* Ithaca: Cornell University Press, 1965. 65-16500. 69

YORBURG, BETTY, ed. *Utopia and Reality.* New York: Columbia University Press, 1969. 72-79573. 96

YOUMANS, EDWARD LIVINGSTON, ed. *The Culture Demanded by Modern Life; A Series of Addresses and Arguments on the Claims of Scientific Education.* New York: D. Appleton, 1867. 6-29636. 24

YOUNG, A. N. *The Single-Tax Movement in the United States.* Princeton, N.J.: Princeton University Press, 1916. 16-12744. 60

ZINK, HAROLD. *City Bosses in the United States: A Study of Twenty Municipal Bosses.* Durham, N.C.: Duke University Press, 1930. 30-31996. 18

ZUEBLIN, CHARLES. *A Decade of Civic Improvement.* Chicago: University of Chicago Press, 1905. 6-674. 56

Subject and
Title Index